THE BATTLE OF THE OTRANTO STRAITS

Twentieth-Century Battles

Spencer C. Tucker, editor

THE
BATTLE
OF THE
OTRANTO
STRAITS

Controlling the Gateway to
the Adriatic in World War I

PAUL G. HALPERN

INDIANA UNIVERSITY PRESS

BLOOMINGTON AND INDIANAPOLIS

This book is a publication of

Indiana University Press

601 North Morton Street

Bloomington, IN 47404-3797 USA

http://iupress.indiana.edu

Telephone orders 800-842-6796
Fax orders 812-855-7931
Orders by e-mail iuporder@indiana.edu

Library of Congress Cataloging-in-Publication Data

Halpern, Paul G., date
The battle of the Otranto Straits : controlling the gateway
to the Adriatic in World War I / Paul G. Halpern.
    p.   cm. — (Twentieth-century battles)
Includes bibliographical references and index.
ISBN 0-253-34379-8 (alk. paper)
1. Otranto Straits, Battle of the, 1917. I. Title. II. Series.
D584.O8H35 2004
940.4'57—dc22
                                                2003025349

1 2 3 4 5 09 08 07 06 05 04

CONTENTS

ILLUSTRATIONS

Maps

Sketches

Photographs

The object of the raid: British drifters sailing from their base

HMS *Bristol*

SMS *Helgoland* on trials, 7 May 1917

SMS *Saida:* View from crow's nest

HMS *Dartmouth:* Crew of six-inch gun wearing anti-flash hoods

HMS *Dartmouth* at speed during the action

K.195, an Oeffag-built Weichmann (in IV. Gruppe during the action)

An Austrian aircraft (probably K.153 or K.154) makes a low pass
over the crippled *Novara*

SMS *Sankt Georg* cleared for action steaming to reinforce Horthy

Saida towing *Novara* followed by *Helgoland*

PREFACE

THE BATTLE IN THE Strait of Otranto on 15 May 1917 is hardly a household name, even among those with more than a passing interest in naval history. It was hardly a large action as far as naval battles go, but it has certain interesting characteristics. It was the largest encounter between warships at sea in the Adriatic and Mediterranean area during the First World War. It also involved on one side the navy of Austria-Hungary—the *k.u.k. Kriegsmarine*—a force that ceased to exist after the collapse of the Habsburg Monarchy in 1918. Students today, even those with a higher knowledge of geography, find it hard to realize that the two apparently landlocked countries of Austria and Hungary were once together as a great power with access to the sea and control of most of the eastern shoreline of the Adriatic. Adriatic operations had certain peculiarities imposed by the constraints of geography. This was a very different area than the North Sea, the locale familiar to most historians of the war. This is possibly another reason why for a long time the *k.u.k. Kriegsmarine* was able to contend with the naval forces of the much stronger traditional maritime powers Great Britain, France, and Italy. It was hard for the Allies to bring the full weight of their maritime power to bear in the Adriatic. Otranto is also one of the first encounters at sea where aircraft play a definite role, certainly not yet decisive but perhaps an indication of things to come.

For convenience, the term "Austrian" is used in the text rather than the more cumbersome "Austro-Hungarian." The geographical names in use during the First World War are also used rather than the Slavic names that generally replaced most of them after the disappearance of the Habsburg Monarchy. These are also the names that are most familiar to historians. As a matter of policy, documents available in print such as those in volumes published by the Navy Records Society are generally used rather than the archival citation of the original. This is intended to facilitate the reader who might be inclined to do further reading on the subject. For uniformity, times are given according to the twenty-four-hour clock and those given are those cited in the documents which were originally presented in a wide variety of styles. In theory but not always in practice all navies operating in the Adriatic were using the same central European time (GMT + 1). Naval ranks are given in their original form to avoid controversy about exact equivalents about which authorities disagree.

As this study is based on research done over the years for a variety of subjects dealing with the naval history of the First World War, there are many people, some unfortunately no longer with us, who deserve to be acknowledged. However, for the specific purposes of this volume there are some who deserve special recognition. Mr. Erwin Sieche, author of numerous works on the Austrian navy, has been indefatigable in answering my queries and has generously provided me with photocopies of documents from his own collection as well as copies of photographs and charts. Diplomingenieur Nikolaus A. Sifferlinger has also been a source of much information on the Austrian navy and its procedures. I am grateful to the late Inge Baker for putting at my disposal a copy of her translation of her grandfather Kontreadmiral Erich Heyssler's memoirs and to Mrs. Nicola Martin for permission to quote this material. For their assistance I would also like to thank Mr. Roderick Suddaby, keeper of the Department of Documents at the Imperial War Museum, for calling valuable manuscript material to my attention, as well as the late Dr. Peter Jung, Marinereferent and his colleague Mag. Dr. Robert Rill at the Österreichisches Staatsarchiv/Kriegsarchiv in Vienna. The staff of the Public Record Office, Kew, has as always been most helpful although the fact that they do not wear identification badges makes it impossible to give adequate thanks to those who deserve it. Capitaine de vaisseau (r) Robert Feuilloy, Secrétaire Général of ARDHAN [Association pour la recherche de documentation sur l'histoire de l'Aéronautique Navale] graciously answered my queries on French naval air participation in the battle. The Ufficio Affari Generali e Relazioni Esterne, 1° Ufficio (Ufficio Storico) of the Stato Maggiore della Marina, Rome were kind enough to provide copies of material from the *Cronistoria documentata della Guerra Marittima Italo-Austriaca 1915–1918*.

For making available and granting permission to publish photographs from their collection, I should like to thank Dr. Lothar Baumgartner and Mr. Peter Schupita. Those photographs identified as IWM with negative numbers are used with the permission of The Trustees of the Imperial War Museum, London. Crown copyright material appears by permission of The Controller of Her Majesty's Stationery Office.

The maps, sketches, and scanning of photographs are the work of Peter Krafft, Director of Cartography at the Florida Resources and Environmental Analysis Center, Florida State University. The maps are based on a synthesis of British, Italian, and Austrian sources. The sketches are extracted from Linienschiffsleutnant Konjovic, "Fliegertätigkeit anläßlich des Vorstosses der Kreuzerflottille über die Otrantostrasse am 15 Mai 1917," 16 May 1917, Österreichisches Staatsarchiv/Kriegsarchiv, Vienna (File OK/MS-VIII-1/1 ex 1917, No. 2716).

I should also like to thank the History Department of Florida State University for financial assistance in travel and research for this study.

Paul G. Halpern
Tallahassee, Florida
March 2003

THE BATTLE OF THE OTRANTO STRAITS

The Adriatic

CHAPTER ONE

THE NAVAL WAR
IN THE ADRIATIC

THE NAVAL WAR in the Adriatic was shaped by certain peculiar geographical features. The Adriatic Sea is really an arm of the Mediterranean in the rough shape of a long narrow rectangle. The Strait of Otranto forms the entrance to the Mediterranean and is roughly sixty miles wide. The distance between the eastern and western shores of the Adriatic is usually not much more. Consequently, after the entry of Italy into the war on the side of the Entente, the opposing naval forces were really only a few hours steaming distance apart. The Strait of Otranto seemed a convenient place to prevent exit from the Adriatic into the waters of the Mediterranean as well as to block access by sea to the Habsburg Monarchy from the rest of the world. The Austrian field for potential maneuver was therefore relatively limited. On the other hand, within the Adriatic, geography compensated the Austrians for this handicap. The eastern or Austrian side of the Adriatic has a large number of islands forming a protective offshore defensive chain endowed with internal passages that the Austrians could navigate at least partially sheltered from outside attack. In contrast, the western or Italian side of the Adriatic was open, making the Italian coast much easier to attack, particularly at dawn when the rising sun would be in the eyes of the defenders. The two major Austrian naval bases were located near the extremities of the Adriatic, notably Pola at the tip of the Istrian peninsula in the north and the Gulf of Cattaro in the south. The latter was usually referred to as the "Bocche" by the Austrians, and the term appears in the majority of both private and official correspondence. The leading Austrian commercial port and shipbuilding center—Trieste—was virtually in the front line once Italy entered the war, and its shipbuilding yards were largely unusable. The major Italian naval bases were at Venice in the north and, with limited capacity and primarily used by light forces, Brindisi in the south. The Italian battle fleet was not in the Adriatic but was located at Taranto, in the arch of the Italian boot.

The talk of an *Austrian* fleet might puzzle a reader not familiar with nineteenth-century European history. It has been more than eighty years since the Dual Monarchy of Austria-Hungary disappeared from the ranks of the great powers. After 1918 both Austria and Hungary were separated, drastically reduced in size, and limited to the Danube River for access to the sea. Matters were quite different at the outbreak of the First World War. Austria had direct access to the sea through possession of Trieste and the Istrian peninsula in the north and Dalmatia on the eastern shores of the Adriatic. Hungary's link to the sea came through rule over Croatia and possession of the port of Fiume, today Rijeka. The navy enjoyed some success in the nineteenth century. The Austrian naval victory at Lissa in 1866 provided one of the few bright spots in that otherwise disastrous year for Habsburg fortunes.

However, until the turn of the century, the *k.u.k. Kriegsmarine*—the navy of Austria-Hungary—remained essentially a coast defense force. The Austrians had made good use of the invention of the automotive torpedo, and the famous Whitehead torpedo factory was located at Fiume. Torpedo boats operating in the maze of Dalmatian islands were a common feature of Austrian naval maneuvers. Outside of the Adriatic, the navy was represented by cruisers of one sort or another in events like the 1900 Boxer Rebellion in China.

This situation changed after the turn of the century, and the Austrians began building larger ships to form a true battle fleet. The phenomenon of navalism had reached the Habsburg Monarchy, and among other things the navy had the support of the heir to the throne, Archduke Franz Ferdinand. By the outbreak of the First World War the Austrian navy had three semi-dreadnought *Radetzkys* and three *Tegetthoff*-class dreadnoughts, with a fourth on the stocks. A second class of four dreadnoughts had also been approved. Austrian naval power was now something that naval staffs had to take into account.[1]

The primary motivation for the Austrians was probably fear of their traditional nineteenth-century rival Italy. Italy and Austria-Hungary were both allied to Germany by the Triple Alliance of 1882, but the question of *Italia irredenta* or "unredeemed Italy," meaning those Italian-speaking territories still under Habsburg rule, might someday provide the excuse for war. It was a common saying that Italy and Austria must either be bound in an alliance or at war with each other. One never knew what the future might hold and it was best not to fall too far behind the Italians at sea. However, the Austro-Italian competition created a paradox. Both were allies of Germany and even though they were to a large extent building against each other, after their fleets had grown to a certain point a tantalizing prospect arose. If they combined their fleets they might counter the usually far more powerful French fleet. If they did not, they stood the danger of being defeated in detail. The result of these conflicting emotions was the secret Triple Alliance naval convention of 1913, formed with Germany's obvious blessing. The convention provided for the Austrian and Italian fleets to unite in the event of war in Sicilian waters, initially under an Austrian commander in chief, Admiral Anton Haus. The Austrians and Italians would be joined by whatever German ships were in the Mediterranean. The naval convention had actually been pushed by the Italian navy, who felt vulnerable and exposed to French and potential British naval power as the bonds of the Anglo-French entente of 1904 were tightened. Furthermore, the Italian naval leaders were kept in the dark by the Italian foreign office as to the strictly defensive nature of the Triple Alliance. The Italians, however, had excellent reasons for remaining neutral when the war broke out in 1914, and with the Italian declaration of neutrality the Triple Alliance naval convention became a historical curiosity.[2]

The Austrian fleet could now have no realistic expectation of a victory in a classic naval engagement with the French fleet. Initially, however, the French commander in chief was preoccupied with protecting the transport of troops from North Africa to France. This created a window of opportunity when the Austrian fleet might have escaped from the Adriatic to the Dardanelles and then carried on the war against the Russian fleet in the Black Sea. Kontre-admiral Wilhelm Souchon, commander of the German *Mittelmeerdivision* (the battle cruiser *Goeben* and light cruiser *Breslau*), decided to abandon any plan of joining the Austrians in the Adriatic and, after a feint to deceive his British pursuers, made for the Dardanelles. Admiral Haus, commander of the Austrian fleet, did not know this at first and actually put to sea to cover the German escape in Austrian waters if necessary. The uncertainty over the action of the Austrian fleet weighed heavily in British calculations—Britain and Austria were not at war until a few days after Anglo-German hostilities—and contributed to the escape of the *Goeben* and *Breslau*. The Germans wanted Haus to follow with the Austrian fleet to Constantinople, but Haus resolutely refused. Even if he succeeded in reaching the safety of the Dardanelles, the logistical problems of maintaining the fleet in Constantinople would have been substantial. Furthermore, it would have left the Austrian coast bare of its most powerful warships, and few, least of all Haus, had much trust now in the future actions of the Italians. The latter consideration alone would have been decisive.[3]

The French battle fleet eventually appeared at the entrance to the Adriatic, but future French actions would be hampered by the lack of a suitable base in the vicinity.[4] The British allowed the French fleet full use of Malta, but that was hundreds of miles away. The pro-Allied Greek prime minister Eleutherios Venizelos eventually bent the rules of neutrality enough for the French to use the Ionian islands. However, significant practical problems remained, one of them a lack of targets. A French sweep into the Adriatic caught the Austrian cruiser *Zenta* on blockade duty off the Montenegrin coast. The small cruiser was sunk by a hail of gunfire that even though uncoordinated served as a stark warning of what might happen to the Austrians if they were caught by the superior firepower of the French battle fleet. Haus had no intention of letting anything of the sort happen. The Austrian fleet did not come out. The French bombarded the outer fortifications at the Gulf of Cattaro but the Austrians did not rise to the bait. The French, in turn, did not consider it prudent to push their fleet all the way up to the north of the Adriatic. There were the obvious dangers of mines and torpedoes, especially since the Austrians had a small number of submarines. The possible gains were not worth the risk, especially if the Austrian fleet still did not come out.[5]

The French had obligations in the Adriatic, notably the supply of their allies Montenegro and landlocked Serbia. The Montenegrin coastline was small, the single port Antivari primitive. The difficulties of road transport meant that only a trickle of supplies might eventually reach Serbia. Moreover, the proximity of Cattaro to the Montenegrin ports meant transports were always exposed to potential Austrian raids. Furthermore, and this must be emphasized, any naval force venturing into the Adriatic ran the risk of facing the big guns of the major Austrian warships. As intelligence experts would say in a later age, one must take into account Austrian *capabilities*, not *intentions*, for the latter could never be known for certain. This meant operations needed heavy French ships in the covering force and this meant danger. This was demonstrated on 21 December 1914 when the French flagship the dreadnought *Jean Bart* was torpedoed by the Austrian submarine *U.12* while engaged on one of the sweeps. The *Jean Bart* was able to make it back to Malta down by the bows, but the point was taken. The French battleships would not normally venture into the Adriatic. The bigger French ships would be limited to a distant blockade patrolling along a line to the north of Corfu. But even this proved dangerous if they were in range of submarines operating from Austrian bases. This was again demonstrated on the night of 26–27 April 1915 after the French had temporarily moved the patrol line further north in case reports of the negotiations with Italy provoked increased Austrian naval activity. This gave the Austrian submarine *U.5* the opportunity to torpedo and sink with heavy loss of life the large armored cruiser *Léon Gambetta*. The French moved their patrol line further south to the parallel of Cephalonia.

The French navy did what it could to surmount the difficulties. Before the war the French had one of the largest submarine fleets in the world, although many of the boats suffered from design constraints. On 8 December 1914 the

Curie made a daring attempt to penetrate the main Austrian base at Pola only to be sunk and subsequently salvaged and put into service as the Austrian *U.14*. The French also sought in the autumn of 1914 to exploit the vulnerabilities of the Gulf of Cattaro. Batteries on Mount Lovčen in adjacent Montenegrin territory looked over the gulf, and the French landed naval guns and gun crews who with considerable difficulty managed eventually to install a battery of 15cm guns on Mount Lovčen. The batteries commenced fire on 15 October only to face effective counter-battery fire from the 24cm guns of the old *Monarch*-class battleships. These coast defense vessels may have been obsolete for a role at sea, but they were effective in this work. Haus decisively ended the menace when on 21 October he sent the semi-dreadnought *Radetzky* to the Bocche and her 30.5cm (twelve-inch) guns silenced the French batteries and forced the French to evacuate their positions. Cattaro might have been vulnerable to a full-scale expedition, but this was anathema to the French high command, anxious to concentrate on what for them was the decisive theater on the western front.[6]

The beginning of the Anglo-French campaign at the entrance to the Dardanelles in 1915 provoked renewed calls for a more active role for the Austrian fleet, particularly from the Germans and from at least some elements of AOK—*Armeeoberkommando*—and some in the Austrian foreign office. There were also suggestions that the Austrians either send submarines to operate off the Dardanelles or send badly needed munitions to the Turks by means of a fast light cruiser. The handful of submarines available to the Austrians lacked the technical capabilities to operate off the Dardanelles, and it seemed foolish to sacrifice one of the precious light cruisers for the relatively small amount of munitions it could carry.[7] Haus resisted the temptation to court cheap popularity by executing what he sarcastically called a "hurrah" action likely to lead to a disaster, and he had the moral courage to defend his policy against the sharp comments and snide insinuations of both his German allies and some of the army who could not understand the fleet's relative inactivity while the army had been suffering heavy losses.[8] Perhaps most important of all, the uncertain attitude of Italy made it imperative to keep all available forces in the Adriatic.

The inability of the Austrian navy to have any effect on the situation at the Dardanelles led directly to one of the most important developments of the war in the Mediterranean theater. The Germans decided to send their own submarines. The first German U-boats were *UB.7* and *UB.8* of the small *UB.I* class. They were broken down into sections and shipped overland from Germany by rail and then reassembled at Pola. Their ability to operate off the Dardanelles was, however, limited by their range, and in fact the Austrian navy had to tow them through the Strait of Otranto under the cover of darkness in order to save fuel. The Germans, however, quickly demonstrated that it was technically possible for larger submarines to make the long trip directly by sea from Germany. On 13 May 1915 Kapitänleutnant Otto Hersing managed to reach Cattaro with *U.21* and later proceeded to the Dardanelles, where in the last week of May he sank the battleships *Triumph* and *Majestic*. Allied naval operations at the Dardanelles were now immensely complicated and the strategic value of Austrian bases in the Adriatic greatly enhanced. Other large German submarines would follow as well as more capable smaller boats of the *UB.II* class. The real and most damaging effect of the presence of submarines in the Mediterranean would not be against Allied warships. It would be merchant shipping in the Mediterranean as elsewhere that suffered the greatest loss.[9]

After 26 April, when Italy signed the Treaty of London obligating her to enter the war within a month, the question became whether the naval resources of Italy would change the situation in the Adriatic. They would not. The same constraints imposed by the new technology and geography continued. Haus, seeking a psychological advantage, led the entire Austrian fleet out on a sortie on 23 May to bombard various points along the Italian coast, sinking an Italian destroyer in the process. It was the largest single operation by the Austrian fleet during the war, and it was the last. The main Italian battle fleet was far away with no chance to intervene. The Italians soon learned their own lessons about the danger of using large warships deep in the Adriatic. On 7 July the large armored cruiser *Amalfi* was torpedoed and sunk by the submarine *UB.14* while supporting a sweep by destroyers in the northern Adriatic. The submarine was actually German, shipped in sections by rail to Pola and reassembled. At the time of the sinking, the only Austrian in the submarine was a single officer acting as pilot. All other officers and men were German. This raised an awkward point as technically Germany and Italy were not yet at war and would not be until August 1916. To get around the difficulty, the submarine was given an Austrian designation, *U.26*. This practice continued for over a year and caused a considerable amount of confusion and diplomatic complications.

The commander of the Italian fleet, Viceammiraglio Luigi Amadeo di Savoia, Duke of the Abruzzi, a cousin of the King and a well-known and glamorous explorer in pre-war days, had offensive plans of his own. He aimed at seizing the islands of Pelagosa and Lagosta to form a chain of lookout stations extending across the central Adriatic towards the Dalmatian coast, where operations might continue on the Sabbioncello peninsula jutting out from the mainland itself. The *Capo di stato maggiore* (chief of naval staff), Viceammiraglio Paolo Thaon di Revel, was dubious about these plans, and the Italian army, like its counterpart in France, had no troops to spare for operations of this sort. Nevertheless, Pelagosa, in the middle of the Adriatic, was occupied without opposition as a first stage on 11 July. But on the 18th of July the armored cruiser *Garibaldi*, on an operation to shell the coastal railway near Ragusa, was torpedoed and sunk by the Austrian submarine U.4. This was the second major Italian loss within a fortnight, and the operation against Lagosta was cancelled. If they were not going to continue on to Lagosta, retention of the waterless and barren island of Pelagosa became meaningless for the Italians. The Austrians also counterattacked at Pelagosa and, although an Austrian attempt at a landing was repulsed on 28 July, Austrian light cruisers and destroyers returned to bombard the island on 17 August, destroying the fresh water cistern. The island was more trouble to hold than it was worth and the Italians evacuated the following day. The submarine had enforced a form of stalemate in the Adriatic, at least as far as ships larger than light cruisers were concerned.[10]

The policy of the Italian fleet was delineated by Thaon di Revel in a series of letters to Abruzzi in July and August of 1915. It was fundamentally defensive, even in regard to light craft. Italian admirals were warned to avoid excessive activity by destroyers and torpedo boats, which were considered relatively fragile. Italian naval commanders were advised also to refrain from operations in bad weather, which might put a strain on these craft. Ships were therefore to be conserved as much as possible for a long war. Action might eventually come, but only after a long wait, and the Italians would have to be ready for it. They could not have their ships immobilized for lengthy repairs because of excessive wear and tear incurred on operations of little use.[11] The precious battle fleet would be conserved at Taranto in case the Austrians would ever hazard their own capital ships, which were now largely inactive at Pola except for short voyages outside the harbor to the nearby Fasana Channel for sub-caliber shoots. Operations continued in the Adriatic, but they were now increasingly affairs of submarines and torpedo craft. It was hardly heroic, but it was perhaps realistic under the changed circumstances.

There was another flurry of activity accompanying the Austro-German offensive against Serbia following Bulgaria's entry into the war in September 1915. A combined German, Austrian, and Bulgarian offensive began in early October. Heavily outnumbered and virtually isolated, Serbia was eventually overwhelmed. The Bulgarian advance soon cut off a potential route for supplies to Serbia from Salonika, and the Allied expeditionary forces attempting to relieve the Serbians by moving up the Vardar valley were forced to fall back on Salonika, where they established what would become another front. There was also a tenuous and difficult route for Allied supplies to Serbia and Montenegro by means of primitive northern Albanian ports. These were vulnerable to Austrian forces operating at Cattaro, and Admiral Haus, after some arm-twisting from AOK—the Austrian military high command—deployed two light cruisers, the six Tátra-class destroyers, and six T-74 class torpedo boats accompanied by an oiler to the Gulf of Cattaro. These represented the bulk of the most modern and rapid light forces at his disposal. The Austrians executed a series of raids and sank a number of supply ships bound for Serbia and Montenegro. These operations culminated in the action of 29 December. The remnants of the Serbian army accompanied by large numbers of civilian refugees as well as Austrian prisoners made an arduous retreat through the mountains of Albania to the coast where the Allies were presented with the problem of sustaining them and eventually evacuating them. Haus, on reports from aerial reconnaissance that two Italian destroyers had brought troops to the Albanian port of Durazzo, ordered them to be attacked. An Austrian force under the command of Linienschiffskapitän Heinrich Seitz in the light cruiser *Helgoland* and five *Tátra*-class destroyers attempted to catch isolated Allied forces in the area between Brindisi and Durazzo. They surprised and sank a French submarine but failed to find any surface ships, and at dawn on the 28th four destroyers entered the port of Durazzo and sank a steamer along with a large and small schooner. Unfortunately, in leaving the harbor under the fire of shore batteries, two destroyers struck mines, sinking one and badly damaging another. It was taken under tow but under the pressure of the Allied pursuit had to be abandoned. The Allied light forces at Brindisi put to sea and attempted to intercept the Austrians. The Allies were between the Austrians and their bases with a superior force, but after a high-speed chase that at one point saw the Austrians come close to the Italian coast in an attempt to work around their pursuers, the onset of darkness permitted the Austrians to escape.[12] The Allies were dissatisfied that the Austrians had managed to escape with an inferior force, but Haus was even more furious at the loss of two of his precious handful of modern destroyers in return for relatively minor losses inflicted on the enemy. He sharply reprimanded Seitz, the commander of the Austrian naval force, and relieved him of his command.[13] Given the geographical situation and relative balance of forces, Haus realized the Austrians were probably lucky to have gotten away as lightly as they did. This may have influenced his actions during the subsequent evacuation of the Serbian army during the winter months of 1916.

The Austrian navy had an opportunity to attack this World War I version of a Dunkirk-style evacuation. They failed to exploit it.[14] Such efforts as the Austrian light forces made were frustrated by increased vigilance on the part of Allied screening forces, thereby ruining the element of surprise, bad weather, or mishaps. But if Allied light forces could counter their Austrian counterparts, would the intervention of the heavier ships of the Austrian navy have made a difference? The question is counterfactual. Haus, regarding the southern reaches of the Adriatic as a potential trap infested by potentially far superior Allied forces, chose not to risk his major assets.

The big ships were not completely idle. The older battleships and cruisers of the Fifth Division provided heavy artillery cover for the offensive by the XIX Austrian army corps, which succeeded in clearing Montenegrin forces from the heights of Mount Lovčen during 8–10 January 1916. The coast defense battleship *Budapest*, armored cruisers *Karl VI*, *Kaiser Franz Joseph I*, and small cruisers *Aspern* and *Panther* demonstrated that even ships no longer suitable for action on the high seas could still perform useful service under certain circumstances. Within a few days the Montenegrins requested an armistice and dropped out of the war. This was no minor success, for Montenegrin observers had up to then been able to report daylight movements of Austrian ships in the Bocche. The value of the latter as an Austrian base would subsequently be greatly enhanced, and Haus transferred the cruiser squadron from Sebenico to Cattaro. However, more than 160,000 Serbian troops had been permitted to escape, to be reformed to fight again another day. Furthermore, the Austrian army did not push on southward to capture the port of Valona. The loss of Valona would certainly have hindered Allied efforts to close the Strait of Otranto.

With the end of the Balkan campaign by early 1916, the war in the Adriatic, at least on the surface, seemed to settle down. A virtual stalemate prevailed. The Austrian fleet was effectively bottled up in its arm of the Mediterranean and the *k.u.k. Kriegsmarine* was a matter of concern largely for the neighboring Italians. But if the Austrian fleet was not going anywhere outside of the Adriatic, the Entente forces were not venturing inside with major warships. It was simply too dangerous in this relatively restricted geographical area. In March, Haus was able to deflect yet another demand by AOK for a "ruthless action" to accompany Chief of the General Staff Conrad von Hötzendorf's planned *Strafe* or punishment offensive against the Italians. Haus pointed out that the situation had changed considerably from the first day of the war with Italy, when the action of the entire *k.u.k.* fleet had been able to achieve surprise. One could not expect that to happen again. Haus pointed out that his fundamentally defensive strategy had been successful to date. Battleships should not be risked in an operation that could have no real military effect on the enemy. If the sole operational purpose was to damage the enemy, they could accomplish this with far less risk and cost through air raids.[15]

This does not mean there was no activity. The light craft, destroyers, torpedo boats, and submarines of all the navies were active, as were the air forces. There were sweeps and countersweeps, fleeting coastal bombardments, and efforts to ambush ships with submarines. The Austrians ran regular convoys down the Adriatic coast to supply their forces in Albania, sheltering behind the chain of islands on the eastern shore. The Allies, especially the French, attempted to interrupt this traffic with submarines. These actions can be learned of today by resorting to the multi-volume official and semi-official histories published in the inter-war period. This was to use the contemporary term *kleinkrieg*. New weapons and methods of warfare were evident. On 15 September 1916, two Lohner flying boats of the Austrian naval air service, flying from the naval air station at Kumbor in the Gulf of Cattaro, sank the French submarine *Foucault*, which had been reported approximately ten nautical miles southwest of the entrance to the gulf. This was reputedly the first success of aircraft against submarines.[16] In the duel between aircraft and submarines, the Italians claimed that the Austrians enjoyed a natural advantage. The waters of the Adriatic on the eastern or Austrian shore were supposedly relatively clear, allowing the discovery of submarines even when submerged. The waters of the Italian shore were far more opaque.

The Italian navy also developed a weapon well-suited to Adriatic conditions. These were the *Mas* boats, the term coming from *motobarca armata silurante*. The latter was the version optimized for torpedo warfare, while the antisubmarine version was *motobarca anti-sommergibilile*. These were small (approximately sixteen meters) wooden craft powered by gasoline engines, and the early models were capable of a speed of 22–25 knots. They had a crew of eight and could be fitted with two torpedoes. Their relatively small size and short range (approximately 123 nautical miles) made them less suited for the rough waters of the open sea, but in the narrow confines of the Adriatic they were in their element. The Italian navy had ordered the first group in April of 1915. More than a year later they had their first notable success when on the night of 7 June 1916 two *Mas* boats penetrated Durazzo harbor and torpedoed and sank an Austrian steamer. In order to save fuel, they had been towed to the Albanian coast by a pair of torpedo boats escorted by French destroyers. On 25 June, acting on aerial reconnaissance reports of two steamers at Durazzo, the *Mas* boats returned for another raid, escorted this time by an Italian scout cruiser and an Italian destroyer. They again succeeded in sinking an Austrian steamer although the ship was later salved.[17] Here was an example of new techniques and weapons—aerial reconnaissance and *Mas* boats—acting in combination. The Adriatic was an unhealthy place for large surface ships.

The Austrian navy in 1916 periodically gave the Allies a sharp reminder of its existence. On the night of 31 May–1 June the destroyers *Balaton* and *Orjen* and three torpedo boats supported by the light cruiser *Helgoland* raided the line of drifter patrols in the Strait of Otranto, sinking one. Linienschiffskapitän Nikolaus (Miklós in Hungarian accounts) Horthy, in the light cruiser *Novara*, raided the patrol line again on the night of 9 July, sinking two and damaging another two. Horthy was establishing his reputation as an ambitious and aggressive commander. A third raid on the night of 22 December by six older *Huszár*-class destroyers was thwarted by the timely arrival of six French destroyers that had been escorting transports in the vicinity.

That the seaward flank of the army in the upper Adriatic had to be protected, given the relative proximity of the major Austrian base at Pola, meant that the Italians had to maintain fairly strong forces at Venice. In 1916 and on into the winter of 1917, these included the three old battleships *Saint Bon, Fili-*

berto, and *Sardegna*, a squadriglia of five large destroyers, another squadriglia of smaller *Carabiniere*-class destroyers, and a large flotilla of coastal torpedo boats as well as some high-seas torpedo boats equipped for minesweeping. They were backed by a flotilla of fifteen Italian submarines, three suitable only for coastal service. There were also a number of British submarines at Venice, initially old *B*-class boats of declining value.[18] While the exact composition of the Italian forces naturally varied, they were separated from the forces in the Otranto Straits by the length of the Adriatic and even further from the major Italian battle fleet at Taranto. In addition, as the submarine war grew in importance, they represented light craft that were badly needed on the shipping lanes in the Mediterranean.

However important the Adriatic was to those mostly concerned, the Italians who had the enemy fleet on their doorstep, it was more of a backdrop or starting point for the truly important naval event following the Dardanelles and Balkan campaigns of 1915–1916. This was the submarine campaign. The Mediterranean U-boat flotilla grew steadily and German submarine operations in the Mediterranean enjoyed spectacular success. There were a number of reasons for this. The area was rich in targets, and the mixture of nationalities — British, French, and Italian — and lack of unified command hampered efforts to counter the submarines, as did the Allied agreement at Malta in March 1916 to divide the Mediterranean into a number of different national zones. The Allies did not introduce convoys until the late spring of 1917 and their alternate methods, such as patrolled routes, were ineffective. Moreover it was only the British who had anything even approaching adequate numbers of small craft suitable for escort or anti-submarine work. The French and Italians were far behind. The weather was better in the Mediterranean than in the Atlantic or in the North Sea, which gave the submarines a larger opportunity to work. The Mediterranean also offered another advantage to the Germans. They were less likely to encounter American ships in this region and thus had fewer inhibitions about pursuing the submarine campaign with greater vigor.

The Mediterranean in 1916 was the scene of the most successful submarine cruise of the war. On the cruise from 26 July to 20 August, Kapitänleutnant Lothar von Arnauld de la Perière in *U.35* sank in the western Mediterranean a total of fifty-four steamers and sailing craft, a total of 90,150 tons. On his preceding cruise from 6 June to 3 July he had accounted for forty ships or 56,818 tons. It is small wonder that by August the total tonnage sunk by Mediterranean submarines during the war exceeded one million tons. The number of submarines available to the Mediterranean U-boat flotilla as of late October 1916 included ten large submarines (including one in the Black Sea and four on their way from the north); two large minelaying submarines; and five *UB.II*-class, one *UB.I*-class, and eight *UC*-class minelayers.[19]

In January 1917 the German government succumbed to pressure from the military and the navy and took the momentous and ultimately fatal step of agreeing to the resumption of unrestricted submarine warfare. Their Austrian allies were hesitant with the exception of Haus, who was among the strongest supporters in the Dual Monarchy of the principle of unrestricted submarine warfare. Haus, with a navy far smaller than that of the Germans and with the odds far more heavily against him in surface warships, looked to submarines as possibly the only hope for victory for the Central Powers. The Austro-Hungarian government eventually reluctantly agreed with the general sentiment that if the war had to continue there was probably nothing else that could be done. A meeting between Kaiser Karl and the German high command to settle the details of the question took place at Schloss Pless on 26 January. Haus and his chief of staff were with the Kaiser, and Haus promised all possible support to German submarines operating from Austrian bases, even to the point of taking old warships out of service to provide workers for refitting the U-boats. This initially involved the old armored cruiser *Kaiserin und Königin Maria Theresia* and the torpedo cruiser *Panther*, but Haus promised other old ships would be taken out of service when the submarine war required it. The Austrians also promised that their own submarines would act against Allied shipping outside of the Adriatic, notably on the transport route between Malta and Cerigo.[20]

The Schloss Pless conference may have had at least some effect on the subsequent action in the Otranto Straits. On the return journey in bitter cold winter weather on unheated railway trains, Haus apparently caught pneumonia and died aboard his flagship at Pola on 8 February. He had been a truly commanding presence in the *k.u.k. Kriegsmarine*, its first and only *Grossadmiral*. His successor, Vice Admiral Maximilian Njegovan, intended to follow Haus's essentially defensive policy, but Njegovan lacked Haus's great authority, and one suspects there was now more scope for offensive raids and greater risks.[21] Horthy would profit from this in coming months.

April 1917 proved to be the record month for sinking ships by German and Austrian submarines. The total would never be repeated, largely because the Allies were driven to introduce the convoy system. In April, German submarines throughout the world sank a total of 860,334 tons, of which 254,911 tons (3,724 tons by submarine-laid mines) could be credited to the U-boat flotilla in the Mediterranean. The same month Austrian submarines sank 23,037 tons, a far smaller contribution but reflective of the fact that as of 2 April there were only two Austrian submarines operating at sea in the Mediterranean compared to fourteen German U-boats, including one *en route* from northern waters.[22] Although Njegovan urged that construction of Austrian submarines be hastened as much as possible, it was obvious that the great majority of submarines operating in the Mediterranean would be German. However, whether the submarines were Austrian or German or whether they operated out of Cat-

taro or Pola, they all had one thing in common. The geographical configuration of the Adriatic forced them to pass through the Otranto Straits in order to
reach the Allied shipping lanes in the Mediterranean. Those straits consequently were a choke point, and this had been recognized by the Allies early
in the war. Consequently, from mid-1915 they had been grappling with the
problem of how to prevent submarines from passing through them. There
were destined to be numerous schemes during the war, and none of them
would be successful. However, for obvious reasons the Italian port of Brindisi
in the southern Adriatic would, because of its strategic location, assume considerable importance for the Allies by 1917, and in waters near the Strait of
Otranto a heterogeneous collection of Italian, British, and French warships
would be assembled with all the difficulties and complications that command
and control of a multi-national force of this type implied.

CHAPTER TWO

THE ALLIES IN THE
SOUTHERN ADRIATIC

B Y THE SPRING of 1917 the waters of the southern Adriatic and Ionian Sea were home to many diverse Italian, British, and French warships. The command arrangements were equally complex and, unfortunately, sometimes acrimonious, and Allied dispositions were sometimes made according to diplomatic or political considerations rather than strategic necessities. Many thought this was a waste of resources. Moreover, while the Allies enjoyed unquestioned superiority in large warships, they did not always have superiority in light craft, which were not always as strong as desired at the critical place and time.

After the Italian government committed itself to joining the war in the Treaty of London, signed 26 April 1915, a conference took place in Paris to settle the details of naval cooperation among the Allies. The conference was the scene of some hard bargaining. The Italian naval staff did not consider Italy's numerical advantage over the Austrians to be adequate. True, the Italian fleet was superior on paper, but it was not greatly superior, and the Italians demanded reinforcement. Furthermore, in the back of the minds of those on the Italian naval staff—the *Stato maggiore*—there was the belief that with the opposing Austrian fleet almost on their doorstep a few hours' steaming distance away in Pola, it was almost inevitable that should the Austrians come out in force to fight, the Italian fleet would bear the brunt of the battle and any possible losses. Even a victory might leave the Italian fleet weakened vis-à-vis the other combatants and, consequently, Italy's position in a post-war Mediterranean world would be correspondingly diminished.[1] One might have thought this was putting the cart before the horse and that the first objective was to win the war at hand, but one must remember that before the war Italy's rivalry with France in the Mediterranean had been almost as strong as her traditional rivalry with Austria-Hungary, and right up to the moment the Italian government declared its neutrality at the beginning of the war there was every expectation in the Italian navy that they would be fighting against the French.

On the French side in the years just before the war, a possible encounter with the Italian navy had been paramount in the minds of the French naval staff, and the Anglo-French entente of 1904 had the effect in subsequent years of reinforcing the idea that the British would bear the burden of the war in the north against the Germans while the French would assume the guard of the Mediterranean against not only Germany but also Germany's allies in the Triple Alliance, Austria-Hungary and Italy. The minds of the naval staffs in France and Italy did not change immediately, and mutual suspicions remained strong.

There was another consideration. The Adriatic itself was the scene of historic Italian ambitions. The Italians remembered the far-flung empire of Venice and in the period just before the war had come to focus their ambitions on Albania. This meant that the Italians were sensitive about activity by non-Italian warships in the Adriatic—their sea—and were adamant that if anyone was going to command in the Adriatic it was going to be an Italian admiral. In these circumstances inter-Allied relations at the entrance to the Adriatic were bound to be sensitive.[2]

The Italo-French-British naval convention of 10 May 1915 satisfied—at least on paper—the major Italian points. The commander in chief of the Italian fleet would have the initiative and complete direction of operations carried out in the Adriatic by a "First Allied Fleet,"[3] which would consist of the Italian fleet reinforced by twelve French destroyers plus as many torpedo boats, minesweepers, and submarines as the French commander in chief could spare and, if possible, a squadron of aircraft and a seaplane carrier. A codicil to the treaty specified that half the French destroyers should be oil-burning and, if possible, more than 600 tons in displacement. In addition, the French submarines should number at least six. The British obligation was to send a division of four battleships plus four light cruisers, the latter to arrive as soon as they could be replaced by four French cruisers off the Dardanelles, where the Allied campaign was taking place. The French had agreed to increase their battleship contribution to the Dardanelles campaign, thereby freeing the British ships to leave for Italian waters as soon as the French arrived.

There would also be a "Second Allied Fleet," to be formed from the French battleships and cruisers, destroyer and torpedo boat flotillas, plus any Italian or British warships not already under the command of the Italian commander in chief. This was a hypothetical force, to come into being only if the "First

Allied Fleet" was obligated to proceed to the northern Adriatic for an important operation involving all Allied forces. It would be in theory under the command of the French commander in chief and would be ready to respond to
the appeal of the Italian commander in chief. The question of who would
then command this combined force was not answered and never would be.
The French fleet was potentially larger than the Italian fleet, and the French
commander in chief was, by virtue of an Anglo-French treaty concluded in
August 1914, theoretically commander in chief in the Mediterranean, although British operations off the Dardanelles escaped his direct control.
Command arrangements in the Mediterranean were complicated, and inclu-
sion of the Adriatic would make them even more complicated. It would be naive, however, to think that the French commander in chief would ever have
submitted to an Italian commander in chief in the Adriatic or that the Italians
would ever willingly accept a French commander in chief in the Adriatic.

Article V of the naval convention placed all bases on the Italian coast at the
disposition of the Allies. The "First Allied Fleet" would have Brindisi as a
base, and it was recommended that the "Second Allied Fleet" make use of
Taranto, Malta, or Bizerte. However, should the "First Allied Fleet" move
north to use Venice as a base, the "Second Allied Fleet" might follow it to
Brindisi. In actual fact, as the war progressed, the French battle fleet established itself first at Argostoli on the island of Cephalonia, and eventually and
for the duration of the war at Corfu. The British and French also pledged
themselves in Article VI to provide, as far as possible, enough naval support
to the Italian fleet to assure that Allied naval power was clearly superior to the
enemy. There is a good deal of the purely hypothetical in this, for as the war
went on the prospect that squadrons of large warships would move to the
northern Adriatic for an encounter with their Austrian counterparts became
increasingly remote. The question of command in this case was also less of a
problem for the British. Their major naval interests were elsewhere and their
attitude toward the Adriatic was to limit their commitment as much as possible. This tended to make Anglo-Italian relations easier than Franco-Italian relations, unless of course the Italians asked for reinforcements from northern
waters. That was another story.

The division of British battleships that first arrived under the command of
Rear Admiral Cecil Thursby reflected this low priority. They were all—
Queen, London, Implacable, and *Prince of Wales*—pre-dreadnoughts and two,
London and *Implacable,* had a long list of severe defects. *Implacable* and *London* had been launched in 1899, *Queen* and *Prince of Wales* in 1902. Thursby
admitted that the ships in his division were badly in want of a refit. *London*
had not had one in two years. In addition, *Implacable* needed new econo-
mizer tubes.[4] With the irreverence of the young, a midshipman wrote in his
diary: "What their [the Italians'] feelings must have been when this antedilu-

vian quartette [Thursby's squadron] was fobbed off on them can well be imagined."[5] As time went on the British battleships became increasingly redundant and by the winter of 1917 all except *Queen* had left Taranto. By then she was no longer a functioning warship. From December 1916 to February 1917 she had been re-fitted to serve as a depot ship for the anti-submarine barrage patrols, with her six-inch secondary armament removed and only a care and maintenance party aboard. In May 1917 HMS *Queen* had the grand title "Flagship, British Naval Forces" but little else.[6]

The British cruisers that joined the Italians had also already seen hard work. The light cruiser *Dublin* was in good condition, but the light cruiser *Dartmouth* had two boilers out of action, greatly reducing her speed. *Amethyst*, subsequently joined by her sister ship *Sapphire*, was old and comparatively slow — too slow, Thursby pointed out, to outrun the Austrian armored cruiser *Sankt Georg*, which was reported to be at Cattaro.[7] Unfortunately the best ship, *Dublin*, was torpedoed by the Austrian submarine *U.4* on 9 June and, although not sunk, was put out of action. *Dublin* was eventually replaced by the light cruiser *Weymouth*, and the last of the "Gem" class left for good in 1916, replaced by the faster and more capable *Bristol* and *Gloucester*. However, the number of British cruisers remained at four although there were unsuccessful attempts by the Italians to increase their quantity and quality. This type of warship had proved its value in the major theater of the war in the North Sea or at times hunting German raiders on the high seas. A greater number simply could not be spared for the Adriatic.

The command arrangements in the Adriatic were a bit convoluted. All operations in the southern Adriatic were initiated and directed by the commander in chief of the Italian fleet at Taranto. Until February 1917 this was the Duke of the Abruzzi, an officer generally respected and liked by most of his foreign allies. The necessary orders were then given by the Italian commander in chief to the Italian admirals in the Adriatic. Thursby met with the Duke daily and the Duke informed Thursby of what he proposed to do with the British ships and asked if Thursby concurred. The necessary orders were then given to the British ships by the Italian admirals under whom they were serving, but Thursby emphasized that he held the British senior naval officer responsible for seeing that the ships were fit for service, that he understood the orders, and that he considered them reasonable and safe. If he did not, he was not to execute them without reference to Thursby. There was also a French liaison officer at Taranto who met with the Duke daily and kept in contact with both the French commander in chief at Corfu and the French *chef de division* at Brindisi. At sea, forces were to obey the orders of the senior naval officer present. The French *chef de division* and the senior British naval officer at Brindisi naturally attended the local Italian flag officer's meetings.[8] Thursby though made it clear that there was a potential British veto over the orders of

. the local Italian admiral if they were deemed unreasonable or unsafe. The question inevitably arose: How could the possibility of an appeal to a distant Thursby at Taranto be reconciled with the possible need for immediate action in a rapidly developing situation?

The command arrangements, not surprisingly, did not work out well in the long run. Thursby's successor in 1916, Rear Admiral Mark Kerr, was frustrated at having "no executive work or command to do." The British cruisers, submarines, and drifters were all under various Italian admirals and he could "only ask for things that I know I won't get and point out methods which I know won't be carried out."[9] Abruzzi at Taranto invariably accepted Kerr's advice, but it was not always carried out by the Italian commander in chief at Brindisi. Increasingly annoyed, Kerr finally managed by September 1916 to have the drifter base moved to Taranto, where they would work under his direction. Kerr also managed to obtain the use of the old "Gem" class cruiser *Topaze*. Although by this date too slow to work with the cruisers at Brindisi, the ship served admirably as an admiral's yacht and allowed Kerr to run up and down the line of drifters on tours of inspection without having to rely on an Italian destroyer. This was fortunate, for in the autumn of 1916 Italian destroyers and torpedo boats were almost exclusively employed in escorting transports to either Salonika or ports on the Albanian coast. However, in March 1917 the *Topaze* was needed in other areas, notably the Red Sea, and left Taranto, curtailing Kerr's mobility.[10]

The French also had trouble maintaining their commitments to the Italians. They were obligated to provide a dozen destroyers, but the French navy was also deficient in this type of warship. The French in the years immediately before the outbreak of the war had made a strong effort to achieve superiority in capital ships over a potential Austro-Italian combination in the Mediterranean, but the construction of fast light ships in the French program had been deferred to a later period. The war intervened and the French navy found itself without any of the fast light cruisers that were proving so useful elsewhere. There were also too few reliable modern destroyers. In the first month of the war Vice Amiral Boué de Lapeyrère, the French commander in chief at the time, complained that even his new 850-ton destroyers were not reliable, suitable for parades but not as warships.[11] The dozen French destroyers that did go to Brindisi were designated the "Division Française de l'Adriatique" and were divided into two escadrilles. They were the 850-ton *Bisson* class, 800-ton *Bouclier* class, and smaller c.530-ton *Spahi* class, completed in the years 1909 to 1914. They were probably the best the French had, generally regarded as efficient and hard-working but subject to being periodically withdrawn either in whole or part for other emergencies such as the transfer of the French expeditionary force to Salonika in the autumn of 1915 or the transport of the remnant of the Serbian army from Corfu to Salonika in the spring of 1916.

The six French submarines at Brindisi were members of the numerous *"Pluviôse"* class, completed from 1908 to 1911 and generally regarded as good sea boats but hampered by their steam propulsion, which reduced the speed at which they could submerge. The old battleship *Marceau* served as depot ship for the French submarines at Brindisi.[12] The submarines worked to the best of their abilities, suffering some loss and achieving some success. But like the old British *"B"*-class submarines to the north in Venice (finally recalled in October 1916), their opportunities under unfavorable circumstances were few and fleeting. The *Bernouilli* torpedoed the *Csepel* off Cattaro on 4 May 1916, destroying the stern of the destroyer, which, however, survived. This was more than offset by the loss of the *Foucault* to aircraft the following September. The operations of French submarines were not likely to be decisive.

Franco-Italian relations at Brindisi were particularly bad. The *chef de division* of the French flotillas in the Adriatic for most of 1916 was Capitaine de vaisseau Henri de Cacqueray, a particularly strong-willed officer who simply could not get along with his Italian allies and apparently did not conceal his disdain for them. He was finally transferred to another command in November by a reluctant French minister of marine. De Cacqueray's successor, Capitaine de frégate (quickly promoted to Capitaine de vaisseau) Joseph Frochot, proved more amenable.[13] On a larger scale, the problem of a possible reinforcement of the Italian fleet by a division of French semi-dreadnought battleships of the *"Danton"* class remained unsolved, the subject of fruitless talks throughout 1916. Before leaving his Adriatic command in May, Thursby lamented, "The French and Italian fleets should be fully capable of dealing with the Austrian fleet but it is a great waste of strength to employ them as separate units. There are not sufficient cruisers and T.B.D.'s [destroyers] to serve two fleets and undoubtedly if they combine many of the older battleships could either be paid off or used elsewhere."[14]

The question of who would have first call on the services of the French destroyers at Brindisi in case the French commander in chief at Corfu required them for his own fleet in the event of an Austrian sortie also remained unanswered. It was, perhaps, fortunate that the subject was becoming more and more of a theoretical question, as the possibility that the Austrian fleet would come out seeking a decision in the southern Adriatic became increasingly remote. By the spring of 1917 the Allies had more pressing problems to worry about, notably the unrestricted submarine campaign.

The French fleet at Corfu was by itself more than equal to the Austrian fleet. Its core consisted of the 340mm [13.4-inch] gunned dreadnoughts *Provence*, *Lorraine*, and *Bretagne* and the twelve-inch gunned dreadnoughts *Courbet*, *Jean Bart*, *France*, and *Paris*. With neat symmetry, this matched the four *Tegetthoffs* and three semi-dreadnought *Radetzkys* at Pola. However, the French also had the five surviving semi-dreadnought *Danton*-class ships, at the very least comparable to the *Radetzkys*, as well as the five pre-dreadnought *Patrie*-class ships, although some of the latter had been detached for the Aegean. The French could also call on the services of five or six large armored cruisers, although not all of these ships would be available all the time. There were for example detachments caused by interventions in Greek affairs and of course ships were periodically absent for dockyard refits. These movements now involved danger. The battleship *Danton* was torpedoed and sunk on 19 March 1917 approximately thirty miles south of Sardinia while returning from a refit in Toulon. Nevertheless, even allowing for the numbers of older battleships and cruisers on detached service in the Levant, the odds against any Austrian sortie by the Austrian heavy ships were great. Ironically, it was in light ships and flotilla craft that the French were comparatively weak. There was nothing to match the Austrian *Novaras*, and it was also problematic how many destroyers the French commander in chief would be able to gather if he were to take his battle fleet to sea. The French commander in chief since December 1916 was Vice Amiral M. Gauchet who, while theoretical commander in chief in the Mediterranean, was increasingly reduced to a superfluous role. The big French ships remained largely inactive at Corfu throughout 1917. Gauchet seemed preoccupied with trying to keep his men trained for an encounter with the Austrian fleet, one destined never to come, while the submarine war grew in intensity and the British steadily assumed or were forced to assume its direction. The French also felt the inexorably increasing demands for men to man patrol craft to combat the submarine menace, and in 1917 they would be forced to put ships in reserve to economize on manpower. This included two old battleships in April to be followed by two large armored cruisers in August.[15]

Brindisi was the sole port on the Italian Adriatic coast south of Venice suitable for a base. The fast flotilla craft and light cruisers of the Italian navy were usually stationed here, although some were often deployed to Valona. The five Italian dreadnoughts—*Dante Alighieri, Conte di Cavour, Giulio Cesare, Andrea Doria,* and *Duilio*—remained in Taranto, less and less likely to play any important part in the war.[16] The Italian second division, the four fast light battleships of the *Regina Elena* class (*Regina Elena, Napoli, Roma,* and *Vittorio Emanuele*), were more like battle cruisers than true battleships, with their primary armament of only two twelve-inch guns. They alternated, although not necessarily as a complete division, between Taranto, Brindisi, and Valona. The same was also true for the three large armored cruisers (*Pisa, San Giorgio,* and *San Marco*) of the third division.

In May 1917 the senior naval officer at Brindisi and commander of the "Divisione Esploratori" was Contrammiraglio Alfredo Acton. The division consisted of the three *esploratori* or scout cruisers *Quarto* (c.3,400 tons) and the slightly larger (c.4,000 tons) *Nino Bixio* and *Marsala*. The ships, completed in 1913 and 1914, were the Italian counterparts to the Austrian *Novaras,* and

Quarto was judged by one naval historian to have been the most successful ship in the Italian navy, the other two not having attained their planned speed.[17] The numbers of Italian and French destroyers varied because of the frequent detachments for special purposes and the growing demands of the submarine war. The Italians aimed to have three squadriglie of three units each with one always ready for sea, another at a half hour's notice, and the other at six hours' notice. By the spring of 1917 they had received the important reinforcement of three *"esploratori minori"*—*Racchia, Aquila,* and *Mirabello.* These roughly 1,700–2,000-ton ships were larger and more powerfully armed than most destroyers, and they were extremely fast. *Aquila* had originally been one of a class of four ordered by the Rumanian government and taken over by the Italian navy after Italy entered the war. She was designed for 36.5 knots, and the class was considered the fastest in the Italian navy.[18] The Italians also planned to establish a flotilla of smaller torpedo craft at Brindisi consisting of four squadriglie of four ships each of coastal torpedo boats and two squadriglie of five units each of high-seas torpedo boats. These had not been fully formed by mid-May 1917. They were to work off Brindisi, either hunting submarines or furnishing the more than seven escorts per week required for traffic between Brindisi and Valona or Santi Quaranta in Albania.[19]

A substantial share of Italian naval resources were still committed to Venice, where support for the army remained a priority. Besides the three old *Saint Bons*, there was a squadriglia of three *Poerio*-class *esploratori* and two *Nullo*-class large destroyers, a squadriglia of *Carabiniere*-class 400-ton destroyers, and a large number of coastal torpedo boats. The Italians decided they needed the modern *Poerios* and *Nullos* more in the southern Adriatic and intended to replace them with a squadriglia of four smaller and older *Ardito*-class destroyers deployed from the south. However, the ships were retained in Venice temporarily because of the impending resumption of an offensive by the Italian army. Venice was also the base of the majority of Italian submarines, approximately sixteen to seventeen, reinforced by two British *H*-class ships.[20]

The most numerous British contribution to the Adriatic campaign by the spring of 1917 did not consist of purpose-built warships. It instead consisted of the motley collection of drifters and trawlers—the majority former fishing craft—that were employed to establish a barrage in the Strait of Otranto. The idea was apparently first broached by the then First Lord of the Admiralty Winston Churchill at the May 1915 conference in Paris leading to the naval convention on the eve of Italy's entry into the war. At the time Churchill grandly offered fifty trawlers and fifty miles of submarine indicator nets if the Italians would arm and man them. The Italians were not enthusiastic, since arming and manning them would have presented difficulties. British trawlers therefore joined the Dardanelles campaign and proved their worth. In the meantime the Italians learned the harsh realities of the submarine war.

Henceforth there could never be too many small craft of the drifter type. They now fulfilled a multitude of duties such as patrols, escorts, submarine hunting, and minesweeping. Unfortunately the Italians did not have them in sufficient numbers. With the submarine war in the Mediterranean developing as more German U-boats arrived, and with the apparent inability of the Italian navy to prevent those submarines from passing freely through the Otranto Straits, the Admiralty decided to act on its own. On 30 August 1915, it issued orders to various naval bases in the British Isles to make preparations for sixty drifters to leave for the Adriatic as soon as possible.[21] Commander J. O. Hatcher, who was appointed to command them, had once been in the merchant service and had entered the navy through the supplementary list. He had been at the trawler base at Grimsby where he was described as having "by sheer personality, unlimited energy, and driving force . . . managed to extract order out of chaos and defeat any obstructionist."[22] Lieutenant Commander M. E. Cochrane, the second in command, had retired from the navy a decade before the war, and the young divisional officers of the drifters were from the Royal Naval Reserve. The men were for the most part fishermen, and life in the drifters would be far different than life in a regular Royal Navy warship. Cochrane later recalled his first impression before departure to the well-known naval author E. Keble Chatterton: "As to the fisherman crew, one glance sufficiently showed that this was a funny war anyway. No naval officer expected driftermen to be all smartness and spotless in their uniforms, but collectively the [drifter] *Remembrance*'s crew presented a severe shock to their new captain." Cochrane elaborated: there was a skipper who was "distinctly oiled," a sixty-year-old mate wearing a bowler hat, and a "blind drunk" cook in his bunk. Nevertheless the drifters would "within a few short weeks . . . improve beyond all recognition." Regardless of the driftermen's raffish appearance, "[t]he human material was of the best . . . it needed only a period of polishing before it would shine with exceptional lustre."[23]

The first group arrived at Taranto on 22 September to an apparently startled Thursby, who complained, "You can imagine my surprise when suddenly 60 drifters were dumped on me with no organisation, provisions, stores or anything else."[24] Thursby told off so many to each British battleship and as soon as they were ready sent two divisions out to lay nets. The Italians lent a merchant ship, the *Gallipoli* of the Puglia line, to be their parent ship at Brindisi and provided a second ship, the *Adriatico*, in November. The drifters were organized into three divisions with two out with their nets and one in port at Brindisi. Two drifters from each division were normally to be at a subsidiary base at Taranto for docking, boiler cleaning, and repairs. Cochrane also enjoyed the use of a small auxiliary steamer provided by the Italians. The ship was armed with three six-pounders, named the *Mazzini*, and used to inspect the drifters, provide water, deliver mail, and see if the drifters were in the correct positions.[25] The drifters had been sent out unarmed and Thursby had to scramble to make up the deficiencies. By 17 October about twenty were armed, and Thursby hoped to complete the process in a week. He was a bit over-optimistic; the arming was not completed until 8 November. The guns were mostly Italian 57mm and 47mm with some British three-pounders.[26] It was fortunate that the process was completed when it was, for the drifters were extremely vulnerable, and one, the *Restore*, armed only with five rifles, was sunk by the deck gun of the German *U.39* approximately twenty miles southwest of Saseno Island on 12 October.[27] The submarine had been returning to Cattaro.

The idea that the drifters would tangle submarines in their nets in the straits was the sort of thing that was easier on paper than in practice. Thursby quickly discovered the problems: "I am afraid I haven't half enough drifters. The ones out last week reported seeing several submarines but all 2 or 3 miles away. It is a big place to watch & we want more depth to our screen."[28] The area the drifters usually worked lay between the parallels 39° 55′ N and 40° 30′ N, which represented a width of forty-five to seventy miles. The weather worsened as winter approached. The boats frequently had to take shelter and nets were often lost. At other times nets were slipped in order to pursue suspected submarines. The unfamiliar currents in the Adriatic also made it difficult for the drifters to maintain station. The extinguishing of normal lights under wartime conditions added to the problem. Thursby thought they needed forty boats out at a time, and in order to do this, counting repairs and refitting, they would need eighty drifters on station. However, his requests to the Admiralty for more drifters were refused until 15 November, when the Admiralty ordered the dispatch of an additional forty, the first of which began to arrive at Taranto on 7 December. The drifters achieved no success against submarines and despite their light armament remained vulnerable. On 18–19 December the *Lottie Leask,* armed with a three-pounder, was sunk by a submarine (probably the German *U.39*) twenty miles west-northwest of Saseno.[29]

During the winter months of 1916 the drifters were largely taken up with the evacuation of the Serbian army. The drifters played an important role in securing movements or ferrying troops from primitive Albanian ports out to larger steamers. At least two were lost to mines. Thursby reported, "They have rendered magnificent service and are full of enthusiasm" and that Hatcher and Cochrane had certainly organized and run the drifters "in a most efficient manner."[30] However, when the evacuation was completed and the drifters resumed submarine hunting in force, success once again eluded them. In April, Thursby asked the Admiralty for an additional forty to fifty drifters plus forty or more motor launches. He justified the request by pointing out the constant work performed by the drifters since their arrival the preceding September and the extensive area they were patrolling. This extended eighty miles from Brindisi and was forty miles wide at the narrowest point. The strain and wear and tear was beginning to tell and as of mid-March eight drifters had been lost, mostly to mines. The Admiralty, however, found after considerable discussion that they could not spare more than ten from home waters.[31] Unfortunately, in May it was necessary to detach twenty-four drifters to help cover the transfer of the Serbian army from Corfu to Salonika and again Thursby recognized that "the Otranto patrol is practically useless at present."[32]

In the latter part of May 1916, Thursby left the Adriatic to become commander in chief of the Eastern Mediterranean Squadron in the Aegean. His successor was Rear Admiral Mark Kerr, one of the most interesting though controversial admirals in the Royal Navy. He was extremely air-minded and was the first flag officer to qualify as a pilot. He had been head of the naval mission in Greece at the outbreak of the war and was and would remain a strong partisan of King Constantine of Greece, an unpopular stance since the King was considered pro-German or at best neutral and was eventually forced into exile by the Allies in 1917.[33] Kerr's royalist sentiments led one British admiral to sarcastically remark on news of his appointment to the Adriatic, "How happy he will be hobnobbing with the Duc d'Abruzzi."[34] The commander in chief of the Italian fleet at Taranto was a cousin of the King of Italy.

Characteristically, Kerr soon advocated an air raid on the torpedo factory at Fiume by seaplanes carried to within striking distance by cruisers or other ships with a submarine ambush prepared in advance should the Austrians come out. He believed the factory at Fiume was the only torpedo factory in Austria and its destruction would "cramp the future movements of the submarines based on the Adriatic." The plan had the support of the Duke of the Abruzzi but, unfortunately, Kerr could not obtain the forty or fifty seaplanes deemed necessary. Kerr also wanted four British destroyers and either two E-class or four smaller H-class submarines to set an example for the Italians and enable the British to do more aggressive patrolling.[35] Above all, Kerr wanted more drifters. At that time there were not enough to cover the distance and the ones they had were overworked—ten days at sea and two days in harbor— and could not keep as good a lookout as necessary or be maintained in an efficient state. Furthermore, they were extremely vulnerable, as the loss of another drifter to an Austrian raid by the destroyers *Orjen*, *Balaton*, and three torpedo boats on the night of 31 May–1 June seemed to demonstrate. Kerr believed "[t]hey have practically no protection and if they do get a few submarines I expect they will be raided and unless protected they can be wiped out any day or night." He felt handicapped by having to rely on French or Italian assistance for destroyers, submarines, and light cruisers. This was the reason he was so anxious to obtain the four British destroyers as well as submarines to establish two lines of drifters with destroyers on each side of them and submarines to the north. He believed his Allies, both French and Italian, "don't understand keeping a patrol running if there is no excitement."[36]

Kerr was indeed an air-minded admiral, and his suggestions for using aircraft in a strategic manner—to hamper the Austrian ability to carry on submarine warfare by destroying their torpedo-making capacity—were in some respects farsighted. Unfortunately, his intelligence on Austria-Hungary does not appear to have been very good. Within a few days after the outbreak of war with Italy, the Austrians began transferring the manufacturing capacities of the Whitehead factory to St. Pölten, far inland and safe from air attack.[37] Moreover, the Germans who carried on the great portion of the submarine war would have been able to receive their torpedoes by rail directly from Germany and would have been unaffected by Kerr's proposed action.

Kerr had been a quick convert to the idea of an Otranto barrage. Within a month of his arrival he wrote in a private letter to the First Sea Lord: "The Mediterranean seems to me to be an artery of trade which has been cut & will, if not tied up, bleed us to death. All the S.M.s come in & out of Cattaro. We hear them everyday by the Telefunken direction stations near here. An Austrian plane flies over the drifters & reports where they are, & as the water is deep & the gaps large they dive and dodge us with impunity."[38] The requested reinforcements for Otranto, however, came only in a trickle. In mid-September, instead of the desired 150 drifters there were only 96.

The Adriatic received other reinforcements, namely twelve motor launches supported by an armed steam yacht, the *Catania*. The latter, commanded by the Duke of Sutherland, had been fitted with a workshop to serve as parent ship for the launches, initially in Egypt and now Italy. The motor launches, designated by "ML" numbers rather than by name, were seventy-five to eighty-foot wooden-hulled boats powered by gasoline engines. They were manufactured by the Elco Company of the United States, assembled in Montreal, and employed on a wide range of duties, especially anti-submarine work and inshore minesweeping. They were based at Gallipoli, a small port forty-five miles southeast of Taranto with a sub-base at Tricase. Tricase was extremely primitive but was located on the Adriatic coast at the Otranto Straits. The use of the motor launches was likely to be limited by bad weather, and their gray paint and small size made them difficult to see and also presented the danger they might be mistaken for submarines. Consequently, they eventually had white diagonal lines painted on their hulls to avoid incidents. Unfortunately, this method of making the MLs more visible to Italian patrols also had the effect of making them more visible to submarines. The MLs' gasoline engines also represented a distinct fire hazard.[39]

The exact area that the drifters worked was naturally subject to variation and partly dependent on enemy activity and the Allied resources available to protect them. During the summer of 1916 this protection was steadily reduced. Submarines made life difficult for the Allied patrols during daylight hours. On 23 June an Italian auxiliary cruiser, the converted liner *Città di Messina*, was torpedoed and sunk approximately twenty miles east of Otranto by the Austrian submarine *U.15.* The Italian cruiser had been in company with the French destroyer *Fourche,* which promptly launched a depth charge attack on the submarine. The attack seemed to produce results. An oil slick appeared and the destroyer's captain assumed the submarine had been sunk and stopped to rescue survivors. It was a fatal mistake. The submarine was very much alive and the *Fourche* was cut in two by a torpedo, sinking in less than a minute with the loss of nineteen men. The Italians then stopped using cruisers during daylight hours and left protection of the drifter line to a section of destroyers. This did not save the drifters early in the morning of 9 July when Horthy in the *Novara* raided the line west of Saseno, sinking *Astrum Spei* and *Clavis,* damaging *Ben Bui* and *Bird,* and taking nine British sailors prisoner. The Austrians escaped before Italian destroyers arrived, and the next day, 10 July, one of the Italian destroyers, the *Impetuoso,* was torpedoed and sunk by the Austrian submarine *U.17* off Brindisi. The Italians concluded that the drifters could no longer be effectively protected, and the drifter line was accordingly shifted southward to a less vulnerable position.[40] In September 1916 Kerr established a drifter line running from a point five miles north of Santa Maria di Leuca to Fano Island and then turning southward to Samothraki. He had enough drifters to establish a small secondary barrier that was periodically shifted. Nevertheless he was still conscious of the drifters' vulnerability and complained, "We have no protection for our drifters from sea or sky."[41]

On 30 October a special conference concerning the Otranto barrage took place in the flagship of the Duke of the Abruzzi at Taranto. Here a French proposal that direction of the barrage be given to the French *chef de division* at Brindisi in order to achieve unity of command was turned down. It was unpalatable to the Italians, especially since it would at the time have meant that the very unpopular and abrasive de Cacqueray would be in command. The French also proposed moving the drifter line northward with the San Cataldo–Saseno line as the northern limit. There would be a French destroyer patrol to the south of the drifters. This French proposal was unacceptable to Kerr, who pointed out that the line would have been the same distance from the Austrian base at Cattaro as it was from potential support from Brindisi and hence too vulnerable. Moreover, too much time would be lost reaching it from the drifters' base at Taranto compared to the more southerly line. Kerr also argued that the more dangerous line in the north did not really offer any better chance at catching a submarine than the safer line in the south. The result was a compromise suggested by the Duke of the Abruzzi. This would put the drifters on a line running from Otranto to Asproruga, south of Cape Linguetta. The Italians would also lay a minefield running eastward for ten miles and would, if their other obligations permitted, attempt to have two destroyers out on patrol. The compromise was acceptable to Kerr because the most dangerous part of the line would now be some distance south of Valona. The proposed Italian minefield would also reduce the area the drifters would have to patrol. However, beyond this the Italians refused to risk any additional precious destroyers on the patrol—they pointed out that three had already been torpedoed—but offered to transfer twenty-two trawlers from the Tyrrhenian and an additional eighteen coastal torpedo boats to the barrage as well as increase the number of their aircraft at Brindisi and Valona. The additional trawlers would enable the Italians to patrol to the north of the drifter line. Moreover, a light cruiser would always be kept under steam at Brindisi ready to sail at a half hour's notice. Although the promise of Italian reinforcements was actually more than the French had hoped for, there was absolute deadlock over the question of command of the barrage. Abruzzi would not think of placing command of the Otranto Straits under a non-Italian and threatened resignation if the idea was adopted. Kerr was wise enough to remain quiet but his own conclusion was, not surprisingly, that the problem would not be solved until the British sent out sufficient destroyers and seaworthy small craft under a senior British naval officer who could deploy enough drifters to form a double line at all times, taking into account the necessity of the drifters for rest, repairs, and refits.[42]

It is hardly surprising that Kerr was angling for British control of the Otranto blockade. He was hampered by the fact that after the Otranto conference the Admiralty still could not provide more than about twenty additional drifters. There had been the prospect of four *H*-class British destroyers, but these were detained at Malta for the protection of trade. The Italians and the French had been scouring distant countries including Japan and even neutral sources for more trawlers that could be adapted for anti-submarine work. The Italians had some success and were able to provide an additional twenty trawlers, as promised at the conference, drawn from the western coast of Italy. These were to patrol north of the drifter line. French and Italian promises of additional gunboats for the barrage, however, remained merely promises. The Italians needed these more powerful craft to protect traffic to and from Albania and the bases they had established there.[43]

The drifters remained potentially vulnerable and this was demonstrated on the night of 22 December when four Austrian *Huszár*-class destroyers under the command of Korvettenkapitän Bogumil Nowotny in *Scharfschütze*, together with *Dinara*, *Velebit*, and *Reka*, raided the line.[44] Fortunately for the drifters, only one was damaged due to the prompt arrival of six French destroyers (*Casque*, *Protet*, *Commandant Rivière*, *Commandant Bory*, *Dehorter*, and *Boutefeu*) who by chance were in the vicinity en route to Taranto to escort transports the following morning. The commander of the French destroyers, Capitaine de frégate Bréart de Boisanger, in *Casque*, responded the way an enterprising destroyer captain might be expected to do. He proceeded toward the drifters' alarm signals and the sound of gunfire. Nevertheless this was night and the technology for command and control of fast destroyers under these circumstances did not yet exist. Vice Admiral Sir Reginald Bacon, commanding the Dover patrol at this time, described the situation in frequently quoted words: "It is as easy to stop a raid of express engines with all lights out at night, at Clapham Junction, as to stop a raid of 33-knot destroyers on a night as black as Erebus, in waters as wide as the Channel."[45] The Austrians may not have been quite that fast but the circumstances were similar. The six French destroyers, all over 800 tons, were superior in armament to the 420-ton *Huszárs* (two 100mm guns, four 65mm guns, and four torpedo tubes versus six 6.6cm guns and two torpedo tubes), but this was offset by the darkness. Things soon began to go wrong for the French. The second in line failed to see *Casque's* shaded signal to increase speed and alter course and as a result the destroyer was followed only by the *Commandant Rivière*. The other destroyers lost contact with their leader. Next, a shell in the aft boiler room put *Commandant Rivière* temporarily out of action, leaving *Casque* alone although her commander thought he was being followed by the rest of his force. *Casque* slowly gained on the enemy, evaded a torpedo, and fired one of her own, but sustained a hit in the forward boiler room that reduced her speed to twenty-three knots. The Austrians escaped, but more trouble was in store for the French. Admiral Acton at Brindisi had ordered three Italian destroyers led by the *Abba* to sortie in an attempt to cut off the Austrians. They were followed by the British light cruiser *Gloucester* accompanied by two Italian destroyers. The French and Italian destroyers literally ran into each other in the darkness when *Abba* rammed *Casque* and a short while later *Boutefeu* rammed *Abba*. The two damaged destroyers had to be towed back to Brindisi to be repaired to fight another day. During their return, the Allied destroyers spotted the German submarine *UB.36*, which was attacked before it had any opportunity to use its torpedoes. The submarine escaped. In turn, the French submarine *Le Verrier* off Cattaro apparently spotted the returning Austrians in the distance but was in no position to act. The whole affair on the Allied side was a graphic example of the problems involved in commanding and controlling different nationalities and groups of ships at high speed in the darkness, although the Austrians also had little to show for the risks they had run.[46]

The British gained at least some of their objectives in the Strait of Otranto at an Allied naval conference held in London on 23 and 24 January 1917. The Italians agreed to the withdrawal of British battleships from Taranto with, as mentioned, the exception of the *Queen*, which would remain as a depot ship for the drifters.[47] Retention of this ship was necessitated by the desperate need of the Italians for tonnage. They had been compelled to reclaim the ships used until then by the drifter crews as depot ships. The majority of the *Queen's* ship's company were withdrawn for other duties, so the old battleship was now little more than a hulk, certainly not ready to play a role in any potential naval battle. The British had been anxious to withdraw the other old battleships, which served no useful function and whose crews were badly needed for other work and ships. The British also received French and Italian agreement to the withdrawal of all but two of their battleships from the Aegean. The British would be reinforced off the Dardanelles by two French pre-dreadnought "*Patrie*"-class battleships. The price for Italian agreement had been a promise that the withdrawal would only take place if a "substantial" French force was permanently stationed at Corfu and that the British "make every effort" to reinforce the Italians with "a convenient number of light craft when available." The Allies accepted "that major [offensive] operations in the Adriatic were not at present possible, but that minor operations should be carried out with vigor." The Italians also agreed, at least for the moment, that the French commander in chief would assume command if the "greater part of French naval forces in the Mediterranean" ever took part in operations in the Adriatic. This was not likely, which is perhaps why the Italians appeared to agree.

The British won a major concession regarding the Otranto barrage, the command Thursby and Kerr had long desired. The Allies concurred that the means for protection of the drifters was not sufficient, but for a more efficient organization and better defense they agreed that the barrage system would come directly under a British officer who would act as a commodore. He would be directly under the Italian commander in chief and would in these waters be able to call on the services of all French and Italian ships not in use elsewhere. In addition, he could if necessary also ask any Allied warships in the vicinity for assistance.[48]

The officer chosen for the position of commodore of the barrage had already had much experience commanding small craft, primarily in anti-submarine work. Commodore Algernon Heneage had commanded a squadron of minelayers at the beginning of the war and, after a period in command of the old battleship *Albion* in the South Atlantic and at the Dardanelles, had served as commodore commanding small vessels in the eastern Mediterranean.

The majority of the London conference had been concerned with the submarine war, and here a compromise was reached concerning the routing of shipping in the Mediterranean. The British had been anxious to abandon the system of frequently changed but fixed patrolled routes adopted at the Malta conference the preceding year, which had not been a success. The British favored dispersion of ships as offering the greatest safety, and they had already implemented this for their shipping between Cap Bon and the Aegean on 11 January. They favored using coastal routes as much as possible in the remainder of the Mediterranean. The Admiralty at this stage also turned down suggestions from certain British officers in the Mediterranean that convoys be introduced. In the western Mediterranean things remained substantially the same with traffic using coastal routes as much as possible, especially neutral Spanish territorial waters. The British would investigate the possibility of establishing protected "ports of refuge" where ships might shelter in daylight hours. In the eastern basin of the Mediterranean there would be a trial of the two systems. British shipping and any others that cared to join them would use the British system of dispersion between Cap Bon and Port Said while the French system of fixed patrolled routes, frequently changed, would be used for shipping to and from Salonika and the Aegean. After a suitable period of trial, a comparison of the two systems would be made and a future conference would decide on a permanent system.[49]

Within a short time, the introduction of unrestricted submarine warfare by the Germans and Austrians demonstrated that neither system was effective and Allied losses grew to staggering levels in April. By this time there was also considerable discussion of how to make the Otranto barrage more effective, as its lack of success was readily apparent. In the context of the submarine war it is easy to understand how the possibility of restricting entry and exit of submarines from the Adriatic to the shipping routes in the Mediterranean became even more attractive. However, by the time Commodore Heneage took up his duties at the Otranto barrage, there had been important changes in the Italian high command that would render relations among the Allies less comfortable than they had been during the tenure of the Duke of the Abruzzi. The duke had eventually succumbed to the mounting pressure against him caused by widespread Italian dissatisfaction with the conduct of the naval war. On 3 February there was an announcement that he was relinquishing his command for reasons of health. Most observers realized that far more than health was involved. There was a general shakeup in the Italian naval high command and Thaon di Revel emerged at the top as "Chief of the naval staff and commander of the mobilized naval force." A few admirals closely associated with the duke were removed to other commands. Viceammiraglio Cutinelli-Rendina became interim commander of the fleet at Taranto. As the title implies, Revel in theory combined the office of chief of staff with that of commander of the fleet, an arrangement that was probably possible only because of the relative inactivity of the fleet. In practice, Revel spent most of his time in Rome where he had a sub–chief of staff directly under his orders. He was a staunch defender of what he regarded as Italian interests and apt to be far less conciliatory toward Italy's allies. Allied naval conferences for the remainder of the war could at times become caustic. Revel also had little use for the Otranto barrage. Its scant results convinced him that some of the small craft used on the barrage would be better employed on mercantile routes. His outlook was fundamentally defensive. Priority, he believed, should be given to arming merchant ships and to the construction of small craft for anti-submarine duties. Italian overseas commitments, such as the Italian contingent at Salonika, should be reduced as should all unnecessary transport by sea. The real priority was to ensure the supply to Italy by sea of essential commodities such as coal.[50]

The Italians believed the Otranto barrage could be more effective if it was transformed at least partially into a fixed instead of a mobile barrage. Revel outlined a scheme to Kerr for a continuous net running from Santa Maria di Leuca to Fano Island. The top of the net would be about twenty-six feet (eight meters) below the surface and the bottom would be 200 feet below the surface. The distance involved represented approximately forty-seven miles. Drifters would patrol ten miles north and ten miles south of the net. Revel thought the Admiralty should provide the necessary material, notably the nets, and proposed the cost be shared between the British and Italians. He also intended to request the French to supply mines to be placed in the nets. Revel proposed that the British, French, and Italians share the costs in equal parts since all would benefit. The steel would have to be imported, although Revel thought the glass buoys might be manufactured in Venice. Kerr believed, in contrast, that if the net were agreed to, every part of it except the mines should be made in Britain, for otherwise he doubted the Italians would have it ready in time. Commodore Heneage, for his part, was skeptical about maintaining a net of this length.[51] The British, in short, were not enthusiastic.

The French had their own proposal for the barrage. This also involved a fixed rather than a mobile barrage. It was prepared by two officers in the Mining Commission at the Ministry of Marine in Paris. The two, Lieutenants de vaisseau Fromaget and de Quillacq, envisioned a fixed net with mines approximately forty miles in length. Roughly three-quarters of this would be in depths of between 200 and 500 fathoms.[52] The popular naval writer E. Keble Chatterton, writing after the war, summarized these Italian and French projects in pithy fashion: "Just as a wooden barricade stretched across the road will be far more effective than a line of policemen for withstanding a rush, so a less pliable and yielding obstruction than unanchored nets would be more likely to stop those clever U-boats."[53]

The Admiralty in London was as unenthusiastic about the French and Italian projects as were Kerr and Heneage, who were on the scene. The captain supervising submarine defenses thought the French had underestimated the practical difficulties, notably the time and floating plant required for construction. The director of the anti-submarine division was equally dubious, considering the scheme "impracticable" and requiring an "enormous" effort to maintain, and that submarines would easily be able to avoid the nets. However, to preserve good relations with the French and avoid a potential argument, the Admiralty agreed to a practical trial of the scheme in depths approximating those to be encountered in the Adriatic. The trial length would be one mile.[54]

Heneage may have been skeptical of the French and Italian projects for a fixed barrage, but he was nevertheless a strong supporter of the principle of a

barrage in the Strait of Otranto as the best means to stop submarine depreda-
tions. The principle was more attractive to him than the idea of escorts for
shipping. He was, as was eventually demonstrated, on the wrong side of history, but the arguments at the time had a strong appeal. Heneage prepared a
paper for an Allied naval conference scheduled to take place at Corfu at the
end of April and expressed the gist of those arguments in a simple diagram:[55]

Barrage	Escort
Prevention	Cure
Offensive	Defensive
Concentration	Dispersal

The Allied naval conference opened aboard the flagship of Vice Amiral
Gauchet, the French commander in chief, on 28 April. It met in an atmo-
sphere of crisis since April was the worst month of the war for the Allies as far
as submarine losses were concerned. The methods in use to counter the submarine menace were obviously not working. The Allied admirals had little difficulty in reaching unanimous agreement that they not return to the 1916
method of fixed routes and, since losses of ships sailing in dispersed fashion
and in isolation were staggering, the admirals recommended that in open waters far from the coast, ships should sail in convoys with escorts. The convoys
would follow dispersed routes, chosen at the last minute according to circumstances by routing officers at the port of departure. In general, however, navigation should be at night and along the coast whenever possible. The coastal
routes and choke points would be patrolled. The net effect was to establish a
hybrid system of both convoys and patrolled coastal routes. A central authority
for anti-submarine warfare in the Mediterranean was to be established at
Malta. It would contain representatives of the different navies and be responsible for making arrangements for transport routes and escorts. Although nom-
inally under the French commander in chief in the Mediterranean, the commission would eventually become the mechanism for virtual British direction
of the anti-submarine campaign in the Mediterranean. The scattered British
commands in the Mediterranean would also be brought under a British commander in chief who would be assisted by an officer of flag rank to represent
Britain on the Malta commission.

The question of the Otranto barrage probably caused the most disagreement at the Corfu conference. Here Kerr's proposals were rebuffed. Kerr argued that the Allies were unsuccessful in the Mediterranean because they
were simultaneously employing three different systems against submarines:
patrols, escorts, and the Otranto barrage. Kerr considered these to be half measures since no one system was really pushed to the limit. He therefore proposed a trial of two of the systems for one or two months. This would be ac-
complished by, for example, removing about 100 drifters from the Otranto

barrage where for lack of sufficient numbers they were ineffective. The drifters removed from Otranto would be used on patrols. If the results were not satisfactory, the drifters would be returned to the barrage. They would then be reinforced by enough small craft taken from other patrols to make the barrage truly effective. Heneage was reluctant to pull drifters off the barrage for Kerr's trial, but he supported the proposal provided the other preparations for the barrage involving nets, hydrophones, and provision of more aircraft continue. For Heneage, the real problem was lack of numbers, whether the barrage was fixed or mobile. He demonstrated this with simple arithmetic. He had 124 drifters, and approximately 70 were out on the line each day. There were approximately forty-five miles to be covered in the passage but each drifter could only cover one-half mile. There were inevitably gaps, and submarines obviously had little difficulty in passing through them. Heneage believed he could stop this with additional ships, aircraft, a fixed-net barrage, and hydrophones. Nevertheless it is easy to understand that the idea of reducing patrols and escorts for the benefit of the Otranto barrage at that moment of crisis proved unacceptable to the majority of officers at the conference. Kerr's proposal was rejected, although the conference did agree to recommend hastening construction of the fixed-net barrage and in the future establishing fixed barrages off the Dardanelles, at Gibraltar, and in the Gulf of Smyrna, with the distant possibility of an even more ambitious barrage between Cap Bon and the coast of Sicily.[56]

The British had actually moved on their own toward the introduction of convoys on the eve of the Corfu conference. On 27 April the Admiralty ordered the first trial convoy between Gibraltar and Great Britain. The system of convoys would eventually be extended to the Mediterranean. The British were also conscious of the continued vulnerability of the Otranto barrage to Austrian raids. Heneage found no destroyers were to be obtained from his Allies, and he considered his ability to control the drifters crippled. In early April, when what he described as his "slow old yacht" the *Catania* had to go in dock, he was reduced to flying his commodore's broad pendant in a motor launch.[57] As of 26 April, Heneage had at his disposal one yacht, thirty motor launches, and 120 drifters. However, the promises made by the Italians at the London conference concerning small craft to support the drifters had been conditional, and Admiral Revel now argued that he had to send nearly all his small craft to the west coast of Italy because of enemy submarine activity. Revel, according to Kerr, "thought the risk of having the T.B.'s [torpedo boats] and Patrol Trawlers sunk by an enemy raid so great as to make it inadvisable to place any there" although he agreed to eventually send "a few" patrol trawlers to work under Commodore Heneage.[58]

The deputy director of operations at the Admiralty, Captain George Hope, thought that the French and Italians had taken full advantage of their condi-

tional promises made at London about all available craft not needed elsewhere coming under Heneage's orders. The ships were always needed elsewhere. However, Hope had to acknowledge that the British case was
weakened by the fact that the four destroyers the British sent to the Mediterranean for the barrage had never worked there either since they were continuously employed on escort duties. He thought only three courses open,
namely, go on as at present, "which seems of little practical value," take over
the whole barrage and its protection themselves, or else turn the whole thing
over to the French and Italians. He recommended the British take it over
themselves. Admiral Henry F. Oliver, the chief of the naval staff, regarded the
barrage as it was as "probably much better than anything the French or Italians could substitute," and that the British were "well off" as regards aircraft,
which along with the motor launches would assist the drifters. Oliver was inclined to dismiss the fixed barrage schemes, notably the French proposal, as
impractical. The Admiralty pointed out to the French that their experiments
with the scheme had been carried out in depths of only twenty to thirty fathoms, not the great depths they would encounter in the Strait of Otranto, and
he therefore suggested that a trial section of only one mile should first be laid
in the Otranto channel.[59] The schemes for a fixed barrage remained up in the
air in early May, but it is evident the British were far from enthusiastic about
having to bear the heaviest burden of the material expense. Admiral Jellicoe,
the first sea lord, came to the reluctant conclusion that leaving matters as they
stood on the barrage was "the only course possible under existing conditions
however regrettable this is."[60] This then was the situation when the Austrians
prepared their raid. The British had a vulnerable drifter line which was apparently achieving little, and the multitude of demands placed on the British,
French, and Italian navies by the unrestricted submarine war seemed to work
against anything but the weakest and most sporadic protection being given to
the drifters.

The object of the raid: British drifters sailing from their base. (IWM Neg. Q63401)

HMS *Bristol*. (IWM Neg. SP512)

SMS *Helgoland* on trials, 7 May 1917. Note shortened mainmast so as to resemble a *Tátra*-class destroyer. (Dr. Lothar Baumgartner Collection)

(opposite) SMS *Saida*: view from crow's nest. Note torpedo tubes and broadside batteries of 10cm guns so devastating to the drifters. (Dr. Lothar Baumgartner Collection)

HMS *Dartmouth*: crew of six-inch gun at drill wearing anti-flash hoods. (IWM Neg. HU68281)

HMS *Dartmouth* at speed during the action. (IWM Neg. HU68282)

K. 195, an Oeffag-built Weichmann (in IV. Gruppe during the action). (Peter Schupita Collection)

An Austrian aircraft (probably K. 153 or K. 154) makes a low pass over the crippled *Novara*. (Dr. Lothar Baumgartner Collection)

SMS *Sankt Georg* cleared for action steaming to reinforce Horthy. (Dr. Lothar Baumgartner Collection)

Top to bottom: *Saida* towing *Novara* followed by *Helgoland*. (Dr. Lothar Baumgartner Collection)

The Austrians return. Center left to right: *Saida* towing *Novara, Helgoland, Sankt Georg.* Destroyer *Tátra* lower left. Torpedo boat on each flank. (Dr. Lothar Baumgartner Collection)

Dartmouth after being torpedoed. Under magnification men can be seen aft either abandoning or reboarding. (IWM Neg. HU68284)

Dartmouth under tow by *Marittimo*. French or Italian destroyer in background. (IWM Neg. HU68285)

SMS *Saida* arriving at Pola for repairs watched by crew of unidentified battleship. Note temporary repairs to damage near bow. (Dr. Lothar Baumgartner Collection)

CHAPTER THREE

THE AUSTRIANS
PREPARE AN ATTACK

I N THE MIDDLE OF May 1917, the *k.u.k. Kriegsmarine* risked the most modern and effective of its small force of light cruisers and destroyers on a raid on the drifter line in the Otranto Straits. A glance at a map would easily show that this was indeed a risk, for a raiding force would have to pass south of the parallel of Brindisi, where there were considerable Allied light forces, and would consequently be in the potential position of having an avenging enemy force between it and the safety of its base in the Gulf of Cattaro. That the Austrians were prepared to take this risk would seem to indicate that they considered disruption of the drifter line to be worth it, which leads to the assumption that the work of the drifters was at least annoying enough to provoke the action. What effect then were the drifters having on Austrian and German submarine operations?

During the war large numbers of former fishing craft were taken over by the Admiralty for naval service. There were two main types, trawlers and drifters. Trawlers and drifters are frequently referred to in the same context, and to the untrained eye they may appear similar in photographs. There are, however, differences between them due to their different functions. Trawlers are larger than drifters and because of their role in trawling the ocean, that is dragging nets, they are equipped with more powerful engines. Consequently they tend to be better suited than drifters for minesweeping. Drifters, as their name implies, work in a more passive manner after shooting their nets.

At the Strait of Otranto the drifters operated on a deceptively simple principle. They deployed astern wire mesh nets 180 feet deep. This implies a naive notion that the submarine was a giant steel fish to be netted, but that was not the case. The nets were so-called "indicator nets," that is, they were fitted with buoys released by the violent motion of a submarine maneuvering against the nets.[1] The buoys, devised to ignite and burn calcium when fouled, would thereby betray the presence of a submarine under the surface. The alarm would be given and, if suitably armed, the drifter might drop depth charges. The submarine would have lost a large measure of its greatest asset, its invisibility. There might be an added dividend. Should the nets become entangled in the submarine's screws, the ability of the submarine to maneuver or escape might be limited. Submarine commanders would be aware of this nightmarish possibility and the drifters might therefore have a deterrent value, or perhaps might channel submarines toward minefields.[2]

The French and Italians had proposed a fixed mine-net barrage in the Otranto Straits. This would have been a wire net fitted with mines supported by mooring buoys. The objective was for any submarine coming in contact with the net to detonate one of the mines. This was potentially more destructive, although as we have seen in the preceding chapter the Admiralty had reservations about the feasibility of the French and Italian schemes, particularly how such a net could be maintained or the mines serviced or inspected to see if they were still functioning.

By the spring of 1917, indicator nets had achieved little in the way of success in terms of submarines actually destroyed.[3] The drifters had been at work more than seven months before they caught a submarine, and that success was to a certain extent accidental. The Austrian submarine *U.6* under the command of Linienschiffsleutnant Hugo von Falkhausen left the Bocche on the evening of 12 May 1916 to seek enemy traffic along the line from Cape Santa Maria di Leuca to Valona. The submarine was a 240-ton Holland type boat built at the Whitehead Yard in Fiume and placed in service in the summer of 1910.[4] The following night, the 13th, in the middle of the Otranto Straits, Falkhausen spotted a drifter a few hundred meters ahead. He promptly submerged and turned toward the east only to spot a second drifter steering parallel to the first twenty minutes later. He decided to break through the approximately 500-meter gap that he perceived between the drifters at a depth of thirty meters. A short while later there was an unexplained noise of something on the hull but the noise soon stopped and all seemed normal. The noise was almost certainly caused by *U.6* fouling one of the nets laid by the drifter *Calistoga*, whose head was turned round by the strain. Her skipper saw that one of the indicator buoys had fired, fired alarm signals, slipped his remaining nets, and set out after the moving buoy. Eventually Falkhausen, on taking a sight, observed a flare or light in the submarine's wake. He assumed it was an alarm signal but had no explanation for it. However, when it was apparent the submarine was towing the light, Falkhausen surfaced to cut it loose. On opening the hatch his third officer discovered *U.6* covered by a net. The Austrians made every effort to cut away the net, and one of the crew undressed and swam out and cut the line that was apparently towing the signal apparatus. Unfortunately for the submarine, as they frantically began work, a drifter appeared 500 meters off, opened fire on the submarine, and set off alarm rockets. This was the *Dulcie Doris*, who had been approximately 1,000 yards northwest of *Calistoga* and had observed one of her own indicator buoys set off. Her skipper also slipped his nets and set off in pursuit. A second drifter, *Evening Star II*, soon appeared and also opened fire. She was followed by *Calistoga*, who did not fire as the other two drifters were in the line of sight. Falkhausen was caught, unable to submerge and towing a light that was betraying his presence. He tried to escape at full power despite the drag of the net, but the submarine's port shaft was fouled and the port engine would not start. The submarine could not get clear of the drifters even though their gunfire so far had been ineffectual. Falkhausen realized the game was up, ordered his code books and confidential material thrown overboard, and, as the drifters approached, opened the submarine's Kingston valves and scuttled the boat. He and his men, a total of three officers and seventeen ratings, were picked up by the drifters and eventually turned over to the Italians to spend the remainder of the war as prisoners. The Admiralty awarded £1000 to be divided among the men of the three drifters.

Falkhausen reported after the war that while a prisoner he had learned that the drifters that night had actually been forced to cut loose their nets because of bad weather and the net in which his submarine was entangled was therefore floating abeam of the drifters rather than astern as he had anticipated. If this version of events is correct, then the loss of the submarine was to a certain extent accidental. However, this detail is not borne out by British accounts, where there is no mention of nets being slipped because of bad weather, and references to *Calistoga* having just finished towing her nets into position as well as to *Calistoga*'s head being turned by the strain of the submarine on the net would seem to contradict it.[5] Another possible explanation is that Falkhausen may not have realized that the drifters, by definition smaller and less powerful than trawlers, had great difficulty maintaining nets across the straits because of the strong currents which tended despite the drifters' best efforts to move the nets to a southeast-northwest orientation.[6] This had been considered one of the great difficulties of the barrage, but in this case it may have led to the destruction of the submarine. The episode has been described at length because it is the sole clear example of a submarine being accounted for by nets in the Strait of Otranto prior to the raid.[7]

There might have been another submarine victim in the summer of 1916. The German *UB.44* sailed from the Bocche on 4 August 1916 for Constantinople and never arrived at the rendezvous, where the boat was to embark a

Turkish pilot for passage through the Dardanelles. *UB.44* was never heard from again. The submarine might have succumbed to depth charge attacks by the drifters *Quarry Knowe* and *Garrigil* in the Otranto Straits at the position 42° 12′ N, 18° 46′ E. However the submarine's disappearance might also have been due to some mechanical or operational failure, perhaps in the Aegean. The fate and location of *UB.44* remains one of the mysteries of the war.[8]

The sinking of *U.6* took place just over a year before the Austrian raid of 15 May 1917. Had anything happened to make the barrage more onerous? At the beginning of April 1917 the Allies introduced what they hoped would be an element of uncertainty. That is, instead of working on a fixed line, the drifters worked within a belt, changing the exact position of the nets within that belt on a weekly basis. The belt ran eastwards from just off the Italian coast to close to Fano Island. The line was usually just south of 40° N latitude. The MLs working from Gallipoli or Tricase patrolled about five miles from the belt at night with the objective of forcing submarines to dive and, hopefully, become entangled in the nets. Heneage sought to eliminate the weakness caused by the gaps left for Allied transport on either side of the line. The gap extended some ten miles from the Italian coast, and drifters were forbidden to operate in it since transports used it nightly. Heneage arranged with the Italian commander in chief that the commodore commanding patrols be informed when no transports were running so that drifters and MLs could be sent into the area. This had not actually occurred as of 22 April, and it was one of the points discussed at the Corfu conference, where Heneage also proposed that on the eastern side of the straits the nets be extended right up to Fano Island with transports piloted through the nets in daylight hours. As an alternative, sufficient protection should be given to the drifters so that they could set their nets just north of the entrance to Valona and therefore clear of the transport routes. The Allies at the conference agreed that the barrage should be extended from Fano Island to Kephali Point on the island of Corfu, but since the exact position of passages along the Albanian coast was of interest primarily to the French and Italians, agreement on the details would be left to them.[9] The operations of the MLs were of course subject to the vagaries of the weather, although this might be expected to improve as summer approached. Nevertheless, real improvement in the absence of many more drifters and armed craft, preferably destroyers, to protect them was likely to be theoretical.

The actual experiences of German and Austrian submarines transiting the Strait of Otranto varied so widely that it is not possible to generalize. There are frequent laconic entries in logs to the presence of "Fischdampfer," the characteristic reference to the drifters. The experience of *U.39* in May and June of 1916 may be taken as typical. Her commander, Kapitänleutnant Walter Forstmann, was an experienced submarine officer who had been in the Mediterranean since September 1915 and was one of the most successful U-boat commanders. There was an Austrian liaison officer with him on the cruise who described how Forstmann on a clear moonlit night in good weather in the straits boldly broke through two lines of drifters by proceeding at full speed on the surface. The drifters seemed to try pursuit but were too slow and soon left behind. This may have represented one extreme. U.39's return represented another. Hourly sightings through the periscope during daylight hours consistently revealed the presence of a group of three drifters and a destroyer. Forstmann was forced to make a submerged passage of twelve hours through the straits, successfully getting through after the onset of darkness, although compelled to submerge once when a destroyer approached. Linienschiffsleutnant Gaston Vio, the Austrian officer, correctly anticipated Allied intentions by guessing that the Allies realized the nets were not very effective and were therefore patrolling the surface, trying to force a submarine to submerge and exhaust its battery. He considered this possible if the Allies could expand the area they patrolled. Forstmann shared this view and could also foresee the patrols being expanded further north and south, thereby causing serious difficulties for passing submarines.[10]

Another Austrian liaison officer who was with the German *UB.46* on a cruise from 19 July to 12 August 1916 had an even easier time. He reported that the submarine had left and returned through the straits while surfaced and had not been disturbed by Allied patrols.[11] In contrast, however, in the same month the commander of the Mediterranean U-boat flotilla complained to his superiors in Berlin that his U-boats on their return had reported strong patrols in the Otranto Straits that had endangered them and that he had accordingly asked his Austrian allies to raid the straits.[12] For the submarines, passage through the straits seemed to be largely a matter of luck. If they were in the wrong place where the drifters were present, they had a hard time; if they were in the right place where there were gaps, they were not bothered. As long as there was an insufficient number of small craft available to close those gaps, this situation was not likely to change. But even in the best of circumstances for the Allies and the worst of circumstances for the Germans and Austrians, the barrage was a hindrance, added danger, and possible delay. It was not an absolute barrier. The amount of tonnage sunk in the Mediterranean reflected this; if it diminished it was usually due to more U-boats under refit and smaller numbers on the shipping routes, or to other factors such as weather. For example, in January 1917 the majority of Mediterranean U-boats were under refit in Pola or Cattaro as a result of intense activity the preceding year, and as a result, at the beginning of February U-boat activity could not be carried out in all sections of the Mediterranean.[13] Any diminishment in the amount of tonnage sunk was not due to the barrage. The amount of tonnage sunk in the Mediterranean by German submarines or submarine-laid mines rose from 78,541 in January of 1917 to 105,670 in February, fell to 61,917 in March, and rose rapidly to a colossal 254,915 tons in the record month of April.[14] The Germans had many things on their minds when they inaugurated unrestricted submarine warfare in the winter of 1917. These concerns were reflected in correspondence between Berlin and the commander of the U-boat flotillas at Pola and with their Austrian allies in Vienna. They included problems with maintaining and refitting Mediterranean U-boats, their operational areas, the treatment of neutral ships and neutral waters, especially Spain, and the question of the treatment of hospital ships, which the Germans were convinced the Allies were abusing.[15] However there seems to have been no significant pressure on the Austrians or discussion concerning the Otranto barrage.

The lack of significant pressure or at least surviving records of that pressure in the archives means that as far as the action in the Strait of Otranto is concerned, it is far easier to determine *what* happened than *why* it happened. There is no real evidence of a directive on the part of the naval high command in Germany or Austria ordering a plan for action to be drawn up. Apparently, certain active and ambitious Austrian naval officers were not content to swing round their buoys while the submarines did all the work. There were relatively few ways the *k.u.k. Kriegsmarine* could hurt the enemy with surface warships given the array of forces against them in the spring of 1917. Admiral Njegovan, who had succeeded Haus as Flottenkommandant on the latter's death in February, intended to carry on the defensive policies of his predecessor. He regarded the situation in the northern Adriatic as too dangerous for either Italian or Austrian major units to act on the flanks of the armies, discounted any possibility of significant action by major Italian warships in the northern Adriatic, and thought Italian action would be confined to cheap successes with minor craft. Certainly the recent change in the Italian high command, the return of Thaon di Revel as *Capo di stato maggiore,* did not herald a change to an offensive policy by the Italians. He also did not think an Allied action against Cattaro was likely without an advance on land northwards from Albania, and this presupposed a change in the balance of strength and improvement of Allied communications on the Albanian-Macedonian front.[16] What Njegovan really wanted was more submarines, and in a private letter to Kontreadmiral Kailer, now chief of the Marinesektion in Vienna, he urgently asked that submarine construction be hastened as much as possible. Njegovan could also make good use of motorboats with torpedoes. Moreover, the Austrians also needed mines, and nets were lacking everywhere.[17]

Unfortunately for the Austrians, six submarines that had been under construction on their account in German yards in 1914 had been released to the German navy at the beginning of the war on the assumption they would not have been able to reach Austrian waters. In early 1915 the Austrians, once it was apparent it would be a long war, launched their own building program: four of the so-called *Havmanden* class, a generally unsuccessful type; and six boats based on the German *UB.II* design. An additional two were laid down in 1916. Progress was very slow, largely because of the nature of the Dual Monarchy in which orders had to be divided between Austrian and Hungarian firms, the inexperience of sub-contractors, and wartime shortages. The submarines did not begin to enter service until the first half of 1917.[18]

Nevertheless, all this talk by Njegovan about submarines, mines, and nets involved mostly defensive measures, or in the case of new submarines, offensive measures in the distant future. A raid with fast light forces on the barrage was one of the few immediate offensive actions the Austrians could undertake that might hurt the enemy at sea.

Linienschiffskapitän Nikolaus Horthy de Nagybánya played a central role in both the planning and execution of the ensuing action. The Austrian naval list used the German form of his Christian name, while works dealing primarily with Hungarian history usually use the Hungarian Miklós. He was born in 1868 at Kenderes into a Calvinist, landholding family of the middle nobility, and he entered the naval academy after the accidental death of his older brother, who had preceded him. The young Horthy expressed a desire to replace his brother, and with the support of the Hungarian prime minister, the Kaiser was persuaded to award him one of the coveted places in the academy. Horthy was far from an intellectual, but he had an aptitude for languages as well as athletic and mechanical ability. His pre-war career is most noted for the time he spent as aide-de-camp to Kaiser Franz Joseph from November 1911 to May 1914. At the beginning of the war he assumed command of the pre-dreadnought battleship *Habsburg*, flagship of the IV Heavy Division in the fleet. The ship was obsolete and it was not a command with much scope for initiative. His situation changed in December of 1914 when he was lucky enough to receive a plum job, command of the new light cruiser *Novara*. He would make his name in this ship. His fellow captain and friend Erich Heyssler spoke of the appointment in these terms:

> In fact, no better captain could have been found for this fast cruiser. Horthy had always been bottom of his class at the Naval Academy. The rather over-elegant and in his youth irresponsible and frivolous officer had never set much store by studying on school benches. Perhaps just because of that, he had preserved a healthy and natural common sense. He was vivacious, extremely daring, a good horseman, swordsman, yachtsman and shot. He was also a good seaman and maneuvered well under sail and in torpedo boats as well as in ships. Besides, he was always the most pleasant and friendliest of comrades.[19]

In January 1915 Admiral Haus considered Horthy and his ship as most suitable for a daring plan to break through the Otranto Straits on a dark and moonless night and make a dash for the Turkish port of Smyrna to deliver badly needed munitions to the hard-pressed Turks. If the Turks could provide the necessary coal for the return journey, Haus even thought of Horthy surprising the British off the Dardanelles or else cruising along the Malta–Port Said route for a day or two attacking traffic and creating consternation in the Mediterranean. The plan was abandoned for a variety of reasons and probably wisely, for the *Novara* was too valuable to risk for the small amount of munitions she would have been able to carry.[20] It is significant, however, that no less a person than the Flottenkommandant himself considered Horthy the man to carry it out.

Horthy was the man for special missions. In May 1915, shortly before the Italian entry into the war, he was charged with towing *UB.8*, the first of the small German submarines transported in sections by rail to Pola, through the Strait of Otranto. He rigged a false funnel made of cloth and wire to simulate a transport and was authorized to fly a foreign flag if necessary. Horthy got as far south as eight miles west of Cephalonia before spotting French patrols and casting off the submarine, which successfully reached Turkish waters. Shortly afterwards, in the major action by the Austrian fleet against the Italian coast immediately upon Italy's entry into the war, Horthy led the group of destroyers and torpedo boats attacking Porto Corsini. He boldly brought *Novara* as close inshore as depths allowed in order to draw the fire of Italian coastal batteries away from the destroyer *Scharfschütze*, which had penetrated the narrow channel, the *Novara* sustaining hits and casualties as a result. Later in the year, on 5 December he and *Novara* led four destroyers and three torpedo boats in an attack on the harbor of San Giovanni di Medua. Despite the fire of Serbian batteries on shore, the Austrians succeeded in sinking three steamers and some small sailing craft. Horthy tried another raid against Durazzo with *Novara* and two destroyers on the night of 27 January 1916, but this time he was not successful. The two destroyers collided and had to return to base, and the attempt to proceed alone with *Novara* was frustrated when Horthy encountered French and Italian warships and lost the element of surprise. Horthy had better luck on 9 July when *Novara*, as we have seen, raided the drifter line, sinking two and damaging two others. Given the constraints under which the commanders of most surface ships in the Austrian navy worked, it is easy to understand Horthy's reputation.[21] In addition to skill and bravery, he possessed a high degree of initiative. To quote his friend Heyssler again: "He was one of those who always wanted to be at the enemy's throat all the time, he always urged for action. There were some who burned for action and confrontation and thought up new ideas and suggestions, but there were also others who did their duty bravely and faultlessly but remained quiet until orders were given from above."[22]

Horthy's own memoirs are disappointing on the origins of the raid, possibly because they were written long afterwards when he was in exile in Portugal and probably without access to extensive records. His account is relatively sparse: Even though the Austrians could now make full use of the Bocche di Cattaro, a reference to the elimination of Montenegrin positions on Mount Lovčen early in 1916, their operations "were nevertheless considerably hampered" by what Horthy termed the "bottleneck" formed by the narrow exit through the Otranto Straits. Horthy claimed the Allies were obviously making every effort to cork that bottleneck by means of stronger patrols of torpedo boats and destroyers. The result was "the moment a U-boat showed its periscope above water, it was spotted by the destroyers and attacked with depth charges." If the submarine survived the destroyers, it was "always in danger from the drifters." The latter, Horthy observed, trailed "long nets fitted with explosives and warning devices" to a depth at first of seventy feet and later to one hundred and forty feet. He pointed out that this "was the maximum diving capacity of the submarine."[23] Needless to say, this was not an exact picture of the Otranto barrage in the winter of 1917. Admiral Kerr and Commodore Heneage might have wished this was the situation, but at the time they lacked the means to make it a reality.

Horthy is equally vague on the origins of the plan and possible German involvement. He states, "I had talked at length with every U-boat commander who had entered the Bocche di Cattaro. They were all agreed; it was becoming more and more difficult, if not impossible, to break through this blockade. I made up my mind that it was time to make a clearance."[24] In his semi-official history *Österreich-Ungarns Seekrieg 1914–1918*, Hans Hugo Sokol, a former naval officer, not surprisingly gives a detailed account of the 15 May action, including the operational orders for its execution. Sokol says nothing, however, on the genesis of the plan or its motivation. He does recount the great submarine successes in the first quarter of 1917 and says that, despite an increased number of drifters, submarines often broke through the straits while surfaced without encountering any patrols. Furthermore, Austrian destroyers conducted three sweeps in the Strait of Otranto in the month preceding without meeting any enemy patrols. The sweeps were made by the *Uskoke, Streiter,* and *Warasdiner* on the night of 22–23 April, and *Csepel, Tátra,* and *Balaton* on the nights of 25 April and 5–6 May.[25] Once again this does not support the picture of growing crisis that Horthy paints.

Certainly Horthy and the German U-boat commanders talked about the situation and the erratic annoyance of the Otranto barrage, but it is more likely that the operation stemmed from the need to do something. Heyssler later observed, "In my view the Flottenkommando ought to have been more active with the capital ships and sailed out on missions, even if there was no real target to justify the risks involved. Both the captains and the men must get used to warfare conditions and the stokers and engines kept in trim."[26] He was referring to the big ships and an earlier period in the war, but the implications for the cruisers at Cattaro are clear. Nevertheless, Heyssler too spoke of the "increasing throttling effect" caused by the Otranto barrage.[27] As he was chief of staff to the rear admiral commanding the cruiser flotilla in the Bocche during the winter of 1917, he also had frequent contact with the German U-boat commanders. This suggests the possibility that the Austrians and Germans perceived the potential of the barrage even if at that moment it was still ineffective.

The three light cruisers *Novara*, *Helgoland*, and *Saida* would play a central role in Horthy's plan. They were to have their main masts shortened to resemble the silhouette of destroyers at night. The rationale was that if a cruiser was taken for a destroyer the enemy might not immediately summon overwhelming strength. The three cruisers were also to be thoroughly overhauled in preparation for the raid, with turbines and boilers cleaned and a 7cm/50 antiaircraft gun mounted. *Novara* had already been altered when, according to Heyssler, Horthy brought her into the Bocche at the end of February and confidentially informed him that the Flottenkommandant had approved his plan to attack the straits "in order to make a clean sweep" of the barrage.[28] It is interesting to note Heyssler repeats Horthy's phrase "make a clean sweep." Very few people knew of the plan at this stage, although presumably any trained seaman would have spotted the alterations to *Novara*.

There was a change of command in the cruiser flotilla at the beginning of March 1917, with Kontreadmiral Alexander Hansa taking over. Heyssler used this as an opportunity to suggest a replacement as chief of staff and request command of the *Helgoland*, leader of the first torpedo boat flotilla. The change was approved and in April Heyssler, now free of uncongenial staff duties, proceeded north to Pola where the *Helgoland* was in dock. The three *Helgolands*—frequently referred to as *Novaras* by the Allies—played a disproportionate role in the war in the Adriatic. They had been designed as "scouts," a type that preceded the better-known and more heavily armed light cruiser. Their emphasis was on speed. They were 428-foot ships with a designed displacement of 3,500 tons and a speed of twenty-seven knots. They were armed with nine 10cm/50 Skoda guns, and six 45cm torpedo tubes were added in 1917. Their complement was 340–350. *Novara* and *Helgoland* had been built by the Ganz & Co. Danubius yard at Fiume and fitted with AEG-Curtis turbines, while *Saida* had been built at the Cantiere Navale Triestino at Trieste and fitted with Melms-Pfenniger turbines. The latter caused problems, and *Saida* had difficulty maintaining steam pressure and consequently could not reach the top speed of the other two ships. The matter was the subject of endless disputes with the builders over warranties, and the ship suffered frequent turbine problems. These frequent problems with *Saida*'s turbines also made it difficult to employ all three cruisers as a group during the war. The *Helgolands* had been commissioned between August 1914 and January 1915, and for captains used to handling the older cruisers equipped with piston engines, the lack of vibration and rapid acceleration of the turbines were a delight, similar no doubt to the experience of a driver switching from an economy sedan to a sports car.[29]

The preparations continued in great secrecy, and in an attempt to lull the enemy, Austrian activity was reduced to the usual escorts, aerial patrols, the entry and exit of submarines, and what Heyssler called "only insignificant operations."[30] The latter presumably referred to the destroyer sweeps. *Helgoland* left Pola in the early hours of 10 May, and Heyssler took great precautions in traveling through areas likely to be patrolled by enemy submarines. He was also anxious to conceal movements and the concentration of cruisers that would be present at Cattaro. Unfortunately for the purposes of concealment, while proceeding south the *Helgoland* encountered the German submarine *U.35*, the boat of the legendary submarine commander Arnauld de la Perière. A film crew was on board the submarine and the *Helgoland* was filmed in all her glory, complete with shortened main mast. There was, however, little likelihood the film could have been seen by the Allies before the raid.[31] *Helgoland* entered the Bocche on the night of the 11th. This presumably reduced the time any Italian aerial reconnaissance could uncover an unusual—for the Austrians—concentration of cruisers in the Bocche.

Kontreadmiral Alexander Hansa, as commander of the Kreuzerflottillen, signed the orders for the raid, dated 13 May. It was also Hansa's responsibility to fix the exact date for the operation. There would be two parallel actions to confuse the enemy. The main group, the three cruisers, would sail from the Bocche at 1945 in the order *Novara, Saida, Helgoland*. On reaching Punta d'Ostro at 2015 they would steer southwest for ten nautical miles. At 2100, with *Novara* in the lead, they would increase to twenty-one knots and steer for the separation point ten miles west of Palascia light on the Italian coast. If this light was not seen, separation would take place without orders at 0315. *Novara* would steer to a point fourteen nautical miles west of Fano, *Saida* to a point twenty-eight nautical miles west of Fano, and *Helgoland* to a point forty-two miles west of Fano. The cruisers would attack separately, operate to the east, and arrange their timing to arrive at the rendezvous point fifteen nautical miles west of Cape Linguetta at the latest by 0715. They were to return at full speed in the order *Saida, Helgoland, Novara*, making use of smoke if necessary. Radio traffic would be restricted as much as possible. After the rendezvous, the results of the attack would be signaled to *Novara* and the latter would report to the radio station at Castelnuovo—the radio station in the Bocche—on passing the parallel of Cape Rodoni. If the cruisers were under pursuit and the intervention of the armored cruiser *Sankt Georg*—Hansa's flagship under steam in the Bocche—was necessary, *Novara* was to report the situation and position and would repeat her position, course, and speed at hourly intervals.

The old coast defense battleship *Budapest* might also sortie from the Bocche if necessary. During the departure and later on the return of the Austrian forces, torpedo boats and aircraft would secure the approaches to the Bocche and the approaches would be swept for mines in the western passage for a distance of up to ten nautical miles from Punta d'Ostro.[32]

Austrian aircraft would assist the operation. Aircraft from the station at Durazzo in Albania would take off at 0600 and reconnoiter in the direction of Brindisi for seventy nautical miles, but they would approach the cruisers only if they had something important to report. They would then reconnoiter in the direction of Valona. Aircraft from Kumbor—the naval air station in the Bocche—would take off at 0530 and reconnoiter ninety nautical miles in the direction of Brindisi. They were to attempt to report by wireless telegraphy to Austrian ships the approach of any enemy vessels, taking care not to betray the position of the Austrians. The aircraft would then follow the enemy movements and would be relieved by a second group. In case their radios were unusable, there was a pre-arranged code of flare signals.

The second part of the attack would be conducted by the destroyers *Csepel* and *Balaton* under the command of Fregattenkapitän Johannes Prince von und zu Liechtenstein in *Csepel*. Liechtenstein was one of the more glamorous figures in the navy. Tall and elegant, he was a member of the princely family, reported to be wealthy, and he had been naval attaché in Italy from 1912 until Italy's break with the Triple Alliance in 1915. During the war Liechtenstein had commanded the destroyer *Wildfang* in action before receiving command of the more modern *Csepel*.[33] *Csepel* and *Balaton*, completed in 1913, were part of the 870-ton *Tátra* class. They were the most modern and best destroyers in the Austrian navy, armed with two 10cm/60 and six 6.6cm/45 guns and four 45cm torpedo tubes. The original six of the class had been built by Danubius in Fiume, not without delay and considerable difficulty because of the yard's lack of experience with turbine machinery. Four more were ordered (two as replacements for the pair lost 29 December 1915) and were under construction at the time of the raid. They were capable of making over thirty-two knots and saw extensive and hard service during the war.[34] The *Tátra* herself was originally supposed to have been part of the raid. Unfortunately, boiler trouble reduced her speed and she was relegated to escort duties.

The destroyers were to sail so as to be off Dulcigno at 2100 and then sweep along the Albanian coast past Mount Elias to fifteen nautical miles from Saseno and from there steam toward the southwest to seek enemy transports, taking care not to cut *Novara*'s line of advance. They were to arrange their return so they would pass the cruisers' rendezvous fifteen nautical miles from Cape Linguetta around 0615. During the cruisers' return journey the position of the destroyers would be twenty nautical miles ahead to port. They would eventually receive reports from aircraft. The destroyers were, if possible, to draw pursuers on a course toward the Gulf of Cattaro. In case the Allied ships in pursuit appeared too far ahead and the Austrian cruisers and destroyers facing them were inferior in strength, the destroyers were to draw the enemy away from the cruisers. In any case, during the return journey the destroyers should strive to give battle only in company with the cruisers, making use of smoke when necessary. *Csepel* would report results of the sweep to *Novara* around 0800, at the same time giving her position, course, and time, but otherwise transmitting only the most important information.[35]

There was a third naval component to the raid, the action of submarines. For this the Austrians requested assistance from their German allies. Three submarines were to be employed, two Austrian and one German. The Austrian *U.4*, a small 237-ton Germania-type boat commissioned in 1909, was to lie off the southern entrance to Valona by 0400 to attack large or small vessels entering or leaving. *U.27*, the first of the German design *UB.II* boats to be built and enter service in Austria, was to be by 0530 in a position twenty-five nautical miles from Brindisi along the line of communications from Brindisi to Punta d'Ostro. The Austrians also requested the Germans to order their minelaying submarine *UC.25* to lay mines off Brindisi before dawn and then assume a position to wait and observe. All submarines were to make use of their wireless as much as possible. The Austrian request to use *UC.25* was forwarded to Berlin by the commander of the German U-boat flotilla on 11 May, indicating the raid was planned for the following Sunday or Monday. The Admiralstab promptly approved. *UC.25*, commanded by Kapitänleutnant Johannes Feldkirchner, had entered service in June 1916 and had only arrived in the Mediterranean the month before. This would be Feldkirchner's first mission operating from a Mediterranean base. The submarine was capable of carrying eighteen mines and also had two torpedo tubes and seven torpedoes.[36]

The Austrian naval forces in the Bocche were also to be prepared to support the raiding force on its return. The armored cruiser *Sankt Georg*, flagship of Admiral Hansa, the destroyer *Warasdiner*, and torpedo boats 99M, 100M, 88F, and 84P were ordered to have steam up by 0500 ready to sortie if necessary. They might eventually be followed by the old coast defense battleship *Budapest*, escorted by three torpedo boats. *Sankt Georg*, a 7,420-ton armored cruiser first commissioned in 1905, had a primary armament of two 24cm/40, five 19cm/42, and four 15cm/40 guns. She could provide substantial support for the cruisers, especially if only light forces were in pursuit, but her best speed on trials was twenty-two knots. *Warasdiner* was a 386-ton destroyer that had been under construction for the Chinese government when the ship was taken over by the Austrian navy at the beginning of the war. She was slower than the *Tátras*. The high-seas torpedo boats that would escort *Sankt Georg* were 250-ton relatively new (completed 1915–1916) ships armed with two 7cm/30 guns and four 45cm torpedo tubes. They were capable of making twenty-eight knots and were maids of all work in the navy, performing a wide range of duties from convoy escorts to raids on the enemy coast. *Budapest* was an old (commissioned 1898) coast defense battleship, armed with a primary armament of two 24cm/40 and six 15cm/40 guns whose best speed had been seventeen knots. *Budapest* was part of a class that was now useful mostly for shore bombardments.[37]

Admiral Hansa explained in his report of the action that the Austrians had assumed that the alteration of the three cruisers so that they resembled destroyers would buy them time so they would not be immediately confronted with superior force. The assumption seemed to be that if they were reported as destroyers, only destroyer-type vessels would be sent against them. It remains to be seen if this was a valid assumption. Hansa also explained that the purpose of the parallel action by the Liechtenstein group of destroyers, reduced from a planned three to only two because of *Tátra*'s boiler problems, was to create alarm and confusion in enemy reports of Austrian movements.[38] The disadvantage of this plan was that it obviously meant a division of forces.

The three cruisers were topped off with coal and the three captains, Horthy, Heyssler, and Purschka, had a final conference over the impending operation. Ferdinand Ritter von Purschka was commander of the *Saida*. At the beginning of the war he had the uninspiring command of the old armored cruiser *Kaiserin und Königin Maria Theresia*, a thoroughly obsolete ship suitable only for coast defense. This had been followed by a period commanding the predreadnought *Babenberg*, during which he had participated in the general assault on the Italian coast on Italy's entry into the war. *Babenberg* had bombarded Ancona, but the old ship was likely to offer few possibilities for distinction, and command of the *Saida* was also a great opportunity for Purschka.[39]

Some of the captains took prosaic precautions. Heyssler sent a few of his as yet unpacked chests with clothes and linen to a ship destined to remain in port. He reasoned that he did not want to lose all his possessions in case his ship was hit because replacements in wartime Austria would be difficult. The day before the operation was one of rest, and then after dark on the 14th the force sailed, noiselessly and totally blacked out, through the mine-free channel into the Adriatic, increasing speed as planned to twenty-one knots on "a wonderfully tranquil night."[40] The raid was on.

CHAPTER FOUR

THE ATTACK ON
THE DRIFTERS

T HE ITALIAN NAVY by the end of March 1917 appears to have had some indication that the Austrians might have been planning something, although exactly what and where was uncertain. The suspicion seems to have come through intelligence of the refits undertaken in Austrian yards, although exactly how much of this the Italians actually knew is not known. They therefore made a determined effort to increase both the quantity and quality of the British contribution to the forces in the southern Adriatic. Viceammiraglio Camillo Corsi, the minister of marine, requested that these efforts be supported on the diplomatic front by the Italian ambassador in London.[1] Admiral Corsi began a memorandum addressed to the Admiralty with the flat statement: "It may reasonably be expected that the enemy might, at an early date, develop at sea greater activity, and especially in the Adriatic, with its light craft which, we are informed has been thoroughly refitted."[2]

Admiral Corsi used this information to point out the advantage in speed the Austrian light cruisers enjoyed over the British cruisers at Brindisi. He claimed the Austrians could achieve a speed of twenty-nine knots while the best the British cruisers could do was about twenty-five knots, which nullified the advantage their admittedly heavier armament might give them. Corsi therefore requested that the British substitute three light cruisers of the *Calliope* or a later class. These ships, joined to the Italian *Aquila* class just entering service, would "form a powerful and fast group of scouts, the want of which up to the present has been very badly felt, and without which it is impossible to hope to

obtain decisive results against the molesting fast units of the Austrian Fleet."[3]
The Italians also asked that the four "H"-class British destroyers that had been
promised but diverted to other duties in the Mediterranean be sent to Brindisi.

The Italian requests had little chance of immediate fulfillment. The Admiralty pointed out that what they termed "the increasing number" of German
light cruisers attached to the High Seas Fleet as well as the "large Fleet of Zep-
pelins" the Germans had for observation work in the North Sea was "causing
serious anxiety" to the Admiralty. This meant that, regrettably, the *Calliopes*
or newer classes could not be spared for the Adriatic. The British did promise
that once the German raider currently in the Indian Ocean had been destroyed, the number of British cruisers in the Adriatic would be restored to
five. As for the "H"-class destroyers, the British claimed that orders had actually been issued for them to proceed to the Adriatic, only to be cancelled after
the Germans had announced their intention to attack hospital ships in the
Mediterranean. The destroyers were now needed to escort the latter.[4]

The British, French, and Italian naval forces in the southern Adriatic potentially outnumbered their enemies, but they had the disadvantage of being divided and, as usual, not all were ready for sea. As the Austrians steamed
through the darkness in the early hours of 15 May, the Allied naval forces that
might come to the support of the exposed drifters were at two different points,
Brindisi and Valona, plus those at sea on different missions. The forces at Brindisi were by far the most numerous. The ships with steam up at 0330 ready to
sail at half-hour's notice were the British light cruiser *Bristol* and the Italian
destroyers *Pilo, Mosto, Acerbi,* and *Schiaffino.* The British light cruiser *Dartmouth* was at three hours' notice and was coming to half-hour's notice at 0500.
The British light cruiser *Liverpool* was at six hours' notice. The Italian ships
that would be ready to sail after raising steam included the scouts [*esploratori*]
Marsala, Racchia, and *Aquila* and destroyers *Insidioso, Impavido,* and *Indomito.* The third division of the battle squadron, consisting of three large armored cruisers, worked under a system of one always on duty and two off. This
meant that the duty ship, *San Giorgio,* was at an hour and a half's notice and
the *San Marco* and *Pisa* were at five hours' notice. Of the Brindisi torpedo
boat flotilla, the 13th squadriglia (four torpedo boats) was due to be outside of
Brindisi at 0630 for exercises; the 11th squadriglia (four torpedo boats) had one
section detailed for guard duties at the port defenses and another section ready
to raise steam, and the squadriglia of four high-seas torpedo boats was not
ready and their fires were extinguished. There were two Italian destroyers in
dock, and the French destroyer *Boutefeu* returned to Brindisi at 0600 with
problems with her steering chain and would not be immediately available.
The Italian naval air station at Brindisi had approximately a dozen seaplanes
ready but only one of them was equipped with wireless.[5] Consequently, of the
sizeable force at Brindisi, the only initial response could come from a British

light cruiser and four Italian destroyers, followed by a second British cruiser and an undetermined number of Italian ships. The 10,000-ton armored cruiser *San Giorgio* with her four 25.4cm/45 and eight 19cm/45 guns might have brought decisive firepower to any encounter, but with a speed no better than twenty-three knots, if that, she was unlikely to be able to intervene, and she demonstrated why for the Allies the large armored cruiser was an outmoded concept unsuited to Adriatic conditions.

Brindisi and Valona were also the locations of Italian naval air stations whose aircraft might intervene in any action. While exact numbers of aircraft actually ready to fly at any given moment are hard to pin down, in the first half of 1917 the naval air station at Brindisi had a nominal strength of seventeen flying boats composed of ten FBAs and seven L.3s. The latter were a later series of Macchi-built versions of a captured Austrian Lohner. There were a similar number of FBAs at Valona and small numbers of aircraft at Otranto and Santa Maria di Leuca.[6] The French had also established in 1916 a naval air station on the island of Corfu. The French material also included FBAs.[7]

The FBA—the initials standing for Franco-British Aviation—was probably the most numerous type of aircraft employed by the Allies in the southern Adriatic at the time. The little flying boat is not well remembered today and certainly lacked the glamour and appeal of other types with higher performance. Nevertheless the FBAs were widely used for reconnaissance and bombing in the French, Italian, British, Russian, and other naval air services, although the Royal Naval Air Service appears to have used the type primarily for training. Starting in 1915, Macchi built under license close to 1,000 FBAs in Italy during the war. The performance of different models naturally varied, but the aircraft had a crew of two, could be equipped with a machine gun, had a speed of 140–145 km/h and an endurance of three to four hours, and could carry 125 kg of bombs.[8]

On the opposite side of the Adriatic the Italians had two light battleships at Valona, the *Napoli* at three hours' notice and the *Roma* with fires extinguished and not ready. *Napoli*'s two 30.5cm/40 and twelve 20.3cm/45 guns could also have added decisive firepower to any encounter, but even if she could reach her trials speed of twenty-two knots she was still at a considerable disadvantage compared to the Austrians. Moreover, few ships were available to escort her. Of the other ships at Valona, the scout *Riboty* had fires out while refueling and the high-seas torpedo boat *Albatros* (216 tons) was taking on stores in preparation for sailing at 0430 to meet an incoming convoy. There were also four "*PN*"-class coastal torpedo boats and the high-seas torpedo boat *Clio* (216 tons), but only some of them were ready to raise steam while the others were taking on stores. The stationnaire *Europa*, an old converted merchant ship used as a seaplane transport and depot ship, had three aircraft ready.

There were other Italian ships scattered at different locations. A *Mas* boat was at Porto Palermo on the Albanian coast and the armored cruiser *Varese*, destroyer *Artigliere*, and auxiliary cruiser *Città di Siracusa* were at Butrino on the northern coast of Corfu. Three French destroyers, *Casque, Faulx*, and *Lucas*, detached from Brindisi, had arrived at Butrino the preceding day and were scheduled to leave at 0830 for exercises. They were potentially important in any pursuit of the Austrians.[9]

There were also other French and Italian units at sea including two submarines. The Italian submarine *F.10* (262 tons), one of a numerous class of small submarines, had sailed on the evening of the 13th to operate in a zone between 18° 25′ E and 18° 45′ E and 41° 55′ N and 42° 05′ N with orders to arrive on station before dawn on the 14th and remain in an ambush position during the day on the 14th and 15th, moving to 18° 25′ E at night to charge batteries. The submarine was due to leave its position the evening of the 15th. Unfortunately *F.10* was not equipped with wireless. The French submarine *Bernouilli* (397 tons) had also left on the night of the 13th to operate in the zone between 18° 55′ and the coast between the parallels 41° 40′ and 41° 50′ (the Gulf of Drin) with orders to wait in ambush during daylight on the 14th and 15th, moving to the eastern limit of the zone to charge batteries at night. The submarine was to begin the return trip on the night of the 16th. The *Bernouilli* also lacked wireless.

A more serious potential threat to the Austrians was a group of fast light craft led by the Italian scout *Mirabello* and consisting of the French destroyers *Commandant Rivière, Bisson*, and *Cimeterre*. The group had originally included the destroyer *Boutefeu*, but as we have seen the latter had been forced to return to Brindisi with a broken steering chain. The *Mirabello* group sailed from Brindisi the night of 14th and proceeded in line of file at twenty knots along a line north of the drifters. It was due to reach a position twenty miles west of Durazzo at 0300, then turn north and be off Cape Rodoni at dawn in a position to cut off the return of any enemy group which might have been operating in the straits during the night.

The other group at sea that night was a small Italian convoy bound for Valona. There were three freighters, *Verità, Bersagliere*, and *Carroccio*, escorted by the Italian destroyer *Borea*, a relatively small (330 tons) and older ship completed in 1903 and armed with five 57mm guns and four fourteen-inch torpedo tubes. *Carroccio*'s cargo included fifty tons of munitions as well as fifty torpedoes, and a portion of *Verità*'s cargo included barrels and cases of gasoline and petroleum. The convoy had sailed from Taranto on the 13th, spent the night at Gallipoli, and sailed again at 1000 on the morning of the 14th with the objective of being in a position six miles off Cape Linguetta by 0700 the following morning. The convoy was restricted to a speed of six and a half knots, the best that the slowest ship, *Bersagliere*, could do. A few minutes after 0300 the convoy was approximately three miles from the Albanian coast off Apri Ruga or possibly a little to the north of it. The ships were in a line of file, *Borea*, *Carroccio*, *Verità*, and *Bersagliere* on north-northeasterly course.[10]

The objective of the Austrian raid, the drifters, were organized by divisions averaging six ships per division. However, as seven drifters were under repair at their Gallipoli base, not all divisions were at full strength. The divisions, designated by letter, and the number of drifters actually out that night were deployed from west to east in the following order:

"N" Division (six drifters)
"B" Division (eight drifters)
"C" Division (four drifters)
"T" Division (eight drifters)
"E" Division (six drifters)
"A" Division (eight drifters)
"O" Division (six drifters)
"S" Division (six drifters)

In addition to the eight divisions of drifters, the senior officer of the line that night, Temporary Lieutenant Robert H. Baunton, RNR, patrolled in the drifter *Capella* equipped with wireless. One drifter in each division was also equipped with wireless except for "B" and "E" division, which had none. This made a total of fifty-three drifters actually on the line that night. Another division of drifters, "H" division, did not arrive on the line until after the Austrians had left. Two motor launches, *M.L.182* and *M.L.426*, were patrolling approximately four miles south of "N" division, the westernmost group. "A" division was due to leave for Taranto at daybreak and as a result was the only division to have nets hauled at 0200.[11]

The day's action began when the Austrian diversionary force under Fregattenkapitän Liechtenstein, proceeding at fifteen knots on a course of 241°, met *Borea*'s convoy and commenced the attack. The Austrian and Italian official histories differ on the exact time. The matter of time is a particular source of confusion in reports of the Otranto Straits battle. The Austrians normally followed central European time, or as it was known in German *Mitteleuropäischen Zeit* (MEZ), which was Greenwich mean time plus one. The Italians were supposedly under the same time. However, during the First World War, in common with most of the other powers, the Austrians adopted a form of daylight saving time called *Sommerzeit*. The Italians apparently did not. In 1917, *Sommerzeit* was in force in Austria from 16 April to 17 September, although based on a comparison with times of events cited in Italian reports, the Austrian navy apparently retained MEZ. British ships in the Adriatic were ordered to follow central European time, that is GMT + 1 rather than GMT, although this does not appear to have always been the case, especially with the drifters. Italian reporting was also subject to wide variation, some based on

Italian local time. This was the subject of complaints by British officers after the battle.[12] Nevertheless, the Italian reconstruction of the attack on the convoy, published five years after the Austrian version, seems in this case to coincide better with survivors' accounts and the sequence of events on the Allied side.[13] Moreover, Liechtenstein's report as well as the logs of *Csepel* and *Balaton* support the Ufficio Storico account.[14]

On sighting *Borea* leading the file of ships, *Csepel* and *Balaton* increased to full speed to pass along the starboard side of the Italian ships at a distance of about 1,000 meters. At 870 tons standard displacement and with an armament of two 10cm and six 6.6cm guns and four 45cm torpedo tubes, the Austrian destroyers were far superior in armament to the Italian destroyer. The *Borea* sighted the Austrians and flashed the recognition signal. There was no reply and at 0326 *Csepel* opened fire on the destroyer while *Balaton* fired on the next in line, the freighter *Carroccio*. *Borea* was caught in the Austrian searchlights and was at a distinct disadvantage. The destroyer had just commenced a zigzag ahead of the convoy and was proceeding with only two of her three boilers lit in order to conserve fuel. The practice was prescribed for destroyers and torpedo boats on escort service because of the fuel shortage, but it meant *Borea*'s speed was limited to twenty-four knots. It would have required ten minutes for her third boiler to be lit and become fully effective, but the destroyer did not have the time. Her bow at this moment was at an angle of 30° to the left of the route. Although the destroyer's captain ordered the helm hard to starboard and full speed, his ship was exposed and it may have been only the second of the Austrian shells that ruptured the main steam pipe, leading to a complete loss of steam pressure, which immobilized the engines and generators and rendered *Borea*'s wireless unusable. Communications between bow and stern were cut off, hampering efforts to shut off the escaping steam. The *Borea* was hit at least twice again and began to take on water and list to port. In the meantime *Balaton*'s fire had started a noticeable blaze on the *Carroccio*, laden with munitions, and as the Austrian destroyer continued on past the stricken destroyer, she shifted fire to the *Borea* and fired a torpedo, which missed. The Italian destroyer could only return feeble counterfire. The *Carroccio*'s captain, conscious of the explosive nature of his cargo, ordered the ship abandoned. The Austrian destroyers, recognizing that the *Borea* was helpless, shifted their fire to the two remaining ships and each also launched a pair of torpedoes. The *Verità* sustained a hit in a steam pipe, rendering her motionless, and a blaze erupted from small cases of gasoline stored at the stern. Her crew fired ineffectually at the Austrians. The third ship, *Bersagliere*, also sustained hits but none were serious.

This first phase of the attack had lasted approximately five minutes, followed by a lull of approximately eight minutes. During this interval, the *Verità*'s captain, observing that the gasoline fire appeared to be spreading and his

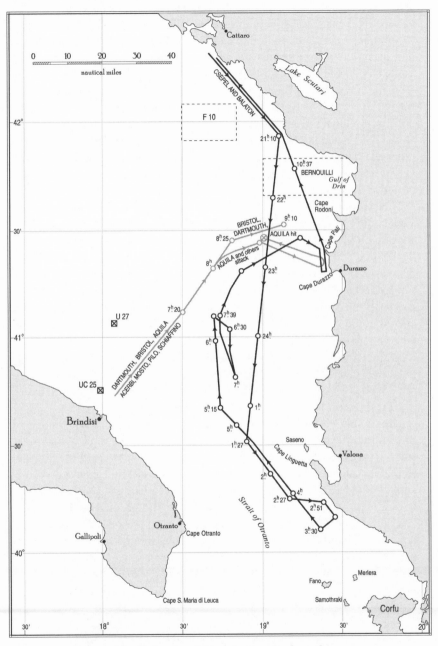

Action of the *Balaton* and *Csepel* —the attack on the convoy

ship was immobilized, gave the order to abandon ship. The *Bersagliere* was able to steam ahead slowly, but her crew, not knowing the course of the action or that the damage was slight, lowered the pinnace and prepared to embark, the pinnace being tied to the ship and towed along with it. The two Austrian destroyers, having reversed course, reappeared, this time passing down the opposite side of the convoy. They resumed fire for a little more than five minutes, illuminating the Italian ships in their searchlights. *Bersagliere* was not hit, but one of her lifeboats, with some of the crew aboard, sustained damage, possibly from machine gun fire. This caused the boat to take on water and created the danger it might sink. The *Verità* escaped further damage during the renewed attack, but the *Carroccio* was hit again in the stern and the *Borea* sustained additional hits forward, and her torpedo room flooded. The action ceased at 0345.

The Austrians were convinced that at least one of their torpedoes had hit the *Verità*. They also observed dense clouds of smoke rising from the Italian destroyer and the *Carroccio* ablaze and apparently sinking by the stern, her lifeboats filled with survivors. It was time to go. Liechtenstein had intended to take survivors of the sinking ships on board but decided against it because of the possibility the glare from the burning ships might permit enemy units to approach the Austrians undetected. Moreover, he reasoned that the calm sea and proximity of land assured the safety of the shipwrecked Italian sailors. He anticipated an enemy reaction and his preoccupation was now to get away from the vicinity of Valona as quickly as possible. As the Austrian destroyers passed the parallel of Saseno Island they could detect a column of smoke from the direction of Valona, indicating that the enemy was indeed putting to sea. At 0445 they had reached a point fifteen miles west of Saseno.

The captain of the *Borea*, Capitano di corvetta Franceschi, who had been thrown into the water along with some of the crew by the force of the explosions, managed with another officer and some sailors to board the stricken ship. They attempted to save the wounded with makeshift rafts and destroy confidential books, but they eventually had to abandon the ship, which sank at 0522. The *Verità* remained adrift and ablaze, the fires fed by the gasoline and oil. Her surviving crew headed for the coast in lifeboats. The *Bersagliere* was in good condition, but the captain and crew who had taken to the boats were frustrated in their attempts to climb back aboard. They had drifted some distance away during the action, and the waterlogged and overloaded condition of their lifeboat made progress very slow. The first ships coming to their rescue arrived a little after 0600.[15]

The Austrian attack had been so rapid that the only two ships equipped with wireless in the convoy, *Borea* and *Carroccio*, were unable to make any signals before they were disabled. Consequently, the first warnings the Italians had was at 0330, when the lookout station at Saseno heard the rumble of gunfire and shortly afterwards observed the gleam of fires from the burning ships. They reported their observations to the Italian naval command at Valona. Further south along the Albanian coast, the lookout station at Porto Palermo also observed and reported a fire at sea at 0350. The high-seas torpedo boat *Albatros* had steam up and was ready to sail by 0430 but was ordered to wait until dawn to avoid the danger of blundering into a superior force in the darkness. This, fortunately for survivors of the convoy, was not long. There was sufficient light at 0440 for the *Albatros* to sail at full speed to the scene of the apparent action. Simultaneously, the coastal torpedo boats 33.*PN*, 34.*PN*, and 35.*PN*, followed shortly afterwards by the high-seas torpedo boat *Clio* and tug *Luni*, were raising steam. The scout *Riboty* had been anchored off Ducati in Valona bay and at 0440 received orders to raise steam. But this took time and it was not until 0800 before she came alongside the *Europa* to take on necessary fuel, and it was 0945 before she was actually ready to sail. The *Riboty* had not been under notice for sea and her bunkers were empty as a result. Nevertheless, that it required more than five hours after receiving the order to make ready before she was able to sail explains why strength on paper did not necessarily translate into force at sea when and where it was necessary. This was even more evident in the case of the light battleships at Valona, the *Napoli* and *Roma*. Both were ordered to raise steam. *Napoli* was ready around 1000, *Roma* not until 1115. They played no part in the action that day.[16]

The Italian "new weapons," aircraft and *Mas* boats, were much quicker at responding to the alarm. It was only twenty minutes after the alarm was given before *Mas.28* left Porto Palermo heading toward the glow of the fires. Dawn also permitted the handful of aircraft at Valona to be employed, and at 0500 an FBA flying boat took off, followed by a second at 0525. Probably because of the morning mist, the first FBA observed nothing except two Italian ships apparently heading back toward the coast. They were the two coastal torpedo boats 34.*PN* and 35.*PN*. The pair had been ordered to sail and reconnoiter to the west, the direction from which the sound of gunfire was heard, apparently coming from the drifter line. At 0645 the aircraft sighted the *Mirabello* group coming from the north. The FBA landed near the *Europa* at 0700, refueled, and promptly took off again with a new crew.

The second FBA, piloted by Sottotenente di Vascello Spagnolo with 2nd Capo timoniere Giuseppe Poggi as observer, had a more productive sortie. The FBA sighted the torpedo boats from Valona coming to the rescue of the convoy as well as the *Mas* from Porto Palermo, and shortly afterwards the remnants of the convoy, both survivors and wreckage. The two aviators signaled the survivors that help was on the way. They then glimpsed very distant smoke in the direction of Cape Santa Maria di Leuca. The FBA investigated and eventually spotted a cruiser with four funnels northwest of Fano Island approximately twenty miles distant steering northwest. The pilot immediately turned toward the ship and arrived overhead at around 0630. He was still not certain of the ship's nationality, for the British *Dublin*-class also had four funnels, and so he circled without dropping bombs until he definitely established it was a *Novara*-class light cruiser. The cruiser was Horthy's *Novara*. The FBA dropped two mine-grenades and a small bomb from an altitude of about 1,500 meters. One of the bombs did not immediately release and required a second pass before it was dislodged. The bombs fell near but did not hit the cruiser, which took evasive action and fired back. The Austrians reported the time of the attack as 0620 from a height of 1,800–2,500 meters with three bombs falling abeam of the bridge and astern to port causing no damage. At that height — over 5,000 feet — and given the relative speed of the ship and the aircraft, both the bombing and anti-aircraft fire were not likely to be effective. The real potential contribution of an FBA in these circumstances was reconnaissance, and the pilot now flew northeast to intercept 34.PN and 35.PN west of Saseno and signal to them the presence of the enemy cruiser. The FBA glided down and the aviators made signs for the ships to follow a course to intercept the Austrians. The FBA also sighted the *Mirabello* group, descended again to furnish information about the Austrians, and then flew off to regain contact with the enemy. At 0715 the FBA observed the rendezvous of the three Austrian cruisers, who then appeared to steam at full speed toward the north. A few minutes later the two aviators watched the first exchange of fire between the Austrians and the *Mirabello* group. (See below, p. 74.) They landed back in Valona bay at 0750.[17] The offensive capabilities of an FBA were unimpressive, but the little aircraft had given a striking demonstration of how naval aviation could gather information well beyond the horizon in a rapidly changing situation.

In the meantime, *Albatros* and *Mas.28*, arriving from different directions, reached the survivors of the convoy shortly after 0600. The *Albatros* picked up the majority of survivors from the three steamers and the *Borea*. *Mas.28* met four lifeboats from the *Carroccio* but the small craft could not embark that many people and could only direct them toward a landing place on the nearby coast. The boat then approached the burning *Verità* and picked up a number of survivors and brought them to the *Albatros*. In turn, the boat received from the latter some severely wounded and took them to Porto Palermo, arriving at 0930. The boat's rescue duties were not over. *Mas.28* immediately put to sea again to gather the survivors of the *Carroccio* from the beach where they had landed and bring them back to Porto Palermo. In the meantime, the *Albatros* attempted to save the remaining ships, transferring the crew back to the *Bersagliere*. The latter was able to raise steam and after forty-five minutes was able to proceed at seven knots, escorted by the *Albatros*, back to Valona, passing the boom at 1325. The Italians were also able to salvage the abandoned *Verità* after the tug *Luni* and coastal torpedo boat 35.PN arrived on the scene at 0800. The tug was able to put a party of four men aboard the bow of the burning ship to attach a cable so that the hulk, still burning, could be towed to Valona, where the fires were eventually extinguished. The final toll of Liechtenstein's attack on the convoy was therefore a destroyer and merchant ship sunk and a merchant ship badly damaged. There were 184 crew or passengers on the ships; the survivors numbered 162. The sunken destroyer *Borea* suffered two dead and nine missing plus twelve of her forty-eight survivors wounded.[18] This was the heaviest loss suffered by any Italian ship that day.

The action of the *Csepel* and *Balaton* was only a diversionary action. The main attack involved the three cruisers on the drifter line itself. Once again there is a problem with reported times. In theory both the Allies and Austrians used central European time as a basis for reporting, but this poses a problem. The senior officer on the line and the eastern divisions of drifters reported hearing the sound of heavy firing to the northeast at 0230. This does not coincide exactly with the time (0326) the Liechtenstein group commenced its attack on the convoy, but the variation of close to an hour would seem to indicate that the British reports used GMT rather than the CET/MEZ of the Italians and Austrians. Commodore Heneage does state in his report that times reported varied considerably, probably due to inaccurate clocks, and this probably accounts for the variations in minutes.[19]

It is now time to return to the main attack on the drifter line. The three Austrian cruisers steaming on a southwesterly course at twenty-one knots went from a line-ahead formation to a line-abreast formation between 1200 and 0100 so as to present less of a target in an area where submarines had frequently been observed. Linienschiffskapitän Heyssler in *Helgoland*, the westernmost cruiser, noted that "not the faintest light could be seen," no signals were exchanged, and the wireless was silent. The beams of Italian searchlights at Valona soon appeared on the eastern horizon and later the lights at Brindisi appeared in the opposite direction. The cruisers separated as planned at 0215.[20] It was a still, moonlit night with good visibility, but the center cruiser, *Saida*, was soon out of sight to those in the *Helgoland*. The three cruisers were now on their own with tension mounting but with no sign that the Allies had been alerted. At 0358 indistinct objects were noticed just starboard of *Helgoland*'s course. The shapes soon became clearer. They were drifters. Heyssler intended to commence the main attack by daylight and, to achieve greater surprise, launch his attack from the south. He therefore altered course to pass to the starboard of the drifters. One of the latter blinked a signal with a message lamp. Heyssler ordered the same signal made in reply. The ruse worked. There was no alarm. British reports confirm that Divisions "N," "O," and "E" at times between 0230 and 0245 observed large ships recognized as cruisers passing them steaming southward. The drifters considered them friendly. The Austrians later confirmed the success of their disguise from interviews with prisoners. In the *Helgoland*, those on the bridge could also discern other indistinct objects further to the east, obviously more drifters. By 0447 Heyssler had brought the ship far enough round Cape Santa Maria di Leuca to be able to see into the Gulf of Taranto. There was no shipping in sight. He turned the ship back toward the drifter line to commence his attack only to hear gunfire further to the east. One of the other cruisers, probably *Saida*, had begun the action.[21]

The drifters in the eastern divisions had been aware of the attack on the Italian convoy. It would be the only warning they had that anything unusual would happen, but obviously at first they did not realize that it would involve them. Lieutenant Baunton, the senior officer in the line in the drifter *Capella*, heard heavy firing to the northeast at 0230 and, in the belief that it was a submarine caught on the surface, proceeded in this direction. He then observed a large flare, which seemed to confirm his assumption, and he continued on this course. However, at a time not given in the report, there was another outburst of heavy firing accompanied by the rockets used as distress signals. This time they came from the southeast, and Baunton now realized it was the drifters that were under attack. He reversed course but by the time he returned to the drifter line the raiders had departed. There remained only the work of cleaning up, the attempt to save damaged craft, tending to the wounded, and attempting to reorganize the line.

It is difficult to reconcile British and Austrian times and the exact sequence of events during the attack.[22] Perhaps this is only to be expected in a night action at different locations and on the British side involving drifters that were improvised warships lacking the formal organization and procedure of a regular naval vessel. Perhaps, too, the exact sequence is not important; the end result was the same. It would probably be expedient for the purposes of clarity to follow the practice of the British official reports and recount events as they unfolded from west to east. The westernmost division, "N," hearing heavy firing to the east—almost certainly *Saida*'s attack—slipped their nets at about 0315. The division then headed for Cape Santa Maria di Leuca. After about fifteen minutes they were attacked by a cruiser coming from the south. This was *Helgoland*, and Heyssler spotted in the first light of dawn a drifter dead ahead and then to the east other drifters apparently on a course for Otranto. Heyssler then asked his gunnery officer at what range he would prefer to fire. Linienschiffsleutnant Alexander Milosević replied, "800 meters." Heyssler accordingly steered to the westernmost drifter at this distance, ran up the battle ensign to the foretop at 0453, and opened fire with the starboard battery. According to Heyssler, it took a while before hits were scored and men were observed taking to the boats, clouds of steam escaping, and the drifter taking on a noticeable list. This procedure was, however, too slow for Heyssler, who feared the other drifters might escape. He therefore closed the range when firing at the second drifter, and the latter's boiler blew up. The crews of the

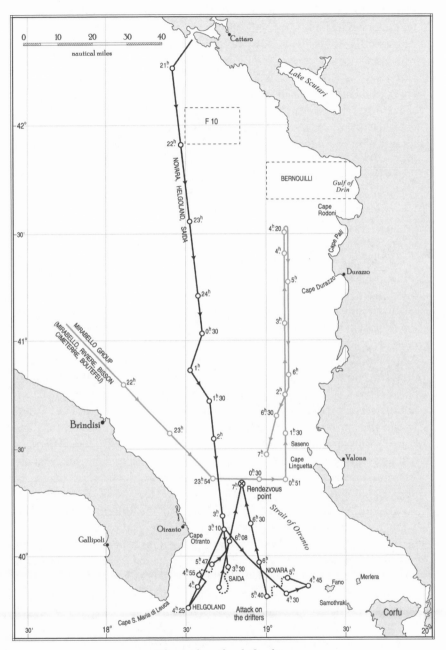

The raid on the drifter line

other drifters by now seem to have taken to their boats, anticipating that their ships would be sunk. Heyssler claimed that he had given orders to fire only after the crews had taken to the boats, for the objective was to sink the drifters with as little loss of life as possible. This is confirmed by the British reports which state that by blowing a siren and dipping her ensign, the enemy cruiser gave all crews a chance to escape before opening fire, and in the case of some crews who had abandoned their ships, headed off the dinghies from the damaged drifters. Heyssler, at ranges closing from 800 to 200 meters, methodically cruised along the drifters, firing alternately with the starboard and port batteries and, after observing a boiler explode and fire raging, moving on to the next drifter. He did not wait for the drifter to actually sink. He did not want to waste ammunition and he assumed the ship was in any case unusable.

Not all drifter men were willing to abandon ship in the face of overwhelming force. Some chose to fight. The sixth drifter in line made a lasting impression on Heyssler. The range had closed to only fifty meters and the crew had taken to their boats save for a lone sailor manning the little gun on the foredeck. The gun seemed pointed directly at *Helgoland*'s bridge waiting to pick off her officers. Heyssler decided he could not wait any longer and gave the order to fire. All six guns of *Helgoland*'s starboard battery opened up with devastating results. The drifter broke up and sank almost immediately, some of the debris landing on *Helgoland*'s deck. This may have been the drifter *Admirable* of "N" division, later included in a list of special recommendations to the Admiralty. The description is a bit different but essentially the same. The drifter is reported to have come under heavy fire, which she returned, but her boiler exploded and the wheelhouse was shot away. The crew abandoned ship but the second hand, A. Gordon, scrambled back on board and ran forward toward the gun with the apparent intention of continuing the fight. He was killed before reaching the gun and the *Admirable* eventually sank. This does not, however, match Heyssler's description of a lone sailor deliberately taking aim, and it is possible Heyssler was describing another drifter whose heroic action was not noted by any on the British side or at least by any survivor.

Division "N" also contained the most famous of the drifters, the *Gowan Lea* and her skipper, Joseph Watt. They quickly became part of the heroic lore of the war in Great Britain. Watt, when summoned to surrender and abandon ship by the cruiser only 100 yards off, chose to fight and reportedly ordered his crew to give three cheers and fight to the finish. He ordered full speed ahead but apparently was able to get off only a single round from his small 57mm gun before an Austrian shell disabled the breech of the gun. The gun crew, under fire, attempted to remedy the fault. During this time a box of ammunition exploded, seriously wounding a deck hand, F. H. Lamb. Lamb nevertheless continued to work with the crew in an attempt to get the gun working again. The cruiser continued on its path, leaving the *Gowan Lea* damaged, but apparently not seriously. Watt was later able to bring the *Gowan Lea* alongside another seriously damaged drifter, the *Floandi* of "O" division, and assisted in removing the dead and wounded.

The image of Watt with his 57mm popgun refusing to surrender and challenging the cruiser caught the imagination of his superiors in the navy. This is reflected in the relevant volume of the official history, where author Henry Newbolt invoked the memory of the Elizabethan age and the heroic fight of Sir Richard Grenville and the *Revenge* against the Spanish fleet off the Azores in 1591: "These encounters recall the immortal fight of 'the one and the fifty-three'; but even the odds against Sir Richard Grenville can scarcely have reached such a height as in the action between the Austrian cruiser and Skipper Watt of the *Gowan Lea*."[23] Watt was subsequently awarded the Victoria Cross. The action of the *Gowan Lea* does not appear to be specifically noted in Austrian reports, probably because her gunfire was ineffectual and, as Newbolt surmised, the Austrians might not have believed the little drifter could survive under the cascade of shells and would succumb the same way as many of the others. They therefore moved on to other targets. This does nothing to diminish the gallantry of Skipper Watt and the crew of the *Gowan Lea*.

"N" division had suffered severe losses. Of the six drifters on the line that night, *Transit*, *Admirable*, and *Selby* were sunk and *Jean* and *Gowan Lea* severely damaged. "B" division, the next to the east, reported being attacked at about 0330 by two enemy cruisers. The second cruiser could only have been *Saida*. This division of drifters did not have time to slip their nets until after they were attacked. This coincides with Heyssler's account of seeing two drifters about 2,000 meters to the east who opened fire on the *Helgoland* but scored no hits. He particularly noted that between the drifters and the cruiser there was a long line of nets towed by the two drifters and marked by floats made of leather, sailcloth, or glass balls. He ordered his bow gun to fire on the drifters while he maneuvered *Helgoland* with engines and rudder carefully through the nets to avoid fouling his screws. The drifting nets may have caused more anxiety to the Austrian cruisers than the drifter's light armament, for should their screws become fouled, as might easily happen in the poor light conditions, any chance they might escape from superior Allied forces would be ended.

The two drifters that Heyssler thought had fired on the *Helgoland* were the *Felicitas* and *Girl Gracie*, although it was probably only the former as the latter is listed as being unarmed. Both were sunk by the guns of the cruiser. Not all the men of the *Felicitas* had life jackets and others could not swim. Hearing their call for help, the first officer[24] of the *Helgoland*, Korvettenkapitän Viktor Klöckner, asked Heyssler if they could stop. Heyssler agreed and a boat from the cruiser was lowered to save eight men. The crews of the cruiser's starboard battery manned the ropes to hoist boat and survivors back aboard in an episode that lasted less than five minutes. The survivors in a boat from the unarmed *Girl Gracie* were also beckoned aboard and as the cruiser moved forward the wash from her screws capsized their empty lifeboat. *Helgoland* had picked up a total of eighteen survivors. Heyssler reported that he could now discern to the south the *Saida* in the early morning light. He also spotted another drifter attempting to escape but refrained from pursuing because the action would have cost too much time. The lucky drifter, identity unknown, therefore escaped. At 0523 the *Helgoland* intercepted a signal from the *Novara* to the *Saida* in reply to an unrecorded query stating that if there was nothing further to destroy they should make full speed for the "battlefield" [*kampfplatz*]. The latter was interpreted as meaning the cruiser rendezvous. *Helgoland* turned away from the drifter line at 0547 and increased speed to twenty-five knots on a course for the rendezvous.

"B" division had eight drifters on the line. *Felicitas* and *Girl Gracie* were its two losses, and the others escaped. "C" division also reported being under fire from two cruisers, obviously the *Helgoland* and *Saida*. Linienschiffskapitän Purschka, commanding the *Saida*, had the least distance to steam after the cruisers separated and apparently was the first of the cruiser commanders to spot the drifters, detecting several at 0345. In order to avoid premature disclosure, the *Saida* stopped engines and remained motionless for about half an hour before Purschka commenced his attack at 0420. The first drifter taken under fire was quickly set ablaze although her crew fired back bravely with their small gun before being compelled to abandon ship. They were picked up by the *Saida*. Purschka reported picking up a total of nineteen survivors and setting another two drifters on fire, one with a heavy list. He observed their boilers exploding. The *Saida* departed for the cruiser rendezvous at 0520. "C" division lost only one of the four drifters out that night, the *Quarry Knowe*. The relatively light loss may have been due to the drifters scattering in all directions as the attack began. The drifter *Garrigill* of "C" division, armed with a six-pounder, was especially cited in reports of the action for being one of the first attacked and immediately returning enemy fire with all members of the crew behaving "in a highly credible manner."

The other drifter division attacked by the *Saida* was "T." The division had been out at its full strength of eight, but lost only the *Young Linnett*. This may have been due to the quick action of the senior officer of the division, Temporary Sub-Lieutenant O'Neill in the drifter *Frigate Bird*, the only one equipped with wireless. O'Neill first heard the sound of firing around 0335 and promptly transmitted an "SOS," then proceeded to move about his division, ordering the drifters to slip their nets and scatter. The *Young Linnett* appears to have been steaming east when it was unfortunate enough to be caught by the *Saida*, although the other drifters in the division were at one time or another under fire also. It is not clear whether it was *Quarry Knowe* or *Young Lin-*

nett that Purschka reported as firing back, but the Austrians were mistaken in believing the drifter's gun was as large as a 7cm. Neither drifter in fact had anything larger than a 57mm.[25] The skipper and crew of *Christmas Daisy* of "T" division were subsequently praised for remaining at their stations while under fire and going to the assistance of other drifters while the attack was in progress. The drifter luckily escaped damage. The timely scattering of "C" and "T" also explains why the *Saida* had the lowest score of the three cruisers.

Horthy in the *Novara* reached the drifter line after the other two cruisers had begun their attacks. He was actually guided to the drifter line by the flash of gunfire and exploding shells and the glow of burning ships. Eventually, by 0455 Horthy could make out twelve drifters ahead, and from a position eight nautical miles northwest of Fano Island in a calm sea, he opened fire at 0507. The brunt of the attack appears to have first fallen on "O" Division, who had slipped their nets at 0325 (0425 Austrian time) and were proceeding toward Fano. They reported being attacked at about 0415 (0515 Austrian time) by a cruiser coming from the south. Of the six drifters in the division actually out that night, three, *Taits*, *Coral Haven*, and *Girl Rose*, were sunk and two, *Floandi* and *Union*, were disabled. The *Novara* was reported as proceeding slowly, perhaps even stopping at times. The drifters of "O" division apparently resisted fiercely. Skipper R. Cowe and his crew in the *Coral Haven* were subsequently cited for behaving "in an extraordinary manner," returning fire with their 57mm from their burning ship until forced to leave as the ship sank. The men of the *Taits* also fought back with their 57mm until the last moment before abandoning the sinking ship. They then noticed that one of the crew had been left on board and rowed back in their lifeboat, reportedly under heavy fire, to rescue him. The *Girl Rose* found her 57mm outranged and was unable to hit back though repeatedly struck and finally abandoned in a sinking condition. The senior officer of the division was in *Floandi*, the only drifter in "O" division equipped with wireless. The ship fought back with her six-pounder but was badly damaged, suffering four killed and three wounded from a complement of only ten. Skipper D. J. Nicholls was wounded in three places but remained at his post until the firing ceased, and he then had to struggle to keep the badly damaged vessel afloat. The engine men also remained at their posts until the steam pipe was shot away. The second engine man was killed and the first engine man wounded, but the latter went below to draw fires immediately after the action ceased. The *Floandi* was actually so badly damaged that had the sea not been calm and the weather good the battered drifter would certainly have sunk. Nicholls was subsequently awarded the Conspicuous Gallantry Medal.[26] The *Morning Star II*, the only drifter in the division to survive without serious damage, was apparently one of the first taken under fire by the *Novara* at a range of 800 yards. The crew returned fire until the cruiser moved off and claimed to have observed several hits.[27] *Novara*, however, reported having received only two "insignificant" hits during the entire encounter with the drifters, a fact that only emphasized the hopeless nature of the encounter between a well-armed cruiser and the lightly armed drifters.

"S" division had been the easternmost group of drifters on the line. They reported being attacked at about 0400 by a cruiser they had observed passing to the south at about 0300. Four of the six drifters were sunk. The *Avondale, Serene, Craignoon,* and *Helenora* were abandoned by their crews. *Novara* stopped to pick them up and reported after the action having thirty-five prisoners. There was one holdout. Second Hand Joseph Henry of the *Serene* did not want to be taken prisoner and refused to leave the ship until forced to do so just before it sank. He then spent about an hour in the water before being lucky enough to be picked up. The drifter *British Crown,* one of the two survivors of the division, was subsequently commended for the actions of her crew in remaining at their posts and later assisting in picking up survivors. Horthy, in the laconic style of his memoirs, acknowledged the resistance: "We gave their crews warning, but not all of them took to their boats; some manned their automatic guns and fired until their boilers exploded or their ships capsized. Crews that had abandoned ship were taken on board by us."[28]

The *Novara* turned away at 0537 to proceed to the cruiser rendezvous. Horthy had sunk seven drifters, the biggest score of the three cruisers. The fact that he was so busy with "O" and "S" divisions probably facilitated the escape of "E" division. This group of six drifters had slipped their nets at 0330 and scattered. At least one of the division, *Bon Espoir,* came under fire, for her skipper and crew were specifically commended for behaving "in an exemplary manner" by not leaving their division and later picking up several survivors and wounded. The drifter escaped damage. The eight drifters of "A" division had been just to the east of the heavily attacked "O" division. They were, however, due to return to Taranto and had hauled their nets and started on their way at 0300. Consequently they were a safe distance to the south when the attacks began. After the firing had ceased they returned to the line to render assistance to the wounded and disabled drifters. The drifters *Mill O'Buckie* and *Endeavour II* of "A" division were especially commended for their service in this work.

After the raid, the surviving drifters were ordered to assemble at Fano Island. Here they were reorganized and given orders for patrol. However, until the necessary protection could be provided, the drifters would not be at sea at night.[29] The Austrian raid had been a success. Fourteen drifters had been sunk, three seriously damaged, and one less severely damaged. Since there were forty-seven drifters out that night, this was not the "clean sweep" Horthy had mentioned in his rhetorical flourish when planning the raid, but it was serious enough for the British to customarily refer to the fate of the drifters as a "disaster." Seventy-two men from the drifters were taken prisoner. The Austrian intent to spare life when possible also appears to have resulted in a low number of killed or missing, possibly as few as nine,[30] and the British appreciated the Austrian conduct. Commodore Heneage noted: "The Austrian cruisers on the flanks of the attack [*Helgoland* and *Novara*] behaved with chivalry in giving the crews of the drifters time to leave their ships, and did not fire at the crews in the dinghies. The behaviour of the centre cruiser [*Saida*] does not appear to have been quite so good, but the evidence on this point is not very clear."[31] In the third year of this bitter war, this acknowledgment of chivalry was becoming less common, but then British-Austrian relations lacked the hard edge of Anglo-German relations. The British and Austrians were in some ways almost accidental enemies.

The Austrians had until then been very lucky. In addition to the damage inflicted on the drifter line, they had also sunk a destroyer and merchant ship off the Albanian coast, all without suffering any casualties themselves. However, the three Austrian cruisers had been as far south as 165 miles from Cattaro. Brindisi, with its potentially superior Allied forces, was actually approximately forty miles nearer to the Bocche. It was daylight by the time the three cruisers left the drifter line, and the Austrians could anticipate that the alarm had been given. They now had to reach the safety of the Bocche, and this was not a foregone conclusion.

CHAPTER FIVE

THE PURSUIT

THE FIRST INFORMATION to reach the Italian naval command at Brindisi that a raid was in progress came from the semaphore station on the island of Saseno off Valona bay. At 0348 (central European time), Saseno transmitted a wireless signal stating that artillery flashes had been observed to the south-southeast. This was obviously the destroyer attack on *Borea*'s convoy, and four minutes later, at 0352, Saseno sent an additional message confirming that it was the convoy under attack. At 0433 Saseno reported the sound of heavy gunfire to the south-southwest, which was obviously the cruiser's attack on the drifters. At 0450 the Italian wireless station at Palascia—the lighthouse on the promontory south of Otranto forming the easternmost point of the Italian mainland—reported the alarm and distress flares fired by the drifters as well as the sound of a heavy bombardment along the barrage. At 0505 Palascia sent a new report stating that a cruiser was systematically attacking the drifter line. The Italian semaphore station at Palascia made similar reports. At 0410 the latter reported the initiation of gunfire in the straits and at 0510 observed two ships but could not establish the type in the prevailing mist. The unknown ships were still in sight at 0555, apparently proceeding northward at approximately fourteen knots, and they only disappeared from sight at 0615.[1] There was yet an additional report of Austrian activity from the French destroyer *Commandant Bory*, which was proceeding from Taranto to Corfu for exercises. Her commander, Lieutenant de vaisseau Cras, at approximately 0430 observed flashes of gunfire far to the north and proceeded to the scene of the

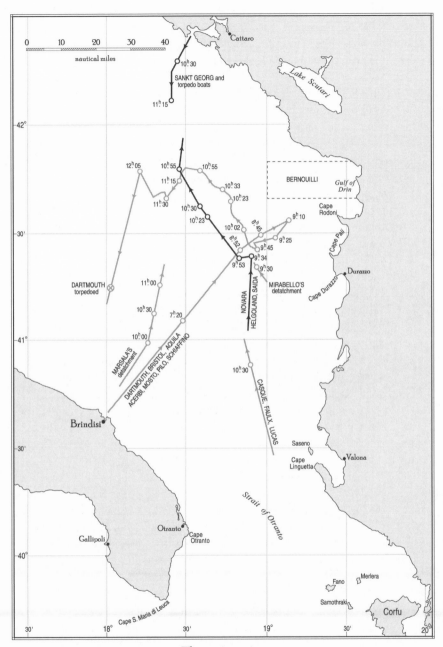

The main action

apparent action. Due to a faulty air pump the destroyer was unable to make more than eighteen knots, but she arrived in time to observe two Austrian cruisers leaving the scene. Unable to follow, the destroyer proceeded to the aid of the survivors, who noted the identification "BR" painted on her bow. Cras, however, spotted an Austrian submarine, apparently the *U.4.* The submarine submerged and the *Commandant Bory*, restricted in speed and therefore unable to follow the cruisers, spent the remainder of the morning hunting the submarine, without success. The mechanical faults that prevented the destroyer from taking part in the pursuit were among a number that would bedevil the French and Italians during the day. *Commandant Bory*'s signal reporting the Austrians was only received by Brindisi at 0530 according to French sources, or 0537 according to Italian.[2]

It was obvious that just before dawn the Italian authorities knew a raid of some sort was taking place in the Strait of Otranto. How did they react? Contrammiraglio Alfredo Acton, the commander of the Divisione Esploratori and senior naval officer at Brindisi, was in his flagship, the old cruiser *Etna*. Launched in 1885, the ship had been relegated to training duties well before the war and now served as a floating headquarters or depot ship.[3] Acton ordered the ships in harbor to raise steam. He also attempted to use those of his ships that were already at sea, notably the *Mirabello* group under the command of Capitano di fregata Vicuna. This force, consisting of an Italian flotilla leader and three French destroyers, had proceeded along its planned patrol route well to the north of the drifter line. It had probably crossed paths with the Austrian cruisers during the night, each side unaware of the other. At 0420 Vicuna had reached the northern limit of his patrol, 41° 30′ north and 19° 06′ east, and turned to the south. At approximately 0435 he had intercepted the wireless signal from Saseno concerning the action against the drifter line and at 0440 received Acton's signal from *Etna* confirming the presence of the enemy in the straits and ordering him to steer to the south.[4]

The British light cruiser *Bristol* had been at a half hour's notice and was therefore one of the first to sail at 0450, accompanied by the Italian destroyers *Pilo* and *Mosto*. Acton ordered the *Bristol* to steer a course of 45°, toward the Gulf of Drin, but at a speed of only twenty knots so as not to distance themselves too far from the *Dartmouth* or the other Italian ships that were raising steam and preparing to sail.[5] Acton's objective was to cut off the enemy coming northward from the Strait of Otranto.[6] The *Bristol*, launched in 1910, was one of a class of five light cruisers of 5,300 tons full load displacement and theoretically capable of twenty-five knots. Her main armament consisted of two six-inch and ten four-inch guns. Her armament was somewhat heavier but her speed slightly less than an Austrian *Helgoland*. The ship had seen action in the West Indies early in the war when she pursued the German cruiser *Karlsruhe* and at the battle of the Falklands in December 1914, where with the armed merchant cruiser *Macedonia* she captured and sank two colliers supporting the German squadron. The class, the first to be considered "light cruisers" rather than "scouts," had been overshadowed by bigger and more heavily armed classes in succeeding years, and there had consequently been a tendency to employ them overseas rather than in home waters.[7]

The *Bristol's* sister ship *Liverpool* was also at Brindisi but had been at six hours' notice and was therefore at a far lower degree of readiness. The ship had just come off her turn as "ready ship" at a half hour's notice and, having been out of a dockyard for almost a year, her captain and engineer officer had taken advantage of the increasingly infrequent luxury of six hours' notice to remedy minor defects. The boilers had just become cool enough to work on and, among other things, the starboard telegraph shafting, which had been causing trouble, was completely parted. Other machinery such as the starboard main circulating engine and the main feed pump in No. 3 boiler room were open for inspection and repair. It would therefore be very difficult for the *Liverpool* to put to sea in a hurry. The ship's captain was also denied the possibility of anticipation, that is, making preparations to sail before the actual receipt of orders from Admiral Acton. *Liverpool's* wireless operators had actually intercepted the "Urgent" signal from Saseno at 0350, but because it was in the Italian cipher they could not read it. They did not attach any particular importance to the "Urgent" designation, for their past experience had shown that Saseno always reported submarine sightings as "Urgent." The *Liverpool* did not receive the order to raise steam until 0515. The lack of the Italian cipher was more than a minor glitch in relations among the Allies. In the opinion of Captain Vivian of the *Liverpool* after the battle, "It is, I think, no exaggeration to say that had we and the other ships *then* [at 0350] started to raise steam the whole result of the action which ensued subsequently might well have been different."[8]

A third sister ship, the *Gloucester*, should also have been at Brindisi, but the preceding month it had been detached to the Indian Ocean to join in the hunt for the German raider *Wolf*.[9] This was another piece of bad luck for the Allies, but not nearly half as bad as the fact that *Bristol* was about to be docked and with her bottom foul could not make her best speed. The two destroyers that accompanied *Bristol*, the *Rosolino Pilo* and *Antonio Mosto*, to cite their full names, were members of a class of eight 806-ton full load displacement destroyers. They had been launched in the spring of 1915 and were armed with four 450mm torpedo tubes and four 76mm/40 guns and capable of a speed of thirty knots. The *Pilo* and *Mosto* were also long-lived, surviving both world wars before finally being struck in 1954 and 1958 respectively.[10]

The principal ship on the Allied side was destined to be the British light cruiser *Dartmouth*, launched in 1910 as one of the four *Weymouth*-class ships, the successor class to the *Bristols*. They were, at 5,800 tons full load displacement, larger and more heavily armed, with eight six-inch guns. They had the same protection as their predecessors and were also capable of twenty-five knots. The *Dartmouth* had participated in the Dardanelles campaign before moving to the Adriatic, and the cruiser and her captain, A. P. Addison, were also veterans of the action of 29 December 1915 and the pursuit of the *Helgoland* and accompanying destroyers after the Austrian raid on Durazzo. *Dartmouth* and *Helgoland* were therefore old adversaries. As a class, the *Weymouths* were slower than the *Helgolands* at their best, but more heavily armed with six-inch guns against 10cm.[11] *Dartmouth* had been at three hours' notice but was due to come to a half-hour's notice at 0500. Addison, however, reported he had received his orders around 0405, and according to the ship's log, hands were called to prepare the ship for sea at 0415.[12]

The Italian accounts are at pains to point out that the Italian reaction to intelligence of the Austrian raid was as prompt as could be expected.[13] This is probably true, and the piecemeal commitment of the Allied ships that day was primarily due to their differing states of readiness. Admiral Acton was understandably anxious to take charge of the operations at sea and, having issued his orders, embarked, to the surprise of Captain Addison, in the *Dartmouth* with his chief of staff Commandante Bucci and others of his staff. According to Addison, he apparently did not fly his admiral's flag in the cruiser, but nevertheless it was an unusual circumstance for an Italian admiral to command an action from the bridge of a British cruiser. It also complicated matters for Addison, who confided to a friend after the battle: "The Italian admiral was very nice but it was very difficult for me as you may imagine, he brought a large staff who got rather in the way, especially when we were torpedoed."[14]

The *Dartmouth* slipped at 0536 and proceeded to sea, and once clear of the outer harbor obstructions increased speed to twenty-five knots on a northeasterly course. She was accompanied by the destroyers *Simone Schiaffino* and *Giovanni Acerbi*. *Schiaffino* was one of the 800-ton *Pilo* class, and the *Acerbi* was one of the four newer *Sirtori* class and had only been launched in February of that year. They were 847 tons full load displacement, thirty-knot destroyers armed with four 450mm torpedo tubes, six 102mm/35 guns, and two 40mm anti-aircraft guns.[15] Acton was reinforced around 0740 by the *esploratori* (scout) *Aquila*, which had raised sufficient steam to sail from Brindisi at 0600.[16] The *Aquila* belonged to a class of four originally ordered by the Rumanian navy at the Pattison Yard in Naples and taken over by the Italian navy when Italy entered the war. They were then classified as *esploratori*, or "scouts," by the Italians; in the Royal Navy they might have been considered flotilla leaders. The ship had been roughly 60 percent completed when taken over by the Italian navy, but wartime difficulties delayed her entry into service until February 1917. *Aquila* was 1,750 tons full load displacement and capable of thirty-four knots. She was armed with three 152mm/40 and four 76mm/440 guns and four 450mm torpedo tubes. The ships of this class were allegedly the fastest ships in the Italian navy. The *Aquila* was also fitted for minelaying. There was, however, a major deficiency in the class. They had a relatively short range as they had been designed for operations in the Black Sea. This fault was offset by the fact they were employed by the Italians primarily in the Adriatic. Their other major defect was their main armament of 152mm guns, which were an older model and for a variety of technical reasons including awkward placement had a relatively low rate of fire.[17]

Acton's forces gradually overhauled the *Bristol, Pilo,* and *Mosto,* and at 0656 *Bristol* was ordered to close the *Dartmouth* group and altered course to the west. At 0712 *Bristol* took station off the starboard beam of the *Dartmouth* making full speed. This caused a problem because the cruiser needed docking and could not reach her full speed. Consequently, Acton's group could not make more than twenty-four knots.[18] The cruisers were deployed in line abreast, the *Aquila* in front and the destroyers guarding the flanks. There are annoying discrepancies between the British logs and the official Italian account as far as exact timing is concerned, but the contemporaries themselves also complained of this problem. Perhaps one should not worry excessively about these particular details. What is apparent is that Acton now had the ships that had sailed from Brindisi that morning together well before contact was made with the enemy. There was now a force of two cruisers, a flotilla leader, and four destroyers seeking to cut the three Austrian cruisers off from their base.

The first contact and exchange with the Austrians was actually made by Capitano di fregata Vicuna and the *Mirabello* group. The *Carlo Mirabello* was designated by the Italian navy as an *esploratori leggeri,* or "light scout." One of a class of three, she had entered service in August 1916 and was 1,950 tons full load displacement with an armament of four 450mm torpedo tubes, eight 102mm/35 and two 76mm anti-aircraft guns, and two anti-aircraft machine guns. The ship was also fitted for laying mines and could reach thirty-two knots.[19] The *Mirabello* led the three French destroyers *Commandant Rivière, Bisson,* and *Cimeterre. Commandant Rivière* and *Cimeterre,* launched in 1912 and 1910 respectively, were members of the twelve-ship, 800-ton *Bouclier* class. They were armed with four 450mm torpedo tubes, two 100mm and four 65mm guns, and had a designed speed of thirty knots. Wartime additions of an anti-aircraft gun, anti-aircraft machine guns, and depth charges increased their displacement to over 900 tons and reduced their speed to around twenty-six knots. *Bisson* was the first of the following class of six 850-ton, thirty-knot destroyers. She had been launched in 1912 with an armament similar to the *Bouclier* class.[20] These ships had already seen much service and had been in engagements with the Austrians. *Bisson* claimed credit for sinking the Austrian submarine *U.3* in August 1916, while *Commandant Rivière* had had her boiler put out of action in the 22 December 1916 clash with Austrian destroyers returning from a raid on the drifters.[21] The French destroyers based at Brindisi and working in the lower Adriatic were probably among the most hard worked ships in the French navy during the First World War, when, because of the strategic relation of forces and the geographical situation, the French capital ships saw relatively little action.

At 0600, Captain Vicuna was twelve miles abeam of Point Semana on the Albanian coast. He had still not seen anything of the Austrians and, concluding it was useless to continue further south, altered course about ten degrees to starboard so that his group was now inclining toward the center of the straits. At 0625 he received a wireless message from the *Dartmouth* with Acton's order to reverse course and head for Cattaro. Almost simultaneously, however, he sighted suspect smoke to starboard and altered course toward it. It was the *Novara*, which had already been sighted and bombed by the Italian FBA piloted by Sottotenente Spagnolo. The FBA approached the *Mirabello* and flew low enough to signal the direction of the Austrians. Vicuna sighted the enemy off the starboard bow at approximately 0700. The Italian and French ships were in line abreast. The Austrians were proceeding at full speed in line astern with *Novara* followed by *Saida* and *Helgoland*. The two groups were on roughly converging courses. *Mirabello*'s position was then 19° east and 40° 27′ north. There was a brief, ineffective exchange of gunfire between 0710 and 0717 at a range of more than 8,000 meters. The Italian and French shells fell short of the Austrian cruisers, but the guns of the latter began to straddle the *Mirabello* group. Vicuna did not think he could close the range in the face of the heavier guns of the cruisers. He therefore decided to merely maintain contact, ordered a starboard turn to a northerly course and brought his formation into line ahead. While executing the maneuver, however, the Italians believed they had spotted a submarine—*Mirabello* actually reported two submarines by wireless—as well as two torpedo tracks. Vicuna accordingly turned even further to starboard to avoid them. It is not clear if there really were any torpedoes or even a submarine. The most likely candidate would have been *U.4*, who had also been reported and hunted by the *Commandant Bory*. The problem with this scenario, however, is that the submarine returned to Cattaro at 2330 that night and reported the only enemy activity observed as being a destroyer off Valona, which it could not get into a position to attack.

The wide turn of the *Mirabello* group to starboard had an unfortunate effect. When the Italians and French resumed their northerly course they were far astern of the Austrians. Vicuna had signaled to *Dartmouth* at 0724 the presence of three *Spauns* (Austrian light cruisers) and two submarines and that he was giving chase and attacking the submarines. He added a second message a minute later giving the enemy course. In order to maintain contact, however, *Mirabello* increased speed to thirty-two knots. This was more than the three French destroyers could achieve and they gradually fell astern.[22]

Heyssler in the *Helgoland* assumed that the enemy destroyers had initially taken the Austrian cruisers for their own because of their altered masts. This was not correct. The Italian FBA had provided ample warning they were the enemy. However, he was correct in assuming that after the Austrian shells had begun to straddle the destroyers, causing them to haul off, they had remained in contact though out of range. This meant that from then on they could assume that the Italians would be informed of the Austrian strength and movements.[23]

The Austrian cruisers were subjected to a second air attack between 0800 and 0900. The first Italian FBA to leave and return to Valona without having seen anything of the Austrians had taken on a load of bombs, changed pilots, and taken off for a second sortie at 0755. Flying northwest, the Italian pilots spotted first the *Mirabello* and shortly afterwards the three Austrian cruisers. They attacked, and one bomb falling around ten meters astern of the *Helgoland* dislodged some rivets from the rudder. Heyssler was inexperienced in countering aerial attacks and, observing the other cruisers on a steady course, took no evasive action. The near miss taught him a lesson. Henceforth a steady course would be something to be avoided when under aerial attack. Horthy ordered his formation into line abreast with *Novara* going to starboard and *Helgoland* to port of *Saida*. That the *Saida* could do no more than twenty-four knots made it easy for *Helgoland*, the rearmost ship, to overhaul her and assume the assigned position.[24] The Italian FBA followed at a distance for a while before leaving and subsequently landing back at Valona at 1005. Heyssler was better prepared for a later air attack. This time when the aircraft was 45° above *Helgoland*, he suddenly altered course, and the bombs fell harmlessly on either side of the ship as a result.

Italian aircraft were not the only ones to attack the Austrians. At least one attack with bombs and machine guns was delivered by a section of French FBAs stationed on the island of Corfu. Enseigne de vaisseau Blutel, flying as an observer with a petty officer as pilot, reported bombing a cruiser. In addition, Enseigne de vaisseau Bragayrac and Second Maître Georges Davin reported bombing a submerged submarine ten miles west of Fano Island.[25] The Austrian reports did not differentiate the nationality of the aircraft attacking them and, given that they were all FBAs, it must have taken a sharp eye to differentiate the red-white-blue cockade and rudder stripes of French markings from the red-white-green of the Italians. Walter Zanoskar, an artillery-observation cadet in the *Novara* during the battle, did make the distinction years later in a letter to a friend. He described the approach of two French aircraft after the first Italian air attack. They had circled the Austrians at first and then made

off toward the approaching Allied ships and finally returned to deliver their attack, a bomb falling between the *Novara* and the *Saida*. The attack apparently
preceded the arrival of Austrian aircraft.[26]

Austrian aircraft now came to the assistance of their cruisers. They were
probably K.177 piloted by Linienschiffsleutnant Konjovič and K.179 piloted by
Fregattenleutnant Klimburg. The planes were Brandenburg flying boats built
by UFAG (Ungarische Flugzeugfabrik Aktiengesellschaft) of Budapest. They
had a crew of two or three, a speed of 135–140 km/h, and an endurance of six
hours. This model was armed with an 8mm machine gun and could carry a
bomb load of 150–200 kg.[27] The two Brandenburgs had taken off from Kumbor, the Austrian naval air station in the Bocche, at 0550 and flew in the direction of Brindisi, sighting the Italian coast at 0655 and the first of the Allied
cruisers at 0701. This was *Bristol* and her escort of Italian destroyers. Within a
few minutes the Austrian aviators sighted the remainder of the Allied ships as
well as their own destroyers *Csepel* and *Balaton* on a parallel course south of
the Allied ships. They then observed the leading Allied ship open fire on the
Austrian destroyers at 0805 and the two destroyers turn southward in the direction of Durazzo, returning fire at 0815. Konjovič reported attacking the leading Allied cruiser with machine gun fire and then turning south looking for
the Austrian cruisers which he spotted around 0820.[28]

The situation at 0805 as reported by I. Gruppe (K.177 and K.179).
Leading ships open fire. *Balaton* and *Csepel* lower right, British
and Italian ships left. (Österreichisches Staatsarchiv/Kriegsarchiv)

After the encounter with the Italian convoy, Liechtenstein, the senior
officer in the *Csepel* and *Balaton*, hastened to escape from possible intervention from the vicinity of Valona and, while attempting to keep in touch with
the cruisers, had turned on a course of 315° at twenty-five knots to detect possible intervention from the direction of Brindisi. He reversed course at 0615,
altered to the northwest at 0700, and at 0730 turned to a course for Punta d'Ostro at the entrance to the Bocche. At around 0735 he sighted several columns
of smoke to the northwest and soon the tops of masts and funnels came into
sight. He estimated there were three cruisers and several destroyers and reported his observations to *Novara*. At 0739 he increased speed to twenty-nine

knots and set a course for Dulcigno, altered at 0812 to Cape Rodoni.[29] Liecht-enstein naturally could not know the exact identity of the ships following him, but he recognized that the leading ship was considerably larger than an Italian destroyer of the *Indomito* class. The *Balaton* identified the ship as a *Quarto*. The lead ship was actually the scout *Aquila*, which opened fire at 0815. The 152mm guns of the *Aquila* outranged the 10cm guns of the two destroyers, and the Austrians at first could not reply. However, as the faster *Aquila* drew closer and hence in range, *Csepel* returned fire. *Balaton* rather than *Csepel* appeared to be the target of most of the Italian fire. The Austrian destroyers, however, would enjoy assistance from the air.

How did things appear on the British and Italian side? The *Aquila* had been lead ship of the *Dartmouth* group steaming at twenty-four knots on a course of 35° with the destroyers acting as escorts on the flanks. The British and Italians sighted suspicious clouds of smoke on a bearing of 140° at 0745. The smoke belonged to *Csepel* and *Balaton*. For a few minutes, the two opposing forces steamed on roughly parallel courses, the British and Italians more to the north and in a position to cut off the Austrian route to Cattaro. The Allies were ap-parently at first unsure whether or not they were dealing with *Novaras* or smaller destroyers. The silhouettes at great distance would have been similar. Both sides had difficulties this day making accurate identifications of the op-posing ships. At 0750 in *Dartmouth*'s report and at 0800 in Admiral Acton's re-port, the latter ordered his ships to increase to full speed and his *esploratori* and destroyers to attack the enemy. *Aquila* and the four Italian destroyers be-gan their approach to the Austrians at 0810. Acton then proceeded on a course of approximately 70° with *Dartmouth* and *Bristol*. His objective in his own words was "to prevent the enemy escaping to the north along the coast of Al-bania."[30] The Italian light craft were initially in roughly a line-abreast forma-tion with *Aquila* in the center and *Mosto* and *Schiaffino* to starboard and *Pilo* and *Acerbi* to port. *Aquila*, steaming at thirty-five to thirty-six knots, drew steadily ahead and opened fire at 0815 at a range of 11,400 meters. She fired a dozen salvoes at ranges varying from 11,400 to 9,500 meters. However, she had difficulty serving her 152mm guns because of their awkward placement and also had difficulty observing the fall of shot because of the dense low clouds of smoke coming from the funnels of the Austrian destroyers. Consequently, as Liechtenstein reported, *Balaton* was bracketed but *Csepel* seems not to have been fired upon.[31]

A second group of aircraft, K.154 piloted by Linienschiffsleutnant Poljanec and K.153 piloted by Fregattenleutnant Zelezny and Fregattenleutnant Lerch, had taken off from Kumbor at 0640 and proceeded on a course of 170°. These flying boats were Weichmann types built by the Austro-Hungarian Albatros Company in Vienna, a subsidiary of the famous German aircraft company. They had been developed from the well-known series of Lohner flying boats by *Schiffbauingenieure 1. Klasse* Theodor Weichmann, hence their name. The Weichmann had a crew of two, a speed of 135–140 km/h, an endurance of six hours, and could carry a bomb load of 150 kg.[32] K.153 was equipped with a radio. They were responsible for the first Austrian enemy contact by wireless that day at 0730 when they had sighted Allied warships and transmitted the message: "2 *Quarto* class, 4 *Indomito* class, course north, 20 nautical miles from Brindisi." This was followed by a second message: "Reported ships are 2 cruisers, 3 destroyers and 2 high seas torpedo boats." They soon observed the *Csepel* and *Balaton* ahead of the Allied ships and witnessed the beginning of the exchange of fire, duly signaling this information at 0815. K.153 did much more, however. The aviators made use of their radio to act as gunnery observers for the destroyers, sending a message that the Austrian fire was 300 to 400 meters short, followed by a second message that the shells were still falling 50 to 100 meters short. This is an interesting early example of aircraft spotting the fall of shells for warships and it foreshadowed a practice that would become widespread in the interwar period. It is impossible to judge the exact extent it may have helped the Austrians, but *Csepel's* stern 10cm gun firing at maximum elevation was observed at 0832 to hit the leading enemy ship. This was the *Aquila*, probably the fastest of the Allied ships at sea that day. The Austrians observed the ship turn away, covered in a cloud of thick dark smoke. One of the Austrian aviators on the scene estimated that the action had taken place at a range of about 6,000 meters. Italian accounts give the range as 9,500 meters, which would have made it an extremely lucky hit indeed. *Csepel's* shell passed through two thicknesses of plating, struck a small stanchion, severed two or three pipes, and exploded in the central boiler room, severing the main steam pipe and killing seven stokers. The numbers two and three boilers became useless. The oil in the foremost boiler room flooded, rising to the level of the fire grates and igniting. At 0830 the ship was immobilized in a location given by the Italians as latitude 41° 30′, longitude 18° 50′.[33]

   The other four Italian destroyers could not catch the enemy. The *Pilo*, less well placed on the outside of the curve formed by the Austrian course toward Durazzo, could not get closer than 10,000 meters, and her captain realized the Austrians would succeed in reaching the protection of the Durazzo minefields and coastal batteries. The *Pilo* therefore altered course and approached the stricken *Aquila* but received no reply to her signal inquiring if *Aquila* required assistance. The destroyer then turned again in the direction of the Austrians. The captain of the *Acerbi*, also badly placed to intercept the Austrians, apparently decided on his own to return to the main group of Allied warships after perceiving suspect columns of smoke to the southwest. The *Mosto* was better placed in regard to the Austrians and managed to close the range to 7,500 meters before opening fire, but her shots still fell far short. The destroyer continued to follow the *Csepel* and *Balaton* to the coast, only to come under fire from coastal batteries at 0900. At 0905 the *Mosto* altered course to the north and proceeded along the coast to make sure the Austrian destroyers had not taken refuge in the Gulf of Drin. The *Schiaffino* had a similar experience, firing eight salvoes, all of which fell short, and then losing sight of the Austrians at 0910 in the shadow of the coast. The *Schiaffino* also found herself bracketed by fire from the coastal batteries and consequently turned to rejoin the Allied cruisers. The commanders of the Italian destroyers were apparently convinced the two Austrians were now secure in the shelter of the minefields and batteries of Durazzo. At 0918 Admiral Acton in the *Dartmouth* signaled for all destroyers to rejoin the main group.[34]

The two Austrian destroyers therefore succeeded in making their escape, turning in the direction of Cape Pali at 0852 and, after reaching Cape Pali around 0900 slowed and circled to port until the Allied ships had passed out of sight to the west. A large Allied destroyer was observed to press on nearly up to the boundary of the Austrian minefields, only to be driven off by the coastal batteries around Durazzo. This destroyer was either the *Mosto* or *Schiaffino*. Their escape to Durazzo ended the active role of the *Csepel* and *Balaton* in the day's action. It did not end their adventures. After the coast was clear of enemy ships, Liechtenstein headed for Point Menders, but approximately ten nautical miles off the point reported that *Balaton* had two torpedoes fired at her by a submarine. Once again the Austrian destroyers were lucky. The torpedoes missed. The torpedoes had been fired by the French submarine *Bernouilli*, which had left Brindisi the evening of the 13th to patrol off the Gulf of Drin on the 14th and 15th and return to base on the 16th. The French submarine commander reported the time of his attack as 1048, but he apparently thought he had fired at *Csepel* rather than at *Balaton*. It would have been an old encounter between the two. Slightly more than a year before, on 4 May 1916, a torpedo from *Bernouilli* had blown the stern off the *Csepel* approximately seven or eight miles south of the entrance to the Gulf of Cattaro.[35] Liechtenstein intended to join *Sankt Georg* and the warships coming out from Cattaro to assist Horthy [see below, p. 93], but on hearing the wireless report that the Allied ships had turned away and abandoned the chase, he proceeded directly to the Bocche and moored at the anchorage off Gjenovič at 1345.[36]

The Austrians continued to be well served by their naval air arm that day, for there were other planes reporting on Allied movements. L.132 (Linienschiffsleutnant Hell) and L.88 (Fregattenleutnant Nardelli) had taken off from Durazzo at 0550 to reconnoiter in the direction of Brindisi. These were Lohner flying boats with a performance similar to the Weichmann although a bit slower with a speed of 110–115 km/h.[37] L.88 was also equipped with a radio and therefore was able at 0625 to report the sortie of the first Allied ships followed by reports between 0700 and 0715 on the sortie of the remainder as well as their course and location. They then headed back to the Albanian coast, where they also witnessed the gunnery duel between the Austrian destroyers and the ships in pursuit and, finally, the escape of the Austrians to the northern entrance of the Durazzo minefield.

The Austrian aircraft as well as *Csepel* had been able to provide Horthy with a series of reports on enemy movements. He acknowledged this in his report after the battle, although he commented that the information he had received on the strength and composition of the enemy units was not consistent.[38] This may have been because *Novara* received the message from *Csepel* reporting the enemy sighting in garbled form, although the full message in correct form appears to have been received in the *Helgoland*.[39] In addition, the Brandenburgs K.177 and K.179 also flew low over the *Novara* at 0832 and signaled the enemy strength and position. At around 0845 Horthy sighted streaks of smoke ahead to starboard and moving toward the east. He assumed this to be the *Csepel* and *Balaton*. At approximately 0905 he sighted further columns of smoke and could soon make out two British cruisers of what he believed to be the *Blanche* and *Liverpool* class, an Italian *Quarto*, and two *Indomito*-class destroyers. At approximately the same time—sources differ on exact timing and sequence—he signaled to Cattaro his position, speed, and course, the presence of enemy cruisers below the horizon, and that "*Auslaufen verspricht Erfolg*," roughly translated as "putting to sea promises success." It was a call for the armored cruiser *Sankt Georg* in the Bocche to sortie and possibly catch the more lightly armed Allied cruisers.[40]

Horthy brought his ships into line-astern formation with *Novara* leading, followed by *Saida* and *Helgoland*. His intention was to close the enemy and engage when in range and draw them away from the *Csepel* group. The main engagement of the day now began at 0928 with the British and Italian ships turning onto a parallel course and opening fire. Horthy soon observed that a British cruiser instead of the *Quarto* was in the lead. Horthy's ship recognition had been off, understandable under the circumstances, for the airmen also had confused *Quarto* with *Aquila* and *Indomito*-class destroyers. It must have been an unpleasant surprise when the leading British cruiser was identified as the more heavily armed *Dartmouth*, not a smaller and more lightly armed *Blanche* class.[41] The latter were 3,300-ton ships armed with only six or ten four-inch guns and only one or one and a half inches of partial plating over the machinery for protection. A 5,250-ton *Dartmouth* had two-inch to three-quarter-inch protection along the full length of the deck and eight six-inch guns. Horthy had underestimated his potential opposition. There was also the possibility that *Novara* never received the wireless message timed at 0850 from *Csepel* announcing her arrival in Durazzo and that she had been pursued by three cruisers and three destroyers. The message, including the familiar error of mistaking *Aquila* for a *Quarto*, was noted in the war diary of the Torpedoflottillen

Kommando but not in the log of the *Novara*. Had he received it, Horthy would have known the destroyers were safe and no longer needed his support and that by following the destroyers so far to the east and so close to the Albanian coast, the Allies had given Horthy the opportunity to break through to the northwest and possibly reach the Bocche without a serious engagement.[42] The very abundance of reports, particularly from aircraft, may have added to the confusion. Airmen in both world wars would be notorious for misidentifying ships, and it would have been difficult to tell the difference between a *Quarto* and an *Aquila*. Horthy's mistake also shows some of the limitations of Austrian intelligence about the enemy order of battle. The *Blanche* class served mostly with the Grand Fleet in northern waters and did not work in the Mediterranean.[43]

"Action" had been sounded off in the *Dartmouth* at around 0900, and at 0910 Admiral Acton spotted the smoke clouds of three ships on his starboard quarter. They were apparently steering north, and Acton, having been warned by the *Mirabello*, knew they were the Austrian cruisers.[44] The two British ships *Dartmouth* and *Bristol* were under the direct command of Admiral Acton and after the battle the senior British naval officer in Brindisi assumed that the admiral at that moment wanted both to cover the disabled *Aquila*, which seemed in the path of the Austrians, and also to cut off the Austrian cruisers from Durazzo. He therefore did not make the more advantageous tactical move of trying to "cross the T" of the Austrian line, that is, place his ships in a position where they could make maximum use of their broadsides while the enemy arcs of fire would have been restricted.[45]

The assumption as to Acton's motives was correct. As he explained after the battle:

> The enemy ships were approaching the *Aquila* who was stopped offering an easy target. The enemy destroyers had by this time got under the guns of the shore batteries near Durazzo and had thus escaped. As my main object [was] the 3 *Spaun* cruisers I altered course together to S.W. to cover the *Aquila*, I got within range and opened fire at 9:30 a.m., the *Aquila* opened fire at the same time. Closing the enemy I got to within 8,500 meters.[46]

Heyssler, in the rearmost Austrian cruiser *Helgoland*, reached the same conclusion that the Italian admiral had decided not to "cross the T" out of the desire to cover the crippled *Aquila*. Heyssler was also conscious of the potentially unequal nature of the fight, given the *Dartmouth*'s larger guns and that Horthy apparently made no attempt to get out of the way and was steaming a steady course.[47] The *Dartmouth*, according to her log, commenced fire at 0929. This corresponds closely to the "about 0928" in Horthy's report. The range according to the *Dartmouth*'s log was 10,600 yards and closing fast. *Dartmouth*'s gunnery officer reported that when he first arrived in the fore control position, the Austrians were at 30,000 yards "bearing red 15," that is 15° to port. He opened fire when the rangefinder range was 14,700. The time of flight of the first salvo was about thirty-five seconds and it fell astern of the leading Austrian cruiser, the *Novara*. He noted that the Austrians opened fire at about 0930. He altered the deflection and the second salvo hit *Novara* right aft, starting what appeared to be a furious fire. Perceptions can be wrong. Austrian records do not record any serious hits to *Novara* at this stage in the action. *Dartmouth* then went into rapid salvoes and observed *Novara* drop astern and for a time remain abreast of the second ship, *Saida*.[48] The second British cruiser, *Bristol*, according to her log, opened fire at 0930, concentrating on the last ship in the enemy line, the *Helgoland*.

Horthy states that he began to use his smoke-making apparatus at around 0930 to conceal his closing the range so that the smaller-caliber guns of the

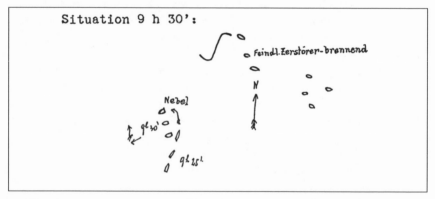

The situation at 0930 as reported by I. Gruppe (K.177 and K.179). British and Italian ships at right with *Aquila* crippled and on fire. Austrian cruisers turning behind smokescreen at left. (Österreichisches Staatsarchiv/Kriegsarchiv)

Austrian cruisers might be more effective. In addition, a shorter range might also give them the opportunity to use torpedoes. Unfortunately, he soon noticed that the enemy destroyers following from the south were now approaching and he considered a torpedo attack from this quarter probable. Horthy emerged from the smoke on a northwest course, and the French and Italian destroyers approaching to port were driven off by the guns of the Austrian cruisers. The ships in question were the *Mirabello* group, that is, the Italian scout and the three French destroyers. The *Mirabello* resumed firing at the Austrians, but it is not clear from reports if the French destroyers were also in position to do so.[49] The *Mirabello's* shooting appears to have had no effect. The Italian and French ships had approached to around 6,000 meters astern of the *Helgoland*. The *Helgoland's* captain was so intent on avoiding collision with the other Austrian cruisers during the nerve-racking maneuvering through the smoke screen that he had not noticed the French and Italians or even that his port guns had opened fire. They had thanks to the initiative of the second gunnery officer, who did not wait for orders to ward off the danger.[50]

The Austrian use of smoke was apparently effective. *Dartmouth*'s gunnery lieutenant observed the Austrians commence creating a dense white smoke screen from the stern of their ships and execute what appeared to be a sixteen-point turn to port. The effect was to completely hide the Austrian cruisers. The only point of aim now available to the British was an ensign at one of the cruiser's mastheads. The *Dartmouth*'s gunnery lieutenant checked fire and ordered a big "down" spotting correction. When he saw this salvo fall short, he increased elevation 400 yards and resumed rapid salvoes, firing four into the smoke. He could not, however, see any splashes. The *Dartmouth* altered course to the south, thereby bringing her starboard guns into action. After about five minutes an Austrian cruiser could be seen emerging from the smoke steering to the north. The *Dartmouth* then altered course about sixteen points to starboard and began steering a course that was roughly parallel to the Austrians'. This had the effect of bringing her port guns into action again.[51]

Horthy's maneuver behind the smoke screen caused the destructive rain of shells to taper off in effectiveness, at least for a time. It also succeeded in another major objective. When the Austrians emerged from the smoke, the range of the British cruisers had been reduced to only 4,500 meters, a much more effective range for the Austrian 100cm guns. On the other hand, Horthy's action nearly caused a catastrophe. Horthy had discussed with his captains before the raid his idea of using smoke in case the Austrians encountered an enemy with superior firepower. They might then anticipate the enemy to make for the Austrian smoke screen. The Austrians would lie in wait behind it, ready to use their smaller guns as well as torpedoes when the enemy emerged from the smoke. That was the theory. In practice it worked out differently. A sudden breeze sprang up from the northeast, blowing the smoke on the Austrians. Heyssler in the *Helgoland* observed *Novara* followed by *Saida* begin making smoke as they veered to port. Contrary to the British impressions, the rear ship, the *Helgoland*, did not make smoke. Heyssler forbade use of the apparatus and concentrated all his attention on following the wake of the ship ahead. He was suddenly enveloped in thick smoke, which penetrated the *gefechtsturm*—the conning tower—and could see nothing. Even when he stepped out of the conning tower, he could barely see beyond the bow. Heyssler was now in what he termed "a miserable position," racing ahead blindly. As he later delicately expressed the situation, "To proceed at a speed of 25 knots, as rearguard in formation and be unable to see much beyond the bow of my own ship, would be against all nautical principles." However, he faced a dilemma. He did not want to lag behind the formation, and he had to assume the leading ship had unimpaired vision and therefore had no reason to proceed slowly. They were in action and some risks had to be taken. *Helgo-land*'s speed did not slacken. What he termed "this eerie situation" lasted eight minutes and suddenly what he feared most nearly happened. Heyssler suddenly saw the masts and funnels of the *Novara* about thirty meters ahead. To his horror, the *Novara* was not directly ahead but at an angle of forty-five degrees to his course. A collision was imminent. He instantly ordered "hard a-port" and actually heard Horthy also bellowing "hard a-port" from the bridge of the *Novara*. The *Helgoland* missed the *Novara* by ten meters, which Heyssler considered "a real miracle." But the danger was not past. Heyssler had been so intent on his progress through the smoke that he did not realize the second ship in line, the *Saida*, had slowed and been overtaken by the *Helgoland*. The result was that now the *Saida* nearly rammed the *Helgoland* from astern, also missing by about ten meters.[52] There must have been some colorful and emphatic expressions in more than one language of the many in the Habsburg Monarchy on the bridges of the three cruisers during those moments. The movements in the smoke screen also had the result of altering the order of the Austrian line which was now *Novara-Helgoland-Saida*.

The Austrian guns were now firing rapidly at the reduced range. They had a characteristic sharp clear crack which some found more unpleasant than the thud of heavier guns. The altered range also meant that *Dartmouth*'s gunnery officer had to make major corrections. The ship was firing salvoes at ten-second intervals, but often only two or three guns actually fired at a time because of the rapid loading. Furthermore, *Dartmouth*'s gunnery officer soon realized that only two or three of his guns were actually firing at the lead ship *Novara*. The other two guns were firing at the second ship in line, now the *Helgoland*. The gunnery officer checked firing, gave new bearings and corrections, and then had the guns "ladder up" on target before resuming salvoes again. According to reports he received from the *Bristol* after the action, the shots fired in error at the *Helgoland* were not wasted, for hits had been observed.

Action took place in three dimensions, that is, in the air as well as on the surface. At roughly the same time the Austrian cruisers had opened fire on the *Mirabello* group, there was a resumption of aerial activity leading to the only real combat between opposing aircraft that day. A section of two Italian FBAs, which had taken off from Brindisi roughly a half-hour before, arrived on the scene and dropped their bombs on the Austrian cruisers from an altitude of 1,200 meters. The bombs missed by thirty meters. The Italian FBAs then spotted the two Austrian aircraft, K.177 and K.179. The two Brandenburgs had, as we have seen, been reporting enemy movements to Horthy. K.179 was being attacked from the rear by the two Italians at 0940 and an aerial duel took place, the Austrian aircraft firing some seventy-five rounds from its machine gun. The engine of FBA No. 7 piloted by Tenente di vascello Orazio Pierozzi with Sottotenente Luigi Lombardi as observer was damaged and the FBA was forced to make a slow glide down to land on the water, a tricky maneuver since the sea had become rough as the wind sprang up. The FBA was now in an awkward position between the Austrian cruisers and the *Mirabello* group as they exchanged fire. The Italian airmen were closer to the Italians and some of the Austrian shells landed nearby, with splinters damaging the left wing. This ended any hope the Italian air crew had of tinkering with the motor and taking off again. They were eventually picked up by the French destroyer *Bisson*, sinking the damaged aircraft before leaving the scene. K.179 received approximately ten hits, two of them serious. Nocchiere Gianelli, the pilot, and Tenente di vascello Casagrande, the observer in No. 429, the second Italian FBA, had to break off the action after their machine gun was damaged — presumably jammed although this was not specifically mentioned — and, short of fuel, they attempted to return to Brindisi. The FBA was forced to land in the sea about thirty miles from Brindisi but was later recovered by an Italian torpedo boat sent out from the base. The two Brandenburgs could claim one enemy aircraft shot down, but they were running short of fuel themselves and had to leave the cruisers at 1000, landing back at Kumbor at 1105.[53]

Horthy was not left without air support. At 0815 the group consisting of K.205, piloted by Fregattenleutnant Rehmann, and K.206, piloted by Fliegermaat Haschke, left their base at Kumbor and by 0915 were over the action. They were newer Brandenburgs with more powerful engines and manufactured by UFAG. With a speed of 140–150 km/h, they were a bit faster and could carry a bomb load of 200 kg.[54] This was probably the most aggressive of the Austrian air groups that day. They reported attacking a British cruiser with machine guns and bombs on their arrival, and at 0950 K.205 again attacked the leading British cruiser (*Dartmouth*) with bombs and machine gun fire. At 1001 the Austrians confirmed the presence of the downed aircraft on the water between the two opposing lines. At the same time they also claimed to have spotted the periscope of a submarine between the lines making for their own cruisers. K.205 believed there was no doubt about the sighting and promptly attacked, dropping a bomb. The presumed submarine submerged and disappeared. K.206 then attacked the second Allied cruiser at around 1015 with one 50kg and one 15kg bomb, claiming a direct hit with the latter on the cruiser's stern. This claim was overly optimistic. Neither cruiser was hit. The aircraft repeated the attack with one 50kg bomb and one 15kg bomb at 1030. For the next twenty minutes the Austrian aircraft attacked the Allied warships with machine gun fire and then dropped their last two 15kg bombs around 1100. K.206 left the scene at 1115, but K.205 remained over the cruisers until 1245. The two Brandenburgs landed safely at Kumbor at 1150 and 1320, respectively. This aggressive group also appears to be responsible for the well-known aerial photographs of the Austrian warships at the close of the action.[55]

The apparent confusion and zigzagging as the Austrians sorted themselves out after the near collisions in the smoke screen made the Allies uncertain at first as to their course. Once this was established, what is commonly referred to as the parallel battle continued with both sides in line-ahead formation on a course to the north-northwest. The two groups by now had also left the stricken *Aquila* astern, safe from surface attack but of course very vulnerable to submarines. The Italian destroyers *Acerbi* and *Mosto* joined the line astern of the *Bristol*, the *Acerbi* opening fire on the Austrians at a range of 9,500 meters. The destroyer in addition to her torpedoes was armed with five 102mm/35 guns, three of which could be used in a broadside. The *Bristol*, as mentioned previously, had a foul bottom and was now having increasing difficulty keeping up with the *Dartmouth*, and she gradually fell behind. The captain of the *Acerbi* then, apparently on his own initiative, moved ahead to the second position behind the *Dartmouth*. It was, consequently, a heterogeneous Allied line consisting of *Dartmouth*, *Acerbi*, and *Bristol*—the *Mosto's* position is uncertain—engaging *Novara*, *Helgoland*, and *Saida*. The range was, however, steadily increasing as *Bristol* fell behind. It was 6,000 meters by 0945 and after fifteen minutes had grown to 7,400 meters. The range increased steadily to 8,800 meters at 1020 and reached 9,800 meters at 1024.[56] The effect of this was to place the major burden of the action on the *Dartmouth*.

There is the inevitable question of why the *Acerbi* under Capitano di corvetta Vannutelli was the only destroyer of all the French and Italian flotilla craft at sea this day still in a position to fire on the Austrians. What had happened to the others? The destroyers *Schiaffino* and *Pilo*, after giving up their pursuit of Liechtenstein's two destroyers, had been ordered by Admiral Acton to render assistance to the stricken *Aquila*, which at one moment was apparently threatened by the approach of the Austrian cruisers. The *Schiaffino* had even turned toward the Austrian cruisers for a brief period of time and fired a few salvoes that fell short. The *Schiaffino* soon returned to the *Aquila* and attempted to take the stricken ship in tow. The fire in the *Aquila* was eventually brought under control and the destroyer *Pilo* arrived to act as escort. While preparing the tow, the Italians reported being attacked and bombed by an Austrian aircraft without suffering any damage. It is not clear from the Austrian reports which plane was involved. The group began the journey back to Brindisi at 1030. The tow parted once but was quickly restored. The three ships were joined by the French destroyer *Cimeterre*, detached from the *Mirabello* group [see below], and eventually by two high-seas torpedo boats sent out from Brindisi. All reached port without further incident that evening at 2030.

The *Mirabello* and French destroyers *Commandant Rivière*, *Cimeterre*, and *Bisson* had, as we have seen, caused concern to the Austrians by their approach and had drawn fire from the cruisers. They received no orders from Admiral Acton, possibly because he was uncertain of their location. This uncertainty was probably caused by the Austrian smoke screen, which might have concealed them from the Allied line. They continued to follow astern and to the starboard of the Austrian cruisers when the latter resumed their rush to the north. The *Bisson*, as noted, altered course and stopped to recover the pilots from the downed Italian FBA. The *Mirabello* also experienced another Austrian air attack in this phase of the action, but suffered no damage. At 1015 Admiral Acton signaled from the *Dartmouth* for the *Mirabello* group to report its position and close on the main group. Unfortunately, any hope that the *Mirabello* group might yet play a meaningful role in the action ended at almost the same moment when *Mirabello*'s boilers shut down because of water in the fuel. The three French destroyers continued on course for a time, but then, led by the *Commandant Rivière*, returned to the *Mirabello*. Shortly before 1100 the *Mirabello* was able to resume normal speed but by this time there was no hope of catching up with the Austrians. Nevertheless, Capitano di fregata Vicuna continued on a northerly course until 1145, when there was more bad luck. The engines of the *Commandant Rivière* broke down. Vicuna abandoned his plans to continue north and decided instead to protect the crippled ships. By noon he had the *Commandant Rivière* under tow. He retained the *Bisson* as an escort and detached the *Cimeterre* to reinforce the ships protecting the *Aquila*. Vicuna was subsequently joined for a time by the French destroyer *Commandant Lucas*, which had come from Corfu, but at 1335 he detached the destroyer to join the *Dartmouth*. *Mirabello*'s little convoy reached Brindisi without further incident at 1900.[57] Admiral Acton was as a result of these events deprived of the services of two scouts and five destroyers, although only one of the ships, the *Aquila*, had actually suffered battle damage.

The *Dartmouth* had intended to concentrate on the leading Austrian cruiser, the *Novara*. Her six-inch guns had their effect. According to her gunnery officer:

> When all guns were firing at the leading ship we appeared to be hitting her all over the place, and all her battery guns and her after gun ceased firing for a time. I could see the hits on her side quite distinctly, and almost every salvo when we were straddling I saw a cloud of grey smoke appear on her deck which I think must have been shell bursting inside. One shell hit her forward under the fore bridge: the burst was quite distinct and for about ten seconds afterwards there was a big glow forward. I think this shell must have set alight some charges on deck, which had been got up for the f'xle gun.[58]

The *Novara* was indeed suffering damage during this phase of the action. Horthy found the British fire "accurate and scientific." *Novara*'s GDO [executive officer] Korvettenkapitän Robert Szuborits was killed when a shell hit the starboard boat winch around 0940. At about 0955 another shell wrecked the chart room. At 1010 Horthy himself was wounded in both legs by shell splinters. He had been in the armored conning tower (*kommandoturm*), but the armored door had been left open for convenience and to avoid restricting his powers of command. The ammunition hoist for the number two and number three guns was just outside and a shell hit, exploding two Austrian shells that had been placed ready for use and badly wounding Horthy and the quartermaster. There were five shell splinters imbedded in Horthy's legs, and a heavy piece of shrapnel carried his cap off without touching his head. Horthy "felt as if I had been felled by a blow on the head with an axe" and was also overcome by poisonous fumes from the shell, briefly losing consciousness. The cold water others poured over him to extinguish his smoldering clothes brought him around. Horthy had himself placed on a stretcher and moved to the foredeck, and, after learning the GDO had been killed, he turned over command to the gunnery officer, Linienschiffsleutnant Stanislaus Witkowski. The most potentially disastrous damage to the *Novara* came at 1035 when a six-inch shell exploded in the aft turbine room, severing a condenser pipe and killing eleven men. The fires in eight of *Novara*'s sixteen boilers had to be extinguished. The ship would not be able to maintain speed.[59]

The heavy punishment taken by the *Novara* may well have spared the *Saida* a similar fate. The ship was rearmost in the Austrian line and, as mentioned before, had held down the speed of the others. Nevertheless, as the battle progressed she began to lag further and further behind. The British concentrating their fire on the leading Austrian ships worked in her favor. It was *Novara*'s situation that most worried the captain of the second Austrian cruiser, *Helgoland*. The *Helgoland* was about 400 meters astern of the *Novara* while the *Saida* was 1,000 meters astern of *Helgoland*. The latter's engines were working well and had revolutions for twenty-four to twenty-five knots. They would have been capable of another two or three knots but could not leave the *Saida* isolated. Heyssler later recalled: "My view ahead was spectacular. *Novara* was surrounded by spouts of water as shells fell around her, some hit her deck and spewed men and material up in to the air. I had the feeling that *Novara* could not hold out against the superior fire-power of the *Dartmouth* much longer."[60] Heyssler therefore ordered his gunnery officer to switch fire from the *Bristol*, now lagging behind, to the *Dartmouth*. However, the *Helgoland* was not unscathed either. Heyssler, like Horthy, had left the door of the conning tower open to occasionally step outside for a better view. He had just done so around 0950 when a shell exploded close by to port and aft of conning tower at the number two gun, wounding some of the crew and producing a tall column of flames. Heyssler was blinded at first by the flash but then realized that the fires threatened to set off ready-use ammunition near the gun. Two officers and a wounded midshipman rushed forward to kick the threatened shells away from the fire. Another shell hit the mechanism of the ship's siren, resulting in "an unholy howl" amid the sharp crack of the guns. This lasted for some time until the engine room crew was able to turn off the flow of steam to the siren. At 1004 a shell hit next to the starboard hawser, destroying a crew latrine and killing one man. A fire erupted but was quickly extinguished by the GDO and his fire-fighting crew. There were several very close splashes, and Heyssler thought it pure chance they did not sustain a direct hit. The ship was indeed hit a third time on the starboard side aft but no one noticed it in the heat of battle and it was only after they had returned to port that the buckled plates below the waterline were discovered.[61]

The *Dartmouth* observed that the Austrians, despite the *Saida*, were slowly drawing ahead. The British cruiser was abreast of the *Saida* but soon became aware that all three Austrian cruisers were now concentrating their fire on her. The *Bristol*, out of range, had been obliged to check fire at 1015.[62] The *Dartmouth* found herself straddled and hit. One shell penetrated the starboard side of the forecastle deck abreast the mast, cutting a ventilating pipe, decapitating a seaman, and finally bursting on the hatch down to the marine's mess deck, killing two and wounding six. Two shells struck aft, one of which entered below the water line but fortunately did not explode. The second burst on striking the deck alongside the after gun, badly scoring but not damaging the latter and not harming any of the gun crew, although one man in the after searchlight platform was wounded by a shell splinter. The Austrian straddles were "most annoying" to the gunnery officer in the spotting top, for his glasses were continually getting wet. Fortunately he had two pairs of glasses with him in the top and handed each to a boy to dry as it got wet. However, the Austrian shells interfered with his spotting, for the shorts caused him to miss spotting the fall of "a great many" of the British salvoes.[63]

Under fire from three ships, straddled, and well ahead of the other British and Italian ships, Admiral Acton at 1045 ordered the *Dartmouth* to haul out to between 16,000 and 17,000 yards. This would permit the *Bristol*, about 6,000 meters behind according to Acton, to catch up. The Austrian salvoes were now falling short of the *Dartmouth*. In the *Helgoland*, the gunnery officer reported to Captain Heyssler at around 1025 that the range was too great for their guns to be effective. Heyssler refrained from checking fire completely and ordered a salvo to be fired intermittently at maximum elevation. He did not want to give the impression the ship had become unable to fight.[64]

Acton ordered speed to be increased again at 1058. The *Dartmouth* slowly closed on the Austrians again and resumed fire, straddling the leading Austrian cruiser at a range of 12,000 to 13,000 yards. Nevertheless the Austrians retained their advantage in speed, and Acton noted he was gradually dropping astern of the leading Austrian cruiser and realized he would not be able to get into a good position with regard to the enemy. Consequently he ordered fire to be switched to the lagging third Austrian cruiser, the *Saida*. Acton's report states that he ordered a turn to starboard at 1100 to cut her off, closing to about

7,500 meters and opening an "intense fire" in which the *Bristol*, having caught up, joined. Acton's report is at variance with *Dartmouth*'s gunnery narrative. According to her gunnery officer, the *Dartmouth* turned toward the *Saida* and at 1030 commenced fire with all three forecastle guns firing directly ahead. Shortly afterwards, according to the same report, *Dartmouth* altered course to port in an attempt to cross *Saida*'s "T" astern. This had the effect of bringing the starboard guns into action. The closest range *Dartmouth* reached in this part of the action was 9,700 yards. *Dartmouth*'s gunnery officer thought they were hitting, and Acton also believed their salvoes "caused serious damages to the enemy."[65]

The discrepancies in timing and even course alterations between the British and Italian accounts are confusing, but the sequence of events is clear. The *Dartmouth* was bearing the brunt of the battle and in drawing ahead of the *Bristol* wound up coming under the concentrated fire of the three Austrian cruisers. Admiral Acton therefore ordered her to haul out and permit *Bristol* to catch up. He would also have been able to use the superior range of the six-inch guns. Upon realizing that he would not be able to catch the leading Austrian ships, he ordered fire to be concentrated on the *Saida*. The sequence of the events that followed is less clear. According to Acton, "at the same time" *Dartmouth* was concentrating fire on the *Saida*, both the *Dartmouth* and *Bristol* were attacked repeatedly by Austrian aircraft using bombs and machine guns. It is not clear from the Austrian reports exactly which aircraft were involved, but it was probably K.153 and K.154, which had refueled and loaded additional bombs at Durazzo before returning to the battle. They had also attacked the *Marsala* group coming from Brindisi (see below) as well as the British cruisers. They reported attacking with bombs and machine guns at 1050 and claimed a "direct hit" on the starboard side of the navigation bridge with a 20kg bomb. This group of Austrian aircraft also reported the cruisers maneuvering evasively at 1100 under the attack of another Austrian aircraft. The latter was probably K.206, piloted by Fliegermaat Haschke, who after delivering an earlier attack had machine-gunned the cruisers between 1030 and 1050. He reported dropping his last pair of 15kg bombs around 1100 before leaving the scene of battle for his base at 1115.[66] As was often the case with aviators, they were overly optimistic in claiming results. None of the British or Italian ships were hit. *Dartmouth*'s gunnery officer reported two bombs falling about 200 yards on the port bow and one close to their stern, although he gives the time as just after they had ceased firing, so it is not certain which aircraft were involved. The *Bristol*'s log also did not differentiate between attacks, merely reporting being attacked "several times by enemy aircraft with bombs and maxims" (machine guns) and being hit by the latter on the forecastle and bridge.[67] The Austrian aircraft may not have inflicted any serious damage but, as Captain Addison of the *Dartmouth* told a friend, they had been "[m]ost annoying!"[68] The aircraft may have had another effect, at least in the opinion of one of the Austrian captains: "Our aeroplanes were a great help, they attacked the enemy cruisers with bombs and machine-gun fire so that they were often forced to take avoiding action which interfered with the precision of their gunnery."[69]

The encounter was now reaching the point of crisis for the Austrians. The Allies' attempt to cut off the lagging *Saida*, now under heavy fire from the two British cruisers, coincided with the *Novara*'s desperate plight, for the damaged cruiser could not sustain her high speed. She had lost the use of half her boilers, and Horthy signaled the other cruisers that *Novara* could only proceed under her own steam for an additional ten minutes. Horthy claimed they could have gone on for a while with sea water but that he did not want to damage the remaining boilers. Horthy ordered the fires raked and the *Novara*'s speed fell off rapidly after 1100. She was soon motionless.[70] However, to the great surprise and relief of the Austrians, it was at this critical moment that Admiral Acton turned away. Why would he do so at a time when the Austrian speed advantage was evaporating, permitting him to use the firepower of the *Bristol* in addition to the *Dartmouth* as well as the destroyer *Acerbi*? There appear to be two reasons. On one hand Acton had learned that Austrian reinforcements had sailed from Cattaro, and on the other hand he knew that reinforcements from Brindisi were now in the vicinity. As Acton put matters in his report: "Two large ships were reported coming out of Cattaro steering south apparently to the assistance of the enemy light cruisers. One of the two big ships had two masts and two funnels. I did not think it was wise to go up north again for fear of being cut off, but the *Marsala* group being quite close I steered in their direction and we met at 11:30 a.m."[71]

At 1104 the two British cruisers ceased fire and on Acton's order turned away. The Austrians had a temporary reprieve. There are problems with Admiral Acton's account. At the moment the British and Italians first turned away there would have been only one large Austrian ship at sea on a southerly course. This would have been the armored cruiser *Sankt Georg*, and this ship had three funnels, not two. The other Austrian heavy ship that came out to support Horthy was the coast defense battleship *Budapest*, but this ship had only one funnel and was not ordered out until after *Novara*'s breakdown was reported. But this was only becoming apparent just as Acton turned away, and a dispatch from *Saida* to *Sankt Georg* stating *Novara* was motionless is timed in the Kriegstagebuch of the I Torpedoflottillenkommando as 1115.[72] An Italian aviator might have observed the ship getting up steam with clouds of smoke or possibly observed smoke from other ships in the Bocche, but this would not explain the report of them "steering south."

The *Marsala* group mentioned by Admiral Acton refers to two scouts and three destroyers from Brindisi. The scout *Marsala*, in company with the smaller scout *Racchia* (a sister ship of the *Mirabello*) and destroyers *Insidioso*, *Impavido*, and *Indomito*, had sailed from Brindisi at 0835 and proceeded at twenty-five knots on a course of 45°. At 0900 Admiral Acton had sent a wireless message ordering the group to support the *Mirabello* group in its attack on the Austrians, although he was apparently not clear about the exact location of the *Mirabello*, apparently believing it to be much closer to the Italian coast. The senior naval officer of the group, Capitano di vascello Ducci in the *Marsala*, however, was able on the basis of intercepted wireless messages to clarify his picture of the situation and alter course to first 25° and then 11° in the general direction of Cattaro and increase his speed to twenty-six and a half knots. At 1030 smoke was observed off the starboard bow, and as they gradually approached this the *Marsala* group altered to a course much closer to north, while to the northeast other ships could be seen along with flashes of gunfire. The *Racchia* signaled *Marsala* at 1050 requesting permission to investigate the enemy, and when this request was answered in the affirmative, *Racchia* increased speed to thirty-three knots and, in company with the destroyer *Impavido*, raced toward the Austrian cruisers. The remainder of the *Marsala* group continued toward the smoke clouds observed off the bow. The smoke was eventually confirmed as belonging to the three Austrian cruisers, while the smoke columns to the right were identified as belonging to the *Dartmouth* group. Austrian accounts note an attack on the *Marsala* and accompanying destroyers by that ambitious pair of flying boats, K.153 and K.154, but there is no mention of this in the Italian account.[73]

At about the same time, a section of Italian FBAs, No. 4 piloted by Guardiamarina Maddalena with Tenente di vascello Davisio as observer and No. 9 piloted by Capo 2nd class timionere Fatini with Capo 2nd class radiotelegraphisti Venturini as observer, flew over the *Marsala*. They had taken off from Brindisi at 1000, reported passing over the *Marsala* at 1020, and subsequently spotted a submarine just to starboard of the Italians' course. They dropped two bombs on the position, without apparent result. The submarine was almost certainly the Austrian U.27, which had been sent to reconnoiter off Brindisi and reported being compelled to submerge by two aircraft. U.27 had already reported by wireless the departure of ships from Brindisi.[74] The two Italian FBAs then turned north, sighted the cruisers in action at 1050, and remained over the battlefield until 1130, confirming the immobilization of the *Novara* and the eventual approach of Austrian reinforcements from Cattaro. There is, however, no indication in the Italian account if they attempted further intervention or if they attempted to pass their intelligence to the Allied ships or even had the means to do so. They were eventually compelled by a lack of fuel to leave. One of the FBAs, No. 4, the section leader, was so short on fuel that it had to land outside of the port. The time of their return and when they could presumably pass on their intelligence was approximately

1220.[75] Nevertheless, Admiral Acton knew that Austrian ships had left Cattaro and knew some rough though erroneous details of their configuration, that is, the number of funnels, etc. It is not clear from either the unpublished or published reports exactly how he received this intelligence, although the most likely source would have been one of the Italian FBAs.

The first Austrian reinforcements from the Gulf of Cattaro consisted of the armored cruiser *Sankt Georg* accompanied by the destroyers *Tátra* and *Warasdiner* and the torpedo boats *84F, 88F, 99M,* and *100M.* They were under the command of Kontreadmiral Alexander Hansa, Kreuzerflottillenkommandant, and had been designated as potential support in the plan for the raid. The *Sankt Georg* and consorts put to sea shortly after receiving Horthy's famous message "Auslaufen verspricht Erfolg." The time given for this message in the log of the I Torpedoflottillenkommando is 0906. *Sankt Georg* signaled *Novara* that she was at Punta d'Ostro, that is, the entrance to the Bocche, at 1020 and ten minutes later signaled her location and that she was on a southerly course. Another message to Horthy followed at 1114 giving *Sankt Georg's* position as of 1100 and informing Horthy that she was making eighteen knots on a course to the south.[76] Hansa had the problem of setting a course that would allow him to reach the hard-pressed cruisers in the shortest possible time, a task complicated by the fact that the British and Italian cruisers were to the east of Horthy's force, that is, between the latter and the Austrian coast. Should the Austrians be pushed too far to the west, a junction might be impossible. In the worst case, if Horthy was forced back south into the Ionian Sea, the Austrian breakthrough would take place the following night, or they might seek to escape by working around the pursuit by approaching the Italian coast, as had been the case on 29 December 1915. This more risky maneuver proved to be unnecessary after a shift of the Allied ships from the east more toward the west had permitted Horthy to assume a northerly course before *Novara* broke down.

As the *Sankt Georg* group sailed, the two Weichmann flying boats K.195 and K.152 took off to reconnoiter, and at 1141, while the ships were steaming at full speed, one of the planes dipped low and dropped a container on the open foredeck of the cruiser with the message: "Nine enemy ships, type not made out, in the vicinity of our cruisers, of which two apparently damaged. Distance approximately 30 nautical miles." At approximately 1154 a message from the *Helgoland* was received announcing that *Saida* was taking *Novara* in tow and that the enemy was renewing its attack. After learning of the situation, Hansa ordered the coast defense battleship *Budapest,* accompanied by the high-seas torpedo boats *86F, 91F,* and *95F,* to put to sea. The ships of the *Budapest* group apparently received the order at noon. The old *Budapest* had four 24cm guns but was slow and not likely to be able to achieve more than seventeen and a half knots. The *Budapest* also spotted a torpedo track not long after leaving the Bocche and fired on it. If the sighting was correct, and this is not certain, it must have been the *Bernouilli*, which had already attacked the *Balaton* unsuccessfully.[77]

After 1100 the speed of the *Novara* had been progressively reduced until by 1115 the cruiser lay motionless. One Austrian historian speculated that Acton's apparent failure to notice the cruiser's plight may have been because he assumed any apparent reduction in speed was designed to allow the slower *Saida* to catch up.[78] The Austrian situation was critical, for at this moment the *Sankt Georg* was estimated to be still twenty-five nautical miles distant. The *Saida*, despite the impressions of the British and Italians, had not sustained a single hit during the last attack. Her captain, Linienschiffskapitän Ferdinand Ritter von Purschka, observed the *Novara* slow, and at a distance of around 100 meters he could discern a man on the bridge waving flag "A," the signal for an engine breakdown. He could also see other officers and men frantically signaling. Purschka decided to take the ship under tow, and he passed slowly down the weather side of the *Novara* and stopped close to the stricken ship. The *Saida*'s towing gear was broken out and Purschka signaled the *Helgoland* to make smoke and cover the maneuver.[79] Heyssler apparently did not see the signal, and *Helgoland*, after turning to avoid ramming the stricken ship, at first raced past. Nevertheless Heyssler quickly grasped the situation and on his own initiative decided to turn and place his ship between the enemy and the other two cruisers, ready to draw and return fire. At 1118 the *Saida* signaled *Novara*'s plight to the *Sankt Georg* but appears to have garbled the message, giving *Helgoland*'s name as the stricken ship instead of *Novara* and erroneously reporting their position twenty miles too far to the north.[80] Purschka assumed command of the three cruisers at 1120 and acted as senior officer until the arrival of the *Sankt Georg*.[81]

As the Austrians moved into their respective positions to begin the attempt to take the *Novara* under tow, they were attacked by a lone Italian destroyer, the *Acerbi*. The *Dartmouth*, as she passed the stern of the *Saida*, had signaled for the other ships to follow her. The *Acerbi* probably saw only the first flag of the signal, with the rest perhaps obscured by smoke. The first flag meant "attack the enemy formation," and the *Acerbi* commenced fire at 1115 at a range of 9,500 meters and continued what *Helgoland*'s log described as a "furious" (*heftiges*) fire at ranges varying between 8,000 and 9,000 meters. Heyssler misidentified the attacking destroyer as a *Quarto*-class scout and reported that the destroyer had gotten as close as 7,300 meters. The *Acerbi*'s captain might have perceived that the situation was opportune for a favorable attack had he been supported by the larger cruisers. He was not. The lone destroyer was subjected to the combined fire of the three Austrian cruisers, although by this time the *Novara* had only two of her seven 10cm guns in action and therefore could only have made a limited contribution. This was another lost opportunity for the British and Italians. The *Acerbi*, unsupported and left on her own, found the

Austrian fire too heavy to approach close enough to use torpedoes. The destroyer then experienced problems with one or more of her guns, presumably a jam, and hauled away to a range of 10,000 to 11,000 meters to rectify the problem. At the same time, the *Acerbi* came under air attack, although it is not clear exactly which aircraft were involved. At 1136 the destroyer received the signal from Acton, by wireless this time, for the other ships to join *Dartmouth*.[82]

The Austrians knew help was at hand. At 1125, just as the *Acerbi*'s attack had been turned away, the *Helgoland*'s log noted that smoke was sighted to the north, presumably the *Sankt Georg* group steaming to their assistance. Would they arrive in time? They knew that additional Allied ships were arriving on the scene as the *Saida* and *Novara* lay close together, now motionless as they struggled with the tow. The *Racchia* and *Impavido*, dispatched from the *Marsala* group to reconnoiter the enemy, had advanced some 5,000 meters ahead of the *Marsala*. At 1130 they were in a position 11,000 meters from the Austrian cruisers. *Helgoland* fired on them. Heyssler again misidentified one of his opponents as a *Quarto* but correctly recognized the other as a *Nino Bixio*–class scout, the class to which the *Marsala* belonged. The Italian ships were reported to have closed to 10,000 meters, with only the *Racchia* actually firing between ten and twenty rounds before turning slowly toward the east. The *Helgoland*'s return fire fell short. Heyssler claimed he could see the bow waves of the attacking ships clearly and wondered why the attacks had not been pressed home when the Italians could see that two of the Austrian cruisers were apparently motionless. In the Kriegstagebuch of the I Torpedoflottillenkommando, he subsequently added a note surmising that the enemy— referred to as "English" [*Engländern*]—were out of ammunition.[83] As the *Novara*'s wireless was out of commission, the *Helgoland* had to send the message to the *Sankt Georg* at 1140 announcing that the *Saida* had taken the *Novara* under tow and that the enemy attack had been renewed. The message was no sooner dispatched than within ten minutes—1150 according to the log—another destroyer was observed to be closing rapidly, apparently to deliver a torpedo attack. The destroyer—possibly the *Impavido*—closed to about 6,000 meters before being driven off by rapid fire from the cruisers, the action being duly signaled to *Sankt Georg* at 1152.[84]

It is not clear exactly which destroyer delivered the 1150 attack on the Austrians. Admiral Acton does little to clarify the point. After joining with the *Marsala* group at 1130,

> I then steered North again having noticed that the three enemy ships had reduced speed and one of them seemed to be stopped. Owing to the *Acerbi*'s misinterpreting a signal she went alone to attack the enemy and was fired at, while [*sic*] she returned brilliantly. I then recalled her. The *Acerbi* reported that one of the enemy ships was seriously damaged. At 12:05 p.m. I decided to return to Brindisi. . . .[85]

However, the *Helgoland*'s log shows that there were three attacks by lone Italian warships during the period *Novara* was stopped. The first at 1124 is misidentified as a "*Quarto*" but is obviously the *Acerbi*, the second at 1130 by a *Nino Bixio*–class (possibly the *Marsala*) and another *Quarto*, the latter the only ship to actually fire. This was probably the *Racchia*. The third attack by a lone destroyer is logged at 1140. Could this have been the destroyer *Impavido*, which had been sent ahead in company with the *Racchia*? Neither the Italian nor Austrian official histories clarify the point.[86] Moreover, it may not have been the destroyer because things appeared slightly different to the *Saida*, whose log indicates that at 1155 the enemy ships came again for an attack, only to be repulsed by the three Austrian cruisers, and that a small enemy unit (one mast, two funnels) listing to starboard and noticeably down by the stern remained for a long time stopped. *Saida* then logged the enemy as turning away to the south at 1207.[87] The destroyer *Impavido* had three funnels, the *Racchia* two. There was not a significant difference in size between the small scout and a destroyer, and the Austrians obviously had difficulty telling them apart at a distance. However, the number of funnels would be a distinct clue to identity, although the Ufficio Storico account has no mention of any damage causing one of the ships in question to list to starboard and be down by the stern.

The details of this phase of the action may be in question but the overall situation was clear. The Austrians could see smoke on the horizon belonging to Allied reinforcements evidently coming from Brindisi. They could even make out the tops of distant masts, and on occasion destroyers or scouts approached and were fired at, but the Allied attacks did not seem to have been pushed home and there were no reports of torpedoes being used. The Austrians realized, however, that they were still in considerable danger. The apparent failure of Acton to coordinate those attacks by the light craft and push them to the limit at a moment when the Austrians were vulnerable and at a disadvantage is another serious error. Had more than one Italian destroyer or scout attacked at the same time, possibly closing near enough to use torpedoes, it would obviously have been more difficult for the hard-pressed Austrians to repel them.

The Austrians actually had considerable difficulty establishing the tow. The steam connection to the *Novara*'s capstan had been damaged and all work had to be done by hand, which slowed the operation. They were always conscious of their vulnerability as they worked with the two ships motionless, and Purschka was later scornful of their enemies' failure to take advantage of the situation, terming the attempts "pitiful" (*kläglichen*).[88] Heyssler in the *Helgoland* during this time moved slowly between the two other cruisers, ready in case of a serious attack to use his smoke-making apparatus to cover them. He described the attack of the *Racchia* and *Marsala*:

Once again the situation became very critical. The joint enemy units made a simultaneous turn towards us so that they were ahead. I could clearly see the bow waves of the rapidly approaching ships. Had they now come up to effective firing distance, had they turned broadside on to us, and developed the full force of their fire, they could have finished us off in a few minutes, especially *Helgoland* which was nearest to them.[89]

The *Saida*'s log indicates, however, that smoke from the *Sankt Georg* group was in sight at 1130, roughly the same time as the attack by what the Austrians perceived as the "*Quarto*" together with the "*Bixio*." At 1145 *Saida* signaled to *Sankt Georg*: "Please proceed with full speed" (*Bitte ganze kraft*).[90] The *Saida*

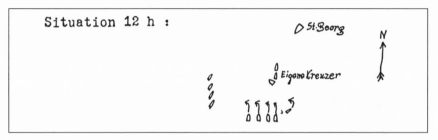

The situation at 1200 as reported by IV. Gruppe (K.195 and K.152). Austrian cruisers center with *Helgoland* screening *Novara* and *Saida*. British and Italian ships bottom center and left. *Sankt Georg* group arriving at right.
(Österreichisches Staatsarchiv/Kriegsarchiv)

recorded the last of the enemy destroyer or scout attacks at 1155 but only noted all the distant enemy ships turning away to the south at 1207. *Saida* was finally under way with the *Novara* in tow at 1229. Horthy's report timed the beginning of the tow slightly earlier at 1225 but agrees (as does the log of the *Helgoland*) that the enemy turned away at 1207. The *Sankt Georg* was now clearly recognizable and close enough for *Helgoland* to signal this information by lamp and radio at 1210, and by 1225 the enemy was out of sight to the south. The actual juncture with the *Sankt Georg* and her escorts took place, according to Horthy, just after the tow began, and *Helgoland*'s log put it at 1230.[91] The crisis had passed, and the Austrian cruisers were saved.

The inevitable question is: What had motivated Admiral Acton to act as he did? Once he had joined with the *Marsala* group at 1130 he by his own account turned north again, heading directly for the Austrians. While the times entered in *Dartmouth*'s and *Bristol*'s logs vary and are confusing because of the frequent changes of course while avoiding aircraft, they show *Dartmouth* on a north-northwest course from 1145 to 1205 and *Bristol* altering course at 1148 to north 25° west and increasing to full speed at 1153 before altering course to the south, thereby breaking off the action at 1205.[92] Acton was now heading back toward the Austrian cruisers, presumably to finish the job. He knew from the *Acerbi*'s report that one of the Austrian cruisers was motionless. He had *Dartmouth*, *Bristol*, *Marsala*, *Racchia*, and five destroyers. He had been engaged in a gunnery duel for more than two hours and had been punishing his opponents with just half this force before turning away the first time. Now he should have been able to inflict further, possibly fatal, punishment in a situation where only the *Helgoland* with her seven 10cm guns was able to maneuver freely and fight back. None of the force now under his immediate command had suffered serious damage. The only ominous note was the distant smoke indicating Austrian reinforcements arriving from Cattaro. Acton made his decision: "At 12:05 p.m. I decided to return to Brindisi for the following reasons—(1) Because of the presence of two large enemy ships far superior to me; (2) because I was near an enemy base and any damage sustained by one of my ships would have meant her certain loss; and (3) because the *Bristol* could not keep up and I wished to avoid an action with large ships."[93]

The decision assured the escape of the Austrians and has remained controversial ever since. Was it correct? A historian writing from the comfort of his home generations later and with the help of hindsight cannot really put himself in the place of an admiral who had the responsibility at the time and did not and could not know all the facts that became apparent after the battle. Acton knew that he was deep in Austrian territory; the naval base at Cattaro was only about thirty-five or forty miles away. He also knew that reinforcements were on their way from Cattaro and that these probably included "heavy ships." He was mistaken as to the number and quality and real fighting force of what might be opposed to him, but full knowledge of this would only come later. The *Sankt Georg* had two 24cm, five 19cm, and four 15cm guns and enjoyed, as her classification as an armored cruiser implies, more armor protection than any of the British or Italian ships. Acton would have known all this. On the other hand, Acton probably could not have known of the likelihood that *Sankt Georg*'s fire-control apparatus would have been inferior to that of the *Dartmouth*, and the British cruiser would have been able to maintain a faster rate of fire.[94] The second Austrian "heavy ship" referred to, presumably the *Budapest*, was slow, obsolete, and had only just left harbor and was still about two hours distant.

Acton has his defenders. Luigi Slaghek-Fabbri, a future admiral in the Italian navy, was then liaison officer in the *Bristol*. He would later write that with the appearance of the *Sankt Georg*, persistence in an attack "would henceforth not offer concrete probabilities of gains but only certainty of losses." Slaghek argued that in the presence of an armored ship "practically unattackable by guns of medium caliber" and protected by a good escort, the "light ships were obliged to give way [*cedere il passo*]." He also pointed out the difficulty of saving any of their own ships which might suffer damage when they were only thirty-five miles from the enemy base and sixty-five miles from their own. Slaghek also raised the specter of submarines having sortied from Cattaro.[95]

The subject is not necessarily an example of differences in British and Italian thinking, the former bold and the latter timid. Captain Addison of the *Dartmouth* wrote to a friend shortly after the battle: "By this time we were nearing Cattaro & 2 at least of the '*St. Georges*' were coming up fast & the Italian Admiral decided to leave it at that & I think rightly."[96] The British also had an exaggerated view of the Austrian opposition. Shortly after the battle there was even the belief in the British Adriatic force that one of the Austrian heavy ships had been a "*Zrínyi*"-class battleship, that is, a semi-dreadnought with twelve-inch cannon. In the year and a half of war remaining after the Otranto action, British intelligence, thanks to the more extensive use of aircraft for reconnaissance, would probably obtain a much better idea of potential Austrian opposition. On the other hand the submarine danger, as we shall see in the following chapter, was only too real, although submarines were not likely to intervene in a fast-moving encounter and were more of a danger when established in waiting positions. They probably would not have been able to interfere had Acton pushed the action. An argument like this can never really be settled. There is no denying the fact, however, that Admiral Acton had missed his chance to go down in history as the victor of a sharp encounter resulting in the loss of one or more enemy warships. The risks, while certainly present, may not in reality have been excessive. Acton's decision made his relegation to historical obscurity inevitable.

CHAPTER SIX

THE FORCES RETURN

THE EXPERIENCES OF THE Austrians and the Allies during their return from the battlefield were very different. The Austrians had far less distance to travel to the Bocche, and after the juncture of the *Sankt Georg* group with Horthy's beleaguered cruisers, a general sense of relief at having survived mingled with a sense of triumph at having safely completed a successful raid. The Allies, in contrast, would feel frustration at the eventual escape of the Austrians and would suffer some of their heaviest losses of the day. Towing the crippled *Novara* slowed the Austrians' return, and there was also a minor mishap. In passing the hawser from *Saida* to *Novara* during the establishment of the tow, the bow of the *Novara* damaged the starboard boat and davits of the *Saida*.[1] At 1210 *Helgoland* signaled to the approaching *Sankt Georg* via searchlight that the enemy had turned away. Ten minutes later *Saida*, with *Novara* in tow, had begun to move, and by 1225 *Helgoland*'s log indicates the Allied ships were out of sight to the south. The *Sankt Georg* group joined the three cruisers at 1230. Admiral Hansa now assumed command. At approximately this time Horthy had a wireless message sent to the radio collection center [*Sammelstelle*] at Castelnuovo in the Bocche addressed to his wife and informing her he had been lightly wounded but that she was not to worry.[2] Although the crisis had passed, the Allied ships had turned away, and the *Novara* was under tow, it is still striking to see a personal message like this transmitted from the battlefield. Admiral Hansa subsequently maintained radio silence so as not to betray to Allied direction-finding stations the rate of their progress.[3] Hansa ordered *Helgoland* to take the lead of the line, followed by *Saida* with *Novara* in tow. The initial speed was only about six knots, increased to about seven after *Novara* received a second hawser from the *Saida* at 1344. The *Sankt Georg* brought up the rear of the line, with the torpedo boats guarding the flanks and zigzagging at full speed.[4] There was additional security from the Austrian aircraft flying overhead. As *Helgoland* moved to the head of the line, she passed only a few meters from the *Novara*, and her captain Heyssler on his bridge waved his cap and called out "hurrah," joined by the smoke-blackened crew of the cruiser. He could see Horthy, who smiled and waved back, sitting beside his conning tower. Heyssler then noticed that Horthy's legs were covered with a blanket and realized that the commander of their raid had been wounded.[5]

The Austrians grew even more secure when the coast defense battleship *Budapest*, together with the torpedo boats *86F*, *91F*, and *95F*, arrived at 1455. The *Budapest* took up a position astern to starboard and the *Sankt Georg* astern to port of the tow. The torpedo boats strengthened the screen.[6] The Austrians also had the potential of additional support from German submarines. At 1455 the German *UC.34* signaled to the Kreuzerflotillenkommando that the boat was off Curzola, ready for action, and could thrust eastward across the Adriatic toward Vieste on the Garignano peninsula. This was well to the north of Brindisi, and consequently the submarine, despite the willingness of her commander, was not really in a position to play any role in the action this late in the day. A week later *UC.34* departed for operations against Port Said and Alexandria.[7]

The Austrians kept a sharp lookout for Allied submarines, but none appear to have been in position to interfere with the return. The only Allied submarine besides the *Bernouilli* on patrol at the time was the Italian *F.10*, which had seen distant smoke on both the 14th and 15th but, lacking a radio, had not been able to pass on the intelligence. The submarine was not near the route of the Austrians on their return.[8] By now the wind had fallen and the sea was smooth as a mirror, and the Austrians had time to take stock of their position and assess their casualties, which, with the exception of the *Novara*, were light. There was also the opportunity to take care of basic needs, and the ovens were lit to provide meals for the men. Heyssler was able to enjoy a belated lunch on his bridge and realized he had not eaten anything since they had sailed the evening before. However, he claimed to feel neither hungry nor tired and attributed this to nerves: "One's nerves are so taut during action all else is forgotten."[9] Not everyone was so oblivious to fatigue. Cadet Zanoskar in the *Novara* relieved a friend at the observation telescope, happy he could sit at the apparatus. He was so fatigued he could hardly stand and was glad there were two aircraft on patrol to alleviate his responsibilities.[10]

Another nineteen-year-old cadet in the *Novara*, Jure Dunay, now had the opportunity to note that the companionways of the cruiser were stuffed with empty shell cases they were not permitted to throw overboard. The hard-pressed Austrians needed to save the brass.[11] The *Novara* had fired 675 shells from her 10cm guns, but this was actually the smallest number of the three cruisers. Her sister ship the *Saida* had fired 832 10cm shells and the *Helgoland* by far the greatest number at 1,052. The *Novara*, however, had suffered the most, taking according to one estimate as many as forty-five hits. This estimate may be excessive, but there is no denying the cruiser had been battered. The ship had been brought to a halt by damage to her boilers and had seven of her ten 10cm guns out of action. The *Novara's* human losses were also the heaviest among the cruisers, with a total of fourteen dead or missing and twenty-four wounded. The other Austrian cruisers, in contrast, suffered remarkably little damage. The British and Italians may have thought they were punishing the *Saida* severely, but in fact the ship had the least damage of the Austrian cruisers. The *Saida* suffered only three hits—one a fierce-looking hole in the starboard bow—and ended the day with three men wounded and two 10cm guns out of action. The *Helgoland* also escaped relatively lightly, suffering five hits that killed one and wounded sixteen, and she had one 10cm gun out of action.[12]

The Austrians were eventually able to use a chain to strengthen the hawser used for *Novara's* tow and this permitted speed to be increased to ten knots at 1641. Shortly afterwards, at 1645, Hansa ordered his ships into line-ahead forma-tion, with *Budapest* at the tail and the torpedo boats closing up on the flanks, and shaped a course for the southwest passage through the minefields for entry into the Bocche. As they passed Punta d'Ostro at 1730 and entered the gulf, Hansa's ships discovered a warm welcome waiting for them. They were greeted with cheers from all the fortifications, ships at anchor, and naval installations on shore. It must have been a proud moment. It was, however, mixed with feel-ings of profound relief at having escaped. Cadet Zanoskar remembered that he had never been so overjoyed in his life as when they had entered the Bocche and he could hear the sound of music and cheering coming especially loudly from Fort Mamula and he could see Mount Lovčen lit by the setting sun.[13] There was also some surprise that the British had not pressed their advantage, enabling the Austrians to escape. The Austrians of course at this stage did not know that an Italian admiral had been in command.

The ships passed slowly through the harbor obstructions to their anchorage off Gjenović, with *Helgoland* anchoring at 1840. The fires in the boilers were drawn and the customary routine of landing wounded, effecting repairs, and writing reports began.[14] There were also prisoners to be landed. There were six-teen of the drifter men in the *Helgoland* where they must surely have spent an uncomfortable time below during the action. They had been kept in the ship's first-aid station where they reportedly spent the time singing hymns and pray-ing. Heyssler requested that a launch be sent from the flagship to take charge of them, but before they left the ship two requested to see Heyssler, who received them in his cabin. He found the pair of drifter captains "decent" and "typical old Salts." They thanked him for rescuing them and the older one complimented him on the way he had maneuvered the cruiser through the nets. Heyssler, in turn, comforted them about their bad luck and wished them good treatment during their internment.[15] There were still lingering traces of old-fashioned courtesy—at least between British and Austrians—in the Adriatic despite more than two and a half years of bitter war, and Heyssler, fluent in English, was married to an Australian of Irish descent.

Horthy was taken to *Dampfer X*, the hospital ship in the Bocche, along with the other wounded requiring hospitalization. They numbered two cadets and thirteen men from the *Novara*, a cadet and two men from the *Helgoland*, and one man from the *Saida*. *Dampfer X*, literally "Steamer No. 10," was the utilitarian name assigned to the former Austrian Lloyd liner *Africa* (4,753 tons) that had been converted at the beginning of the war into a hospital ship. The career of this ship had been symptomatic of the naval war in the Adriatic. Since there had been no major naval action with large numbers of wounded in the first few months of the war, the ship was not needed, and in the spring of 1915 *Dampfer X* was used as an accommodation ship for German submarine crews at Pola. *Dampfer X* reverted to hospital duties in February 1916, presumably because the successful conclusion of the Serbian campaign, the clearing of Mount Lovčen, and the prosecution of military operations in northern Albania opened new possibilities and created additional responsibilities for the navy.[16]

Horthy found his wife Magda, notified of his injuries by his wireless message, waiting for him in the hospital ship. Heyssler, who was a good friend of Horthy, also proceeded to the hospital ship as soon as he had arranged for the departure of his prisoners. He arrived while Horthy was in the operating theater having his wounds treated. The wounds were in both legs but were not severe, and his trousers had been burnt off up to the knees. Horthy, like his ship, received temporary repairs in the Bocche and after a few days when he could be moved insisted on personally bringing the *Novara* north to the dockyard in Pola for permanent repairs. His sentiment was "I could not endure the thought of her [*Novara*] being taken to Pola by other hands than mine." The temporary repairs to the *Novara* were done from the 16th to the 22nd and the ship sailed for Pola on the 26th, in company with the *Saida* and the destroyer *Tátra*. Heyssler, on a farewell visit, found Horthy sitting in a chair on the bridge, and because of the danger from mines and submarines and his own lack of mobility, he actually lay on a stretcher on the bridge throughout the trip north. Horthy eventually had to endure two operations, and it was some time before his hearing, damaged by the explosion, was restored to near normal. It would be months before Horthy returned to duty as captain of the dreadnought *Prinz Eugen*. However, the basis for what would later be considered the "Horthy legend" had been laid.[17]

Among the many details to be handled after the action was the question of a suitable communiqué. This apparently became a matter of some urgency for the Marinesektion in Vienna. Rumors of a naval action in the Adriatic had reached Vienna by the 16th and had assumed "fantastic dimensions" in stock market circles. The communiqué, issued the same day with the information about the actions of the German submarine drawn up in agreement with the German naval authorities, described a successful raid into the Strait of Otranto resulting in the sinking of one Italian destroyer, three merchant steamers, and twenty armed patrol craft with seventy-two prisoners taken from the latter. There had been a hard-fought action during the raiders' return against superior forces from the British, French, and Italian navies, and the enemy had suffered considerable damage with fires observed on three enemy destroyers. Enemy aircraft and submarines had achieved no success while Austrian aircraft had effectively bombed an enemy submarine and had hit two enemy cruisers with bombs. Austrian losses and damage had been small while a German submarine had sunk a four-funneled British cruiser.[18] Needless to say, the claims of enemy losses were a considerable exaggeration and Austrian loss and damage minimized, which would hardly have been unusual for a wartime communiqué.

The men of the three Austrian cruisers received what other officers in the navy with perhaps a trace of envy considered lavish praise and honors. No less a personage than Kaiser Karl I himself visited Pola on June 3rd and personally conferred decorations on officers and petty officers in the *Novara*, then in dockyard hands. The Kaiser was late in arriving, and Fritz Bratusch-Marrain, a former cadet in the *Novara*, remembered how he and the other cadets grew increasingly hungry as they waited. Their superior officers, seemingly sympathetic to their plight, permitted them to have their pudding. When the Kaiser still did not appear, they were allowed to have their meat and when there was still no Kaiser they were given their soup. The result was that for the first time in his life Bratusch-Marrain had his lunch in reverse order.[19] The honors granted the senior commanders all carried the added distinction of "War Decoration and Sword." Horthy received the Militärverdienstkreuz, second class, while Heyssler and Purschka were made knights of the Leopold Order. Liechtenstein received the Order of the Iron Crown, third class, and his fellow destroyer captain, Korvettenkapitän Franz Morin of the *Balaton*, the Militärverdienstkreuz. Hansa, befitting his rank and position as commander of the Kreuzerflottillen, received the Order of the Iron Crown, second class. Although he had not been present during the actual battle, the citation lauded him for his successful leadership of a fleet detachment.[20] The navy had had few opportunities to distinguish itself in surface actions and the lionization of the three cruisers then and after the war is understandable.

Amid the general praise, some Austrian naval officers were conscious that their actions on the 15th of May had not been faultless. Peter Handel-

Mazzetti, then a Fregattenleutnant in the radio collection center [*Sammel-stelle*] at Sebenico, who had been able to follow the action through the wire-less messages, grumbled in a letter to a friend that the *Sankt Georg* had sailed "as usual" much too late and that Admiral Hansa seemed to have great difficulty in deciding to sail, which prolonged the cruisers' peril. At the critical point in the action the wireless signals from the cruisers seemed confused, badly ciphered, and mostly given in the clear, which seemed to indicate in-creased nervousness. The work of the airmen, praised as innovative in one sense, also revealed inexperience in working together with the ships.[21]

Some of the aviators, it was alleged, had been in the air a cumulative total of ten hours on the 15th and their actual airmanship left nothing to be desired. Admiral Hansa praised the skill of Fregattenleutnant Emanuel Lerch and his observer Adalbert Lenti, who had swooped down in K.195 to an altitude of only five meters in a strong wind to drop a container carrying a message onto the forward deck of the *Sankt Georg* while the cruiser was steaming at full speed toward Horthy. This was still a primitive way to pass messages, but Hansa observed that the alternate method of signaling, the use of the *Varta-lampen*—a handheld, battery-powered light—to send Morse signals, worked only moderately well. The aircraft actually equipped with wireless transmit-ters were also far from flawless. Heyssler, for example, criticized the radio work of the aviators. The signals, while loud and clear, could only be partially un-derstood, and he recommended that airmen receive more practice in forming the actual letters, that is, in the transmission of messages by Morse code.[22]

The process of taking the *Novara* under tow was also hardly flawless, seem-ing to take what some considered an inordinate amount of time and resulting in damage to the *Saida* from the *Novara*'s bow.[23]

The lavishness of the praise given to Horthy and his rapid rise to power in the following year no doubt generated further resentments. After the war, Georg Pany, who as a Linienschiffsleutnant had been the navigation officer in the *Novara* in May 1917, was highly critical of Horthy's conduct and belittled his achievements. Some of this may have been personal rancor, perhaps influenced by Horthy's controversial post-war political career. Pany does not seem to have found much support among former officers.[24]

The Allied return to Brindisi was less happy than the Austrian return to Cat-taro, but it was far more eventful. After turning away from the Austrians, Ad-miral Acton in the *Dartmouth* ordered the *Bristol*, *Marsala*, and *Racchia* to form to starboard in line-abreast formation. This placed the *Dartmouth* in the leftmost position. He set a course to the south-southwest, making for the en-trance to the swept channel to Brindisi at a speed of twenty knots, increasing to twenty-five knots between 1225 and 1245. He had the five Italian destroyers—*Insidioso, Indomito, Impavido, Mosto,* and *Acerbi*—ahead as escorts. At approx-imately 1300 Acton was joined by the French destroyers *Faulx* and *Casque*.

The two along with a third destroyer, the *Commandant Lucas*, had been at Corfu and were due to sail for exercises at 0830 that morning. However, Vice Amiral Gauchet, the French commander in chief and titular Allied commander in chief in the Mediterranean, had learned from intercepted wireless messages that the Austrian raid was in progress and had ordered the destroyers at 0630 to make ready to sail. They cleared the obstructions defending the French anchorage north of Corfu at 0800 but were forced to proceed in two groups because the *Commandant Lucas* had a defective boiler ventilator and could not steam faster than twenty-four knots, while the *Faulx* and *Casque* could reach twenty-seven. The faster pair shaped a course for Cape Linguetta and then turned toward the mouth of the Meleda Channel. At 1130 they observed smoke to the northwest. This was the *Mirabello* group with the *Aquila* in tow, about to start back to Brindisi. At the same time, the two French destroyers intercepted Acton's wireless message from the *Dartmouth* calling on all ships to join him. The *Faulx* and *Casque* altered course in compliance. The *Commandant Lucas*, far behind, was ordered to join any Allied warships she might meet and eventually momentarily united with the *Mirabello* group. The *Casque* and *Faulx* were 800-ton destroyers of the *Bouclier* class and part of the French destroyer flotilla at Brindisi. After they joined him, Acton ordered them to take up a position to port of the *Dartmouth* as anti-submarine protection on her exposed side.[25] Unfortunately, Admiral Acton's route back to Brindisi took him directly toward the position where the German submarine *UC.25* was lying in wait.

Kapitänleutnant Johannes Feldkirchner, the commander of the *UC.25*, had been ordered to lay his mines off Brindisi before dawn on the 15th and then assume a waiting position, making use of his radio if the opportunity presented itself. Like the two Austrian submarines employed in the operation, Feldkirchner was ordered to listen at a specified time for a possible recall signal. *UC.25* belonged to the *UC.II* class of 400-ton coastal minelaying submarines. These small boats usually mounted an 8.8cm gun for surface action and had two bow and one stern torpedo tubes carrying a total of seven torpedoes. Their major potential for destruction resided in the eighteen mines carried in six mine chutes. Their normal complement was three officers and twenty-three men. One of the major reasons for developing the *UC.II* class, with its greater displacement, had been the requirement that the boats be capable of reaching the Mediterranean. Their predecessors, the *UC.I* class, had to be shipped by rail in sections and reassembled at Pola. The development of the *UC.II* class also demonstrated that the German navy perceived great opportunities for submarine warfare in the Mediterranean. Feldkirchner had commanded *UC.25* ever since it first entered service in June 1916, operating in the Baltic as part of the Kurland U-Flottille. In March 1917 the submarine was ordered to the Mediterranean, passing through the Strait of Gibraltar on 6 April and accounting for three small sailing craft (two French, one American) off the Spanish and Algerian coasts. The minelaying off Brindisi was the first operation from an Austrian base.[26]

Feldkirchner had left Cattaro the afternoon of the 14th and approached Brindisi during the night, having to pass under a mine barrage previously laid by the Germans and Austrians. At approximately 0410 he had laid his eighteen mines across the safe channel. He then moved off to the north-northeast and two hours later began his period of waiting in ambush. During the morning he spotted a few ships, notably the *Marsala*, but was unable to get into a favorable position to attack. He then moved slightly to the north across the route from Cattaro to Brindisi and after midday spotted numerous columns of smoke on the horizon. This was the *Dartmouth* group returning to Brindisi.[27]

The British and Italians were quite aware that the enemy might attempt to use submarines against them on the return to Brindisi. Captain Vivian of the *Liverpool*, the senior British naval officer at Brindisi, subsequently wrote: "From the reports received and the Telefunken heard, it was to be expected that enemy submarines would endeavor to attack the ships on their way back."[28] Acton's order for the cruisers and scouts to form line abreast was a logical reaction to the submarine danger, since it would, in theory, lessen the opportunities for a submarine commander to make a successful torpedo shot, although naturally placing the ships on the flanks at the greatest risk.

The measures were not enough. Ships in Acton's group began to report submarine sightings, some perhaps erroneous. At 1258 the *Bristol* raised the flag signal for a submarine alarm, although this may have been a false sighting. At 1320 the destroyer *Acerbi* on *Dartmouth*'s port bow sighted a suspicious wake or torpedo track to starboard. Both *Bristol* and *Racchia* spotted it from the opposite side, and the formation sheered to the left while the destroyers *Acerbi* and *Casque* carried out an attack on the submarine's presumed position. It had no effect. Approximately five minutes later there was another submarine sighting, and at 1335 a torpedo thought by Addison to have been fired from a range of about 600 yards struck the *Dartmouth* on the port side forward under the fore bridge and abreast of the conning tower. The explosion blew a large hole approximately thirty by ten feet. The armored deck was torn from the side and badly shattered, with great structural damage resulting. The British thought a second torpedo, which passed astern, had also been fired at the ship. This may not have been the case. The torpedo in question appears to have been fired by the destroyer *Casque* at the submarine and set to a depth of thirty feet.[29] Feldkirchner had managed to slip between the escorting destroyers, and, after checking his position, fired from a range of 500 meters. The submarine appears to have broken surface after firing the torpedo and given the escorts a fleeting glance at its position. The destroyers *Faulx* and *Indomito* followed what they perceived to be the submarine's wake and began to drop depth charges. The depth charges may not have damaged the submarine, but they served to keep UC.25 down and apparently prevented the submarine from making any further attacks. Feldkirchner counted the explosion of twelve depth charges and concluded there were too many escorts to renew the attack. He therefore began his return to Cattaro and arrived the next morning at 0830.[30]

Captain G. Todd of the *Bristol* assumed command of the remaining ships, the *Marsala* and *Racchia*, and proceeded back to Brindisi. He commenced zigzagging shortly after the attack, and at 1430 he ordered the three ships into line-ahead formation before entering the swept channel at 1500, gradually reducing speed. They were not free of danger yet and in fact were close enough to witness the destruction of the French destroyer *Boutefeu* by one of UC.25's mines near the entrance to the harbor at approximately 1520. Nevertheless, the three ships passed safely through the outer and inner booms and secured to their buoys at 1555.[31]

Captain Addison, after the torpedo struck the *Dartmouth*, ordered the watertight doors closed and the ship's boats cleared away. The other destroyers closed on the *Dartmouth*, whose engines had stopped. Addison ordered a rapid inspection of the damage and then attempted to go ahead, a procedure that seemed to make the cruiser's situation worse. He then attempted to proceed stern first but also found this impossible. The ship seemed to Addison to be "quite unmanageable," and the water appeared to be gaining. Consequently, he decided to get his crew safely away before it was too late and at about 1430 gave the order to abandon ship. Acton ordered some of the destroyers to close and lower their boats while the other destroyers formed a protective screen. The ship's company, however, appears to have left in their own boats and were taken aboard the French and Italian destroyers. When the number of men on board had fallen to seven or eight, Acton and his staff left the ship, followed by Addison. They were taken to the destroyer *Insidioso*, where Acton hoisted his flag.[32]

The *Dartmouth* appeared at first to be lost, but as time passed her condition did not seem to be getting any worse. This was probably because Engineer Commander Frank R. Goodwin and Gunner Richard F. Hall had flooded the after six-inch gun magazine before leaving the ship. They hoped this would bring the cruiser up forward and prevent her from going down by the bows. The maneuver succeeded better than Addison had hoped, probably because the compartment was well located in the center line. After about half an hour Addison was encouraged enough to return to the ship with the chief yeoman of signals, Tom Smith. Addison, followed immediately by the engineer commander, inspected various compartments forward and aft. Addison finally determined that the ship could be saved and asked the destroyers to send back men and boats. Because of the danger of further attack, he requested only the number of officers and men he though necessary to do the job, about 300 out of a normal complement of approximately 475. The men scrambled aboard, hoisted in the boats, and proceeded to raise steam while awaiting a tug from Brindisi. They were approximately thirty miles from the harbor. The arrival of tug would take four hours, and in the interim the destroyers formed a protective screen. That no further submarine attack took place was regarded as a "welcome surprise to us."[33]

Admiral Acton, once it became apparent that the *Dartmouth* might be saved, had signaled to Brindisi for tugs and additional torpedo craft. He had to relinquish one of his destroyer screens, for the *Faulx* was now running short of coal. The loss was balanced by the arrival of the *Commandant Lucas*. Back in Brindisi, the harbor authorities cleared the dry dock in anticipation of taking in the damaged ships and also prepared the harbor tugs to assist in maneuvering the ships when they arrived. Acton remained on the scene in the *Insidioso* until 1800 when he ordered the destroyer to head for Brindisi. He wanted to hasten the arrival of the tugs. He met the tug *Marittimo* en route at about 1900 and led her back to the *Dartmouth*, joining the crippled ship at about 1930.[34] The Italian authorities actually had to worry about getting three crippled ships in different groups safely back to harbor. In addition to the *Dartmouth*, there was the *Aquila* being towed by the *Schiaffino* and the *Mirabello* being towed by the *Commandant Rivière*.

The situation at Brindisi also grew more complicated during the morning, for the *Capo di stato maggiore*, Viceammiraglio Thaon di Revel, arrived and took charge of operations on shore. The exact extent of Revel's intervention is not clear and ashore he could have little influence on the unfolding of the action at sea. He was, however, a formidable presence and certainly must have gingered up the Italian officers at the base. The authorities at Brindisi, after the departure of the *Marsala* group that morning, had been following the unfolding of the action as best they could by means of wireless messages, either directly from Acton or from those they had been able to intercept between the ships. There were also more reinforcements ready to sail should Acton call for them. At 1115 Revel had signaled to Acton that the armored cruisers of the *Pisa* division, the *Pisa* and *San Marco*, had steam up, and he asked if Acton wanted their intervention. The two 10,000-ton armored cruisers, each armed with four ten-inch guns, would certainly have matched the Austrian reinforcements coming out from Cattaro, but Acton, after turning away from the Austrians and setting a course back to Brindisi, had indicated that their intervention was not necessary in a signal received at 1250.[35] In the judgment of Captain Vivian, the senior British naval officer at Brindisi, it was probably just as well that they did not sortie because by this time there were no destroyers left in Brindisi to escort them and there were obviously enemy submarines outside harbor. But, reflecting conflicting emotions, Vivian also thought their own cruisers "would have been in a better position if they had a heavy ship or two to support them in the event of their being crippled."[36] There were also potential reinforcements at Valona. The fast battleship *Napoli* with two twelve-inch guns and the scout *Riboty* had been reported to Acton as ready to sail as early as 1000. He apparently did not request their assistance or respond to the message. The Italians that day used only a fraction of the forces available to them, although the benefit of using larger and heavier ships always had to be weighed against the danger of submarines in these relatively narrow waters.

Even before the *Dartmouth* had been torpedoed, a section of two Italian FBAs had been sent out to check on the progress of the groups towing the *Aquila* and *Mirabello*. The Italians also sought to safeguard the approaches to Brindisi. The XI squadriglia of torpedo boats was ordered to proceed to meet the main units, while one section of the XIII squadriglia of *Mas* boats was gathered near the boom defenses, and another section with the remaining *Mas* boats patrolled the approaches. The news about *Dartmouth*'s torpedoing also caused the Italians to institute a nearly continuous patrol of aircraft over the stricken ship. The aerial cover conducted by successive sections of two aircraft each was maintained from approximately 1400 to sunset.

The Italians also deployed a small flotilla of various small craft to assist the returning groups. The high-seas torpedo boat *Calliope* was ordered to assist the *Commandant Rivière*, and Capitano di fregata Guida, the commander of the flotilla in the high-seas torpedo boat *Airone*, led the torpedo boats *Pegaso* and *Pallade*, together with the vedettes (armed fishing vessels) *Capodoglio* and *G.5*, in helping to protect the various groups. Another high-seas torpedo boat, the *Ardea*, guarded the swept channel outside Brindisi. Guida met the *Aquila* group first and detached the *Pegaso* and *Pallade* to assist them. He then proceeded with the *Airone* and *G.5* to the *Dartmouth* where he assumed command of the salvage operations.

The flurry of activity did not save the French destroyer *Boutefeu*, for the *UC.25* had done its work underwater and in the dark. The destroyer had originally been part of the *Mirabello* group and had sailed with them the day before, only to be forced to return because of faulty steering. The fault had been rectified and the ship was in the outer harbor and ready to sail by 1000. The destroyer was anchored close to the British cruiser *Liverpool*, whose captain, Vivian, was chafing at the inaction of his ship. A signal had been made to Acton at 0903 that the *Liverpool* was ready, but there had been no request from the admiral for the cruiser to sail. Vivian had intercepted a 1038 signal made by Acton calling on all ships to immediately rendezvous on the *Dartmouth*. Vivian interpreted this as meaning that the *Dartmouth* might possibly be in trouble and asked Revel's permission to go to sea immediately. Revel refused. Vivian had followed the course of events as best he could by means of intercepted wireless messages, and when the news came that the *Dartmouth* had

been torpedoed he signaled to Revel that the *Boutefeu* was available to render
assistance if required. Revel apparently acted quickly and ordered the *Boutefeu* to join the *Dartmouth* group, together with the Italian torpedo boats *Ardea*
and *Pallade*. His objective was to reinforce the escort around the crippled
ship. Vivian, aware that the *Liverpool* was not now likely to be required, sent
a second message to Revel requesting permission to go out in the *Boutefeu*
himself to see what assistance could be rendered to the *Dartmouth*. Before he
could receive an answer, the destroyer sailed at 1430. Her captain, Lieutenant
de vaisseau Chauvin, rapidly increased speed to more than twenty-two knots,
but at the point where the safe channel turned north, the *Boutefeu*, while passing two Italian minesweepers at work, veered slightly to starboard. Chauvin
then swung back to port to the same course as the two Italian torpedo boats
that were now approximately 2000 meters ahead. He intended to overhaul
them, but just as he started the turn to port the *Boutefeu* exploded one of
UC.25's mines against her port side near the engine room.[37] Captain Vivian
described the scene: "I was watching her at the time and the explosion, which
was very violent indeed, appeared to blow her stern completely off, she then
reared bows up almost vertically and sank; after which two more explosions occurred, possibly boilers, but more probably depth charges."[38] The *Boutefeu*
sank within a minute and a half. The Italian torpedo craft at the outer boom
as well as tugs from the harbor rushed to the scene and together they picked
up seventy-three survivors, seventeen of them wounded. Eleven of the ship's
company were lost. The loss, considering the force of the explosion and the
speed with which the ship sank, was in Vivian's opinion comparatively small.
The *Bristol* now came into sight and Vivian signaled her about the mine danger,
but since the cruiser could not remain outside, she entered harbor close to the
wreckage of the *Boutefeu*. Although Italian sweepers subsequently swept up several mines in the vicinity,[39] the *Bristol* was fortunate not to touch one of them
off. There were, in fact, a total of twenty-three mines swept up after the loss of
the *Boutefeu* according to Acton. Since the UC.25 only laid eighteen, some
must have been the results of earlier Austrian and German incursions.

There remained the task of getting the badly damaged *Dartmouth* back to
port safely. The ship was able to proceed at about 2030, but only stern first with
the assistance of a tug. The damage from the torpedo had made it impossible
to maneuver the ship when going ahead. The cruiser was able to steam under
her own power but had to be steered by the tug and even then maneuvered
only with difficulty. She was able to make seven knots. There was now a sizeable escort: three destroyers to starboard, two destroyers to port, the high-seas
torpedo boat *Airone* ahead, and the vedette G.5 and two coastal torpedo boats
astern. The small convoy reached safety without further incident, assisted no
doubt by the fine weather and the smooth sea. Acton left the group and proceeded back to Brindisi ahead of them in the *Insidioso*. He arrived at 2200 and,

in view of the *Boutefeu*'s fate, ordered the *Insidioso* to remain outside with her searchlights ready for use to guide the returning ships through the safe channel. Vivian, not content to remain in harbor, went out to meet the *Dartmouth* in a motorboat when she finally arrived at 0245. The ship was moored to buoys in the outer harbor for the remainder of the night and eventually, at 0600, shifted to a location in shallow water near the repair ship *Vulcano*.[40] The cruiser would be under repair for months, but she did eventually return to service and participated in the bombardment of Durazzo in October 1918.

The losses in the *Dartmouth* could have been far worse. In the final tally after returning to Brindisi, the executive officer, Commander Fane, and four men were found to be missing, their remains assumed to be in the flooded compartments below. This brought the cruiser's total loss to eight dead and seven wounded. The British had more difficulty accounting for the casualties among the drifters. An interim tally seemed to indicate one officer and five other ranks killed, three officers and ten other ranks wounded (three of the latter severely), four officers and thirty-one other ranks missing and believed to be prisoners, and four officers and thirty-six other ranks missing and believed dead. The number of deaths among the drifter crews fortunately turned out to be much less than feared; of the seventy-five initially listed as missing, seventy-two were prisoners of the Austrians.[41] There were no casualties in the *Bristol*. The French as mentioned lost eleven dead and seventeen wounded in the *Boutefeu*. The Italians had the largest losses, seven dead in the *Aquila*, eleven dead and twelve wounded in the *Borea*, and five dead and nine wounded in the convoy attacked by the *Csepel* and *Balaton*. In contrast, the Austrian casualties were all in the three cruisers; the two destroyers were unscathed. The total Austrian loss was sixteen dead and fifty-four wounded.[42]

The seventy-two prisoners that the Austrians picked up from the drifters were naturally regarded as a potential source of intelligence and were duly interrogated by Austrian officers. They found them to be mostly Scots and, while not stubborn, very reserved. Moreover, the Austrians thought their horizons were limited, and this was also true of the skippers, who were simple former fishermen. There was an exception, a former sailor in the Royal Navy, who answered questions in a precise military manner and with greater intelligence than the others. The Austrians also observed that the English among the prisoners were more talkative than the Scots. Despite the reserve and assumed limited horizons, the Austrians were able to gather a reasonably good picture of the way the drifters worked, their organization, the status of their crews as members of the Royal Naval Reserve Trawler Section, methods of patrol, and a great many other details. They noted with interest the statement of a skipper that the Otranto Straits could be blocked with fifty drifters, but that in general the crews were skeptical about their work and complained about the laxness of the French and Italian destroyer patrols that were supposed to provide protection but were never seen. The motor launch patrols were also seldom seen and then only during the day.[43] There was an amusing story that went around among the Austrians to the effect that one particularly taciturn prisoner, his pipe clamped firmly in his mouth, had finally been stimulated into talk when his interrogator had the bright idea of disparaging the Italians. This was enough to release a torrent of words generally in agreement.[44]

There was a marked contrast in the mood at Cattaro and Brindisi after the battle. The Austrians believed and acted as if they had won a great victory, when in fact they had struck a blow at a relatively unimportant target—the drifters—and had been lucky to escape unscathed. In the Adriatic up to that point, geography and a superior Allied force arrayed against the Austrians had rendered them unable to do much against surface warships. But on this day they the Austrians had conducted a major operation and had been successful, so their feeling was understandable. They had engaged the naval forces of three of their enemies and returned safely after inflicting heavier losses. The mood of jubilation mixed with thanksgiving for having gotten off so lightly was evident. It was enhanced when UC.25 returned the day after the battle with news of the submarine's success, enhanced by Feldkirchner's belief that he had sunk the Dartmouth. On the other hand, the Austrians and Germans remained ignorant of the Boutefeu's sinking for some time. Symbolic of the happy mood, perhaps, was a dinner given by Heyssler in the Helgoland for Liechtenstein and also attended by, among others, Novara's gunnery officer and acting commander while Horthy was still in the hospital, Feldkirchner, and several of Helgoland's officers plus the wife of the cruiser's first lieutenant.[45] The presence of wives such as Magda Horthy at Cattaro deserves comment, since it subsequently became a matter of controversy. As the Allied blockade tightened and shortages increased in Austria during 1917, it became common for many officers, both military and naval, to wrangle permission for their wives and families to visit Cattaro. Here, aside from the warmth of family reunions, the families might obtain naval rations, which were both cheaper and more plentiful than in the hinterlands of the Dual Monarchy. The system lent itself to abuse, and Admiral Hansa, commander of the cruiser flotilla, seems to have become a notable offender. The practice and its abuse were among the sailors' grievances behind the mutiny at Cattaro in February 1918. Heyssler disapproved of the practice and would not permit his family to come. Beyond the bad example, he also cited the case of the wife of a petty officer in the Novara, who together with her small child had watched the triumphant arrival of the three cruisers after the action, only to learn that her husband had been one of those killed. Heyssler was stern: "I was dreadfully sorry for her but wives really do not belong in the front line."[46]

The mood in Brindisi was different and the prevailing sentiment was one of frustration. The British, Italians, and French did not feel that they had been defeated, but there was a general impression that a long-awaited and long-desired opportunity had somehow slipped away. The British and Italians were also inclined to magnify the loss of the enemy. They could observe that one of the Austrian cruisers had sustained what they believed to be severe damage, and Admiral Acton, based on the reports of two different Italian aviators that a cruiser was sinking, believed the reports to be true.[47] Addison wrote a friend, "We knocked them about a good deal [and] I think one sank after." Vivian also judged the report that the third enemy cruiser had sunk as "possible enough," though unconfirmed, for the ship when last seen had been on fire and deep in the water as her consorts attempted to take her in tow. He also thought the submarine that had torpedoed the *Dartmouth* had been sunk by the depth charges of the escorting destroyers. There had been no apparent attempt to renew the attack although *Dartmouth* lay motionless for four hours awaiting the tug and Austrian press telegrams had not initially mentioned the torpedoing of a British cruiser. He was mistaken about this, as Admiral Kerr pointed out a few days later. The report that a British cruiser had been torpedoed did indeed appear shortly in the Austrian press. Nevertheless, Kerr still believed the submarine had been sunk.[48] These sentiments about the enemy cruiser and submarine turned out to be wishful thinking.

The action in which ships of three very different navies operated together revealed a number of problems in cooperation, which should not be surprising. Similar problems plague most alliances, and relations between the three, especially the French and Italians, could be touchy. Nevertheless, appearances had to be maintained. Acton was lavish in his praise, assuring Thaon di Revel that "everyone showed the greatest enthusiasm during the engagement" and that "everybody carried out their duties brilliantly, Commanding Officers, Officers and men both Allied and Italian." He particularly singled out the conduct of Addison, "who throughout the action showed the greatest coolness under trying circumstances" and the ship's company of the *Dartmouth* who carried out all orders "in the simplest and easiest way." The circumstances by which an Italian admiral commanded the action in a British warship were unusual, and Acton concluded his report with a touch of enthusiastic hyperbole: "I must also add that I was so at home in the *Dartmouth*, that to direct operations from her was as easy for me, as if I had been in an Italian ship. So that I can truthfully say that on no occasion have the Allied Flags worked together with perfect accordance of thought and feelings of duty as on this 15th May 1917."[49]

The Italian plaudits continued in a telegram from Admiral Corsi, the minister of marine, to the first sea lord in London. Corsi conveyed his "warmest admiration for the way in which *Dartmouth*, fighting against superior forces, nobly upheld the finest traditions of the British Navy." Revel sent his "hearty congratulations for brilliant action fought by *Dartmouth* which, although torpedoed, was able to return safely to port." Admiral Jellicoe acknowledged these telegrams in suitably appreciative tones along with orders they be communicated to the captain, officers, and ship's company of the *Dartmouth* "together with an expression of Their Lordship's high appreciation of the manner in which the ship was fought."[50] It was all a bit embarrassing to Addison, who told a friend, "I quite blush to read the telegrams, etc. they have sent home."[51]

The real sentiments of the British and French beyond the flowery exchanges deemed necessary to maintain the cohesion of the alliance were rather different. The French, who had lost a destroyer, were predictably critical. Capitaine de frégate Le Sort, commanding the 6ème escadrille of destroyers at Brindisi, had been in the *Commandant Rivière* in the patrol led by the *Mirabello*. The British liaison officer with the French fleet reported after a conversation with Le Sort that he, together with other French officers, were convinced the Italians had advance intelligence of the Austrian raid and this was why the *Mirabello* patrol had been out, but the patrol as executed had been "useless as is proved by the results." The French were also very critical of the administration and organization at Brindisi and particularly cited the "dribbling-way" warships had been sent out on the 15th of May. At the heart of the matter was probably that the French objected "intensely to being under the Italians" at Brindisi, because in their opinion "the Italian does not want to fight and thus they are deprived of a fight when a fight was possible."[52] The French specifically criticized certain maneuvers of the *Mirabello*, which they thought were to avoid action. Le Sort's remarks also revealed difficulties in signaling between French and Italian ships and, perhaps inadvertently, French failures as well. The *Mirabello* group had been at the far eastern end of their patrol close to Cattaro when at 0400 the *Mirabello* had turned southward and increased speed to twenty-five knots instead of steering toward Brindisi as the French expected. Le Sort subsequently discovered that a wireless message had been sent to him but was never received because his wireless operator was a new man apparently on watch for the first time. That an inexperienced man would have been placed in such an important position on a patrol that went close to the enemy coast does not speak highly of the destroyer's procedures. The signaling did not improve, as later *Mirabello* subsequently made a signal to the *Commandant Rivière* by semaphore "in the Italian method." Le Sort could not understand it and made repeated demands for its repetition. The only thing he could understand was that something had happened and that the *Dartmouth* and *Bristol* had left Brindisi. Consequently, when he sighted three four-funneled cruisers in the distance, he assumed they were British light cruisers and had a rude shock when they turned out to be Austrian and opened fire at a range of about 9,000 yards. The Austrian fire in this case had been indifferent, and the *Mirabello* maneuvered to keep out of range, then attempted to keep the enemy in sight, which proved to be difficult. The French destroyers followed the *Mirabello*.[53]

The British also had trouble with the Italian signals. They found that hardly any ships used the squared chart sufficiently and many signals came through without any position given. Again, the *Mirabello* was one of the culprits. *Liverpool*'s signals officer stated that *Mirabello* gave both her own position and the enemy's position wrongly on several occasions. Trying to follow the action by wireless intercepts at Brindisi, Captain Vivian complained, "*Mirabello* either had her squared chart wrongly numbered or else her signals very badly coded, for she completely deceived everybody, including the *Etna*, as to her position."[54] The system of squared charts divided the Adriatic into squares of equal size and was designed to facilitate rapid signaling by which a ship could indicate its position by citing the square and corner of the square in which it was located. It was shorter and hence faster than giving a position by latitude and longitude. The Austrians used a similar system. Unfortunately, some ships like the *Marsala* insisted on giving their positions by latitude and longitude, thereby greatly lengthening their signals. Then there were ships like the *Aquila*, who had reported herself totally disabled and needing to be towed but failed to give any position either by square or latitude and longitude. This might have posed no problem to Admiral Acton in the *Dartmouth*, who knew her position and was for a time in visual contact, but it would have created great difficulties for the authorities in Brindisi who did not. Had, for example, the *Liverpool* been sent out to bring her in, Captain Vivian would not have known where to find her.[55]

The difficulties were compounded by the fact that the Italian ships used Italian call signs among themselves and the British had not been provided with this code. Vivian had repeatedly attempted to obtain this information and the Italian authorities had habitually replied that he was trying to learn their secret call signs. Vivian protested that he had no interest in their secret call signs and that if they did not want the British to read a signal they should use their own cipher, which the British did not have. On the other hand, Vivian argued, if they used a code supplied to the British they ought to use call signs provided to the British. There was one occasion when the Italians did give the British their call signs, but the signs were promptly changed. This resulted in a situation where, to give an example used by the British, they intercepted a signal, "UX to FU: Ships in sight Otranto Straits," without any idea of who UX and FU were. Some of these problems might have been mitigated by the presence of Admiral Acton and his staff in the *Dartmouth*, but for ships not in visual contact with the admiral, there were great difficulties in following the action and anticipating the measures they themselves might be called on to take. There was also what *Liverpool*'s signals officer termed "considerable confusion" resulting from the difficulties of spelling in three languages added to the errors in coding. Nevertheless, he did conclude that, considering the large number of signals, the general wireless signaling work "was good."[56]

These questions suggest that the difficulties of ships of more than one nationality working together may have been underestimated, but they were
probably not insurmountable and could be mitigated in the future provided
there was goodwill and a cooperative spirit on both sides. There was a final,
perhaps minor, source of confusion that continues to plague historians today.
This was the question of time. The *Dartmouth* and *Liverpool* followed the orders of the Malta wireless office and used central European time [GMT +1] as
the "time of origin" for messages. Italian ships, and for reasons not clear, the
Bristol used Italian local time, and this produced variations that the commanders had to reconcile when preparing their final reports.[57]

The cooperation between Allied aircraft and ships does not appear to have
been as extensive or effective as it was on the Austrian side. Italian FBAs had
provided invaluable cover after the *Dartmouth* had been torpedoed and was
motionless waiting for a tow. Nevertheless, Captain Todd of the *Bristol*, in a
supplementary report on the engagement, remarked, "It is suggested that this
action is a case where the co-operation of our own aircraft would have been of
the greatest value, both for warning us of the near approach of the enemy ships
and for spotting at long ranges."[58] This situation was likely to improve for the
British. Before the end of the following month a Royal Naval Air Service station at Otranto became operational.

The resistance of the drifters caught the imagination of many in the Royal
Navy. The spectacle of the plucky little wooden ships armed with "popguns"
resisting a modern cruiser with 10cm guns had all the aspects of the underdog
fighting back against heavy odds that naturally appealed to the British. In his
interim report on the action, Rear Admiral Kerr quickly concluded, "From
the accounts which have come to hand it appears that most of the Drifters behaved with exceptional gallantry and actually fought the cruisers with their
one small gun and I shall have the pleasure of forwarding some names for special commendation."[59] In a private letter to Jellicoe, Kerr brought up the
name of Skipper Joseph Watt of the *Gowan Lea* and expressed the hope that
Watt and the wounded man of the trawler's gun crew would be awarded the
Victoria Cross.[60] Kerr's flag commander, Murray Pipon, was equally enthusiastic. Forwarding a copy of the detailed report that accompanied Kerr's recommendations for awards to a friend, he exclaimed, "It is good reading, isn't
it." Pipon found it "impossible" to express his "admiration for these very gal-
lant fellows, nearly all uneducated fishermen and officered by uneducated
men, fighting what must be to them a rather foreign war out here, where they
are surprised at dawn in their little wooden ships with one 6 pounder gun each
and six knots of speed, by fast well-gunned enemy vessels."[61]

Kerr duly nominated Skipper Joseph Watt and his deck hand Frederick H.
Lamb for the Victoria Cross. Watt was cited for replying to the Austrian demand to surrender by calling for three cheers from his crew, attacking the en-

emy, and then saving his ship when all means of offense had been destroyed. Lamb was cited for continuing to fire his gun throughout the action under hot fire after his leg had been shattered by the explosion of a box of ammunition. Kerr sent a long list of other recommendations that aroused the displeasure of the Admiralty because of its generosity. When the recommendations for the *Dartmouth* and *Bristol* were added the total came to five Victoria Crosses, four Distinguished Service Orders, nine Distinguished Service Crosses, forty-five Conspicuous Gallantry Medals, and fifty-nine Distinguished Service Medals. J. W. S. Anderson of "M" Branch, the Department of the Secretary of the Admiralty (one of the civil departments), pointed out that only fifty-four Conspicuous Gallantry Medals had been given out in the whole course of the war and that the medal was never intended to be awarded on the "wholesale scale" Kerr had put forward. He recommended that Kerr be held to a "scale" of honors and mentions, that is, a total number would be approved, and Kerr would be instructed to select names in order of merit within this scale. Kerr's recommendations went "a good deal beyond" any scale the Admiralty had hitherto approved.[62] Commodore Allan Everett, the naval secretary to the first lord, agreed and did not think the two recommendations for the Victoria Cross came up to the standard required for that award. He also recommended a scale for the drifters of six decorations and six mentions in dispatches for officers and fourteen decorations and fourteen mentions for the men. This would have made a total of forty awards or roughly 6 percent of the numbers engaged, a proportion he considered "liberal for a rout." The second sea lord, who was responsible for matters dealing with personnel, agreed with the scale but thought that when the conditions were considered—a cruiser attacking a drifter—both Skipper Watt and Deck Hand Lamb deserved the Victoria Cross.[63] In the end, Admiral Jellicoe, the first sea lord, suggested the Victoria Cross for Watt and the Conspicuous Gallantry Medal for Lamb and, after First Lord Sir Edward Carson and the King approved, both men received their awards.[64] The Otranto Straits action on the British side had its heroes.

The awards to the *Dartmouth* and *Bristol* generated less controversy. Addison was made a Companion of the Order of Saint Michael and Saint George, and Captain Todd of the *Bristol* and Engineer Commander F. R. Goodwin of the *Dartmouth* were made Companions of the Distinguished Service Order. In addition, the Admiralty laid down a scale of eight medals and eight mentions for petty officers and men, the names to be submitted in order of merit.[65] The entire question of awards seems to be a subject that aroused much resentment. This was particularly true of the Admiralty practice of "awards by scale," that is, setting a maximum number in proportion to those involved and then ordering names to be submitted in order of merit. The officers involved in campaigns such as the Dardanelles or the Battle of Jutland tended to regard this as grossly unfair, not taking account of local conditions and leading to many deserving men going unrecognized and at times less deserving individuals being rewarded.[66]

Even the award of the Victoria Cross to Skipper Watt was not free from this suspicion of at least some error. Watt's citation read:

> When hailed by an Austrian cruiser at about 100 yards range and ordered to stop and abandon his drifter the *Gowan Lea*, Skipper Watt ordered full speed ahead and called upon his crew to give three cheers and fight to the finish. The cruiser was then engaged, but after one round had been fired, a shot from the enemy disabled the breech of the drifter's gun. The gun's crew, however, stuck to the gun, endeavouring to make it work, being under heavy fire all the time. After the cruiser had passed on, Skipper Watt took the *Gowan Lea* alongside the badly damaged drifter *Floandi* and assisted to remove the dead and wounded.[67]

Long after the war, the skipper of the drifter *British Crown* and chief of "S" division of drifters that night, Andrew Lyall, wrote to the popular naval author David Masters about the latter's account in one of his books of the *Gowan Lea* rendering assistance to the *Floandi*. Masters had based his account on the *London Gazette*. Lyall thought Masters should "in the interests of accuracy" be "fully informed of all the circumstances." The *British Crown* had been in "S" division, the easternmost division of drifters, and Lyall, without wishing to detract from the heroism of Watt in defying the Austrians, pointed out that the *Gowan Lea* in the westernmost division had been a long way from the *Floandi* and it had been the *British Crown* that had gone to the assistance of the crippled *Floandi*. Lyall claimed that the first time Watt saw the *Floandi* was some fifteen hours later when the *British Crown* towed the crippled drifter into Brindisi.[68]

The statement about the *Floandi* formed only the last sentence and a minor portion of Watt's citation. The major part concerned his conduct in the face of the Austrian cruisers and there was no dispute about this. The error in reporting may have originated in Appendix V, "Recommendations sent to Admiralty respecting Action of certain Drifters," to the report of Commodore Heneage, the commodore of patrols, to Admiral Kerr.[69] The *British Crown* (but not Lyall) was mentioned here as being fired on, with the crew remaining at their posts and subsequently assisting in picking up survivors. Lyall's name does not appear among those mentioned in the *London Gazette*. One might indeed question how a drifter in the westernmost division of drifters wound up coming alongside a drifter in the easternmost division, about thirty miles away and in a direction away from its base. No one thought to question this at the time. All the same, a confused action at night with the drifters scattering after the attack does not lend itself to neat explanations. There was no question, however, about Watt's courage, and Watt by all accounts was a most shy and reticent individual who did not speak of his wartime exploits.[70] The linking of the *Gowan Lea* and the *Floandi* has become enshrined in even recent accounts.[71]

Another individual who was awarded the Conspicuous Gallantry Medal for services on 15 May 1917 did not in fact perform those services on that occasion and was apparently not even present. Engineman Walter Watt, RNR, was cited for jumping overboard and attempting to escape while being taken to an Austrian cruiser. He was recaptured but, when the boat was alongside the cruiser, he jumped overboard a second time and escaped. He was picked up by a drifter an hour and a half later. It is a stirring story and it did happen, but it refers to the sinking of the drifter *Astrum Spei* in May 1916. Watt, then a trimmer, was rewarded by being advanced to the rank of engineman. The Admiralty subsequently discovered in November 1917 that although Walter Watt's name had not been included in Kerr's original submission of recommendations, it was added to the revised (and reduced) list of recommendations the admiral submitted in accordance with the Admiralty "scale." Kerr, now back in London, explained that he considered the first award inadequate and had informed Watt he would try to obtain a medal for him, and he justified this by claiming Watt's act set an example to the men in the drifters and led to an entirely new spirit among them. Kerr also claimed that his own flag captain had raised the matter at the Admiralty with certain sea lords and that Kerr had referred to Watt in a semi-official letter to Jellicoe.[72] Commodore Everett, the naval secretary, was particularly annoyed, as he considered himself "more or less responsible" to the first lord that recommendations submitted to him were in order. He felt "as if some deception had been practiced" and that there was no justification in this case for a name "to have been officially smuggled in a list which obviously was only intended to refer to a particular occasion."[73] Everett was so incensed at what seemed to him the "sharp practice" that he recommended and Jellicoe initially approved an Admiralty letter of reproof to Kerr, which was duly drafted but later, and under circumstances not clear in the file, marked "cancelled." Kerr had escaped official rebuke but obviously had won no friends at the Admiralty. Engineman Watt kept his medal, which was after all well earned and probably never knew anything of the minor storm surrounding the circumstances of its award. The incident, while small in itself, is an example of the pitfalls that accompanied the granting of honors, medals, and mentions.

There was also a potentially darker side to the subject of the drifters at the Strait of Otranto and certainly not one that the Admiralty would have been happy to see made public. In his covering letter with the recommendations for awards, Admiral Kerr may have been lavish in his recommendations and praise for those drifters that fought, but there were others that had slipped their nets and scattered when the Austrians attacked. These names were naturally not included in Kerr's list. But what of the drifters that had surrendered to the Austrians? Kerr used their action to justify his recommendations for awards:

> Other drifters' crews undoubtedly abandoned their ships when called upon to do so by the Austrians, and some were taken prisoners. It is considered that this conduct, though disgraceful, should not be dealt with officially, as to give honours to the men who fought, will be a great incentive to future gallantry and will have more effect in making all do their duty, than Court-Martialling those who surrendered or escaped, for these men are not brought up to discipline or warfare.[74]

Sir Edward Carson, the first lord, was not, however, willing to leave it at that and asked to be advised as to whether some action should be taken with regard to the drifter crews who had abandoned their ships. Carson thought it "very important to show that we expect the traditions of the Navy as to fighting to the last to be observed."[75] Admiral Burney, the second sea lord, was less harsh: "If these men had been active service ratings I should certainly have proposed some action, but as they are only drifters' crews who have not been under any kind of disciplinary training (as all men in the army have) and the obvious inutility of a drifter pitting itself against a cruiser, I think that the matter is better left alone." Burney did suggest that a letter be sent to Kerr "expressing their Lordship's regret" that while some of the drifters displayed great gallantry, there were other drifters that "were too readily abandoned and surrendered to the enemy thus failing to uphold the traditions of the Navy by holding out and fighting to the last." Jellicoe agreed and the letter was duly sent with Kerr instructed to inform the officers and men concerned.[76] Since a sizeable number of those concerned may have been prisoners of the Austrians, it is not clear how this would have been applied. The potentially disagreeable episode passed, and if contemporaries thought of the massacre of the drifters, they thought of Skipper Watt and the *Gowan Lea* and not of the drifters that had been readily abandoned. The episode raises the delicate question of how much resistance could be expected when the odds were suicidal, especially from men who were not in the regular navy, and in this case Admirals Kerr, Burney, and Jellicoe showed they were more flexible and conscious of the realities of warfare than the civilian lawyer Carson.

The immediate aftermath of the Otranto Straits action would be a change in the way the drifters were employed. Despite the flowery words of Admiral Acton, the event not surprisingly placed an additional strain on British and Italian relations. French and Italian relations did not change; they remained as troublesome as ever. Ultimately, additional British and Australian forces would be deployed to the southern Adriatic. The effects of this would be to make it increasingly difficult for the Austrians to repeat their success of 15 May. However, the actual effects of the Otranto battle on the submarine war itself were debatable. These subjects will be examined in the following chapter.

CHAPTER SEVEN

THE RESULTS OF
THE BATTLE

T HE MOST IMMEDIATE RESULT of the battle of 15 May was Admiral Kerr's decision to withdraw the drifters at night. For the present, they would patrol only during daylight hours, a restriction which would only change when British reinforcements could be spared. In practical terms this meant that the drifters would now lay their nets between 5 and 10 A.M. and then commence taking them up again at 3 P.M. in order to put in to Otranto, Port Palermo, or Fano Island for the night. The drifters were also moved southward to a less vulnerable line along the parallel 39° 40′. These measures obviously reduced their effectiveness, but the Italians could not provide any protection until July and then only at irregular intervals. Moreover, even then the night patrols remained south of the parallel of Cape Santa Maria di Leuca, which may have rendered them less exposed to Austrian raids but also less effective.[1] In Kerr's opinion, "It is quite certain that until some British destroyers are attached to the barrage for purposes of defense and some "E" type submarines for purposes of offence, that the barrage can be raided by the Austrians in the same manner as heretofore."[2] He was also disillusioned with his allies and did not regard their temperament as suited for patrol work, with even their fast cruisers as a rule taking "some time" to get to sea when the alarm was raised. As it was the Italians who had the fast cruisers at Brindisi rather than the French, he obviously had them in mind. Kerr's solution was simple. He wrote the Admiralty: "A proper British force under a British Admiral would put an end to these raids."[3]

Kerr's action in withdrawing the drifter patrols at night had the full support

of the Admiralty. Captain George Hope, the second director of operations, believed that the Italians had a sufficient force of light cruisers, destroyers, and
submarines at Brindisi to institute proper patrol if they wanted to, and Admiral
Henry F. Oliver, the chief of naval staff, thought that "experience does not
warrant us trusting in Italian assurances alone." He wanted Kerr to receive
"definite orders to withdraw the drifters at night when he is not satisfied that
adequate steps are taken to protect the drifters." The first sea lord agreed. Admiral Jellicoe directed that the Italian Ministry of Marine be informed by
means of their naval attaché in London that the order canceling the drifter patrol at night would not be withdrawn until the British had information regarding the strength of a regular patrol of destroyers to protect the drifters and
when such a patrol would be instituted.[4]

The British were therefore insistent on proper protection being given to the
drifters, but there was no question in their minds about the effectiveness of the
drifter patrol itself. If anything, the Austrian raid worked to strengthen this belief. Kerr pointed out that the Austrians never raided the line until after they
had lost a submarine, and since they had taken a bigger risk this time and used
a larger force in the raid, he thought it probable that the submarines reported
in the nets during May really had been destroyed, although he admitted "the
evidence was not convincing."[5] This was all part of the wishful thinking about
the Otranto barrage that persisted to the end of the war. In reality neither the
Germans nor the Austrians had lost a submarine in the Otranto barrage during
May. The exaggerated belief in the barrage had echoes at the Admiralty. Captain Hope recognized that when the drifters were withdrawn at night the net
line was "of little use" but that the drifter line was "of use if properly patrolled."[6]

There was also a certain amount of wishful thinking about the results of the
encounter. Captain Addison of the *Dartmouth* wrote to a friend: "We knocked
them about a good deal & I think one sank after."[7] Captain Vivian of the *Liverpool*, although not present himself, gathered from reports that the third Austrian ship had been badly hit and on fire when last seen deep in the water. It was
"said to have finally sunk" and though there was no confirmation of this, it was
"possible enough." Vivian, as indicated previously, believed at first that the
submarine that had torpedoed the *Dartmouth* had been sunk by the depth
charges of the escorting destroyers because there had been no resumption of
the attack while the cruiser remained stopped for four hours and there had
been no immediate claim by Austrian sources that a British cruiser had been
torpedoed, which probably would have been the case had the submarine survived.[8] Vivian was incorrect in this assumption. By the 21st of May Admiral
Kerr had noted the Austrian radio report claiming a British cruiser had been
torpedoed, although Kerr still thought the submarine had been sunk. Kerr was
strengthened in his belief by an Italian seaplane report that an Austrian cruiser
had sunk while being towed into Cattaro.[9] It is not clear when the Allies real-

ized the discouraging fact that the enemy had suffered no serious material loss in the action. By the time they did, they probably had already taken steps to rectify the situation in the straits.

The unsatisfactory ending of the battle provoked a certain amount of self-analysis. Kerr gave four reasons why the action was not more decisive. The first and probably the most important was the want of speed of the British ships compared with the Austrians. To this he added that the *Bristol* was armed with only four-inch guns compared to the six-inch guns of the *Dartmouth*. The third and fourth reasons concerned the conduct of Admiral Acton, notably that he had initially gone too far to the northeast and then discontinued the action "a little too soon." The British could do little about Acton's conduct, but Kerr did repeat earlier recommendations that the four-inch guns of the *Bristol* be replaced with six-inch guns and that cruisers with sufficient speed to catch the Austrian light cruisers be substituted for those currently at Brindisi.[10]

There was understandable frustration on the British side over the Austrian advantage in speed. The *Bristol*, due for docking, had been hampered by a dirty bottom, but although *Dartmouth* had "made more revolutions than she has ever done before" and according to her captain "certainly developed a surprising speed," it was clearly not enough to overhaul the Austrians, who "went like hell as before."[11] The original report of *Dartmouth*'s action estimated the Austrian speed as twenty-nine knots, an exaggeration probably caused by overestimating *Dartmouth*'s speed. However, the quibbling over exact speeds did not matter to Vivian, who wrote, "But whether the Austrian Light Cruisers really did or did not reach 29 knots is not material, but what is very material is the fact that they undoubtedly out steam our ships here by 1½ to 2 knots an hour."[12] As speed was so critical in the narrow waters of the Adriatic, Vivian also recommended that if possible the Admiralty avoid drafting to the Adriatic large numbers of untrained or partially trained engine room ratings, especially in big batches. Under local conditions there was little opportunity to give them practice in hard steaming, and until the men could be fully trained, a ship was likely to be handicapped in action. In a similar vein, Vivian recommended that experienced senior engineering officers should be relieved only after an interval of six months. Furthermore, in the southern Adriatic and especially during the summer months, marine growth was "extraordinarily rapid." Consequently, ships ought to be docked as far as possible at intervals of four months.[13]

There was also an erroneous belief among at least some of the British officers that the Austrian cruisers had a heavier armament than they were reported to carry, possibly mounting six-inch guns fore and aft in place of their original lighter armament.[14] This would explain Admiral Kerr's request to replace *Bristol*'s four-inch with six-inch guns. Vivian, on reflection, did not think the Austrians had larger guns than originally reported, although he admitted they outranged British four-inch guns in that class of ship and had repeatedly straddled *Dartmouth* at ranges of 12,000 yards whereas British four-inch guns were only sighted up to 11,600 yards. Vivian attributed this to a possible high muzzle velocity but more probably to the Austrian gun mountings. He therefore asked if the Admiralty could consider altering the mountings of the four-inch guns in his light cruisers so that they could be sighted up to 12,500 yards and open fire at practically the same range as the present British six-inch guns. His gunnery officer had also recommended, if available, replacing the present six-inch guns with a more modern model of gun and mounting (Mark XII six-inch on P.VII[x] mountings). This would increase their guns' offensive power, which at long range was not "as good as it might be." The real answer to the Austrian light cruisers, however, would be the newer "C"-class British light cruisers, which were fast, reached their speed quickly, and were "sufficiently gunned to take care of themselves and make things unpleasant for the enemy."[15] These were the *Calliope*-class cruisers that the Italians had requested without success just before the raid. (See above, pp. 49–50.)

The "C"-class light cruisers, highly prized in the Grand Fleet for operations in the North Sea, were, as Vivian correctly suspected, not likely to be forthcoming. Destroyers, worth their weight in gold as the campaign against the submarine developed, were also hard to obtain. The Admiralty well before the Austrian raid had looked to other sources for this type of warship. In the north, as is well known, the first significant American naval contributions after the United States entered the war were destroyers that operated out of Queenstown. In mid-April 1917 eight Japanese destroyers arrived at Malta to work with the British, especially in escorting troopships. The Admiralty also turned to the Commonwealth of Australia and on 6 May requested the services in European waters of the destroyers *Parramatta*, *Warrego*, and *Yarra*. The Australian government promptly agreed and, recognizing that any potential danger in Australian waters was likely to come from raiders rather than submarines, they offered the services of an additional three destroyers, the *Swan*, *Torrens*, and *Huon*, which were currently at Singapore, on the understanding that a British cruiser might be sent to replace them. A cruiser was obviously of greater value than a destroyer in protecting trade against raiders along the lengthy routes in the Indian and Pacific Oceans. The Admiralty was only too happy to accept and on 4 June informed the British commanders in the Mediterranean of the eventual arrival of the six Australian destroyers. They were "intended primarily to be utilized for the patrol of the Otranto Barrage." This was welcome news to Kerr and Heneage, but the requirements of the submarine war caused the Australian destroyers to be diverted to other escort duties, and they did not actually assume patrols on the barrage until October. In practice, this meant that after the Australians' arrival the British were able to usually keep two or three on patrol to protect the drifters.[16]

The British air operations in the southern Adriatic also improved. At the time of the battle in the Otranto Straits, the Royal Naval Air Service was in the process of forming a base at Otranto. By the end of April the majority of the stores and personnel had arrived for what would become No. 6 Wing. The strength of the wing, composed of two squadrons and a flight, was set at six two-seat Short 184 seaplanes and six Sopwith "Baby" single-seat seaplanes for work over the barrage, and twelve Short 310 seaplanes (when available) capable of carrying a torpedo for attacks on the Austrian fleet or bombing naval targets. The wing also had Sopwith 1½ Strutters, fast land planes that were used mainly when a quick response to a U-boat sighting was necessary. The headquarters were located at Otranto and there were two wireless stations, a direction-finding station, and a lookout post manned by the RNAS at Cape Palascia. All of this had come too late for the 15 May battle. The first patrols by No. 6 Wing did not begin until June 1917.[17]

While Admiral Acton might have heaped praise on his British allies after the encounter, the events of 15 May definitely strained Anglo-Italian relations. The first sea lord was blunt in a minute he added to Kerr's report on the attack on the drifters. Jellicoe ordered that the Italian Ministry of Marine be asked whether the British might expect a regular patrol of destroyers in the future to protect the drifters at night. In addition, the British would require information as to the strength of the patrol before the order to withdraw them at night would be canceled.[18] The statement, communicated to the Italian naval attaché in London on the 30th, caused considerable irritation in Rome. Admiral Thaon di Revel, the *Capo di stato maggiore*, was a staunch champion of Italian rights as he interpreted them and believed his allies were not appreciative of Italian efforts or the special conditions of Adriatic warfare. Revel promptly replied by cable on 1 June that it was impossible to establish a destroyer patrol to protect the drifter line owing to a lack of destroyers. The Italians followed up with a much longer memorandum transmitted through the Italian ambassador in London on 26 June. It was not likely to please or influence the Admiralty. The Italians pointed out that at the beginning of 1917 they had voluntarily consented at an Allied naval conference in London to the withdrawal of the four pre-dreadnought "*Queen*"-class battleships at Taranto although the support of these vessels had been promised when Italy consented to enter the war in 1915. The Italians, in agreeing to their withdrawal, had requested that they be replaced by "an adequate number of light cruisers and torpedo craft" and the British had replied they had none available but would reinforce the Adriatic by "a convenient number of light cruisers and destroyers when available." This had not yet occurred, according to the Italians, and the British had also rejected Italian requests for more modern cruisers of the "C" class. Nevertheless, since the London conference, the Italians claimed that the Royal Navy had been reinforced by no fewer than twenty-six Allied destroyers, that is, eighteen Americans in the north and eight Japanese in the Mediterranean. The Italians attributed the escape of the Austrians on 15 May to the lack of speed of the *Dartmouth* and *Bristol* and claimed that if the British sent a few cruisers of the "C" class or *Arethusa* class, the result of another Austrian raid would be quite different. Revel argued that with the drifters returning to port at night the efficiency of the barrage was greatly diminished. He recognized that the British intended to attach the cruiser *Weymouth* to Brindisi, thereby increasing the number of their cruisers there from three to four, but he argued that the ship was the same class as the *Dartmouth* and therefore too slow.[19] Revel asked the British to reconsider their decision and send two or three cruisers of the latest class as well as at least eight destroyers. He also requested that should any further reinforcements be received from the United States or Japan, they be directed to the southern Adriatic.[20]

The Italian requests did not generate much sympathy at the Admiralty. First and foremost in British opinion, the Italians in their memorandum had taken no account of the French fleet at Corfu. The combined French and Italian battleship strength was overwhelmingly superior to the battleship strength of the Austrians, and this had been the reason the four British pre-dreadnoughts had been withdrawn from Taranto. As for the American and Japanese destroyers, the Americans were employed in the Atlantic defending British, Allied, and American trade, and the Japanese were fully employed escorting troopships in the Mediterranean. The increase in submarine activity meant that even more destroyers were required. The British did not believe the events of 15 May demonstrated that there were insufficient numbers of Italian destroyers to protect the drifter line, provided the destroyers were employed for this purpose. The British claimed that even without considering French destroyers, the Italians possessed "an immense superiority" in destroyers over the Austrians. The British pointed out that the Italians had a large number of destroyers in the northern Adriatic and suggested that the Otranto barrage was important enough to strengthen that area even at the expense of the northern Adriatic. To the Italian suggestion that Italian destroyers might have been shifted from the Otranto barrage to protect trade, the British replied that the very same reason prevented them from sending more destroyers to the Mediterranean and it could "hardly be expected that British trade should be specially chosen to be denuded of protection in order to provide the force required at Otranto."[21]

The British then proceeded to rebut the Italian claim for additional British cruisers. The Admiralty reiterated that under present conditions light cruisers of the *Arethusa* or "C" class could not be sent to the Adriatic and hinted that if the fast light cruisers available to the Italians were properly utilized, they were not necessary. That is, the Italians had the *Marsala, Nino Bixio,* and *Quarto,* and these ships were apparently at least as fast as the four Austrian light cruisers. In addition, the Italians had seven of the *Mirabello* and *Aquila* classes that had no counterparts in the Austrian navy. When added to the four British light cruisers assigned to Brindisi, the Allied superiority was "infinitely greater, in fact, than that possessed by the light cruisers of the Grand Fleet over those of the High Sea Fleet, and this is the reason why it is not possible to weaken the Grand Fleet in order to strengthen the Italian Fleet." The Admiralty added a pointed remark, observing that only one of the three Italian light cruisers was in action on 15 May. If the Italians placed such great importance on this type, "the reasons which permitted of the absence of two out of the three Italian vessels must have been very strong."[22] The best the British could offer was to order the weight carried by the British light cruisers at Brindisi to be reduced as much as possible in order to increase their speed, and to promise that, when ready, four "S"-type patrol boats would be sent from Malta.

The British note irritated Thaon di Revel when it eventually reached the *Capo di stato maggiore*, and he scribbled on his copy that he thought Jellicoe was trying to pull their leg and "use their wood to make a fire."[23] The allocation of destroyers would be the subject of a long-running and acrimonious dispute among the Allies, but the Admiralty, after analyzing reports from the Adriatic, was convinced the Italians were not making the best use of what forces they had. The Italians managed to provide a patrol of three destroyers on the drifter line the night of 5 July, but at that time there had been, according to the Admiralty's calculations, twenty-one Allied destroyers (nine of them French) ready at Brindisi in addition to the three *Mirabellos* and three larger destroyers of the *Pepe* class. Employment on escort duty accounted for seven of these destroyers (five of them French), leaving available for patrol of the barrage no less than fourteen destroyers, three *Mirabellos*, and three large *Pepe*-class destroyers. The Italians apparently could only provide three of these twenty for the barrage patrol on three nights out of six, with two *Mirabellos* standing by at Valona. This translated into nine nights spent at sea out of 120, compared to the British destroyers in the Mediterranean who "had no difficulty" in keeping six out of ten constantly on patrol, thereby spending seventy-two nights at sea out of 120. Captain Charles Coode, the second director of the operations division at the Admiralty, emphatically declared: "In the face of these figures it appears farcical for the Italians to say that they cannot maintain a sufficient and regular destroyer patrol on the barrage without British assistance. Even if the numbers employed on escort duty have to be considerably increased, there should be no difficulty in maintaining a constant barrage patrol of at least six."[24]

Jellicoe was due to attend an Allied naval conference in Paris the last week in July where Thaon di Revel was scheduled to be present. Consequently, he asked the naval staff to prepare a memorandum that would include these facts and deal with the whole subject of the employment of Italian light craft. The conference, lasting from 24 to 26 July, according to Italian accounts included "harsh" discussions between Thaon di Revel and the other Allies, but ended with an agreement that the British admiral in command of the Allied patrols in the Mediterranean would include in his command the Otranto barrage from Cape Santa Maria di Leuca to Fano Island to Corfu. The area to the north of the Leuca-Fano-Corfu line would be under the command of the Italian commander in chief in the same way that the remainder of the Mediterranean was under the command of the French commander in chief. The latter was the theoretical arrangement that had been in effect since August 1914. In practice, the far-flung British forces in the Mediterranean from Gibraltar to the Aegean were basically independent of each other, and to coordinate them, the Allies at the Corfu conference in April 1917 had agreed that a British Mediterranean commander in chief should be appointed. As for the light craft necessary for anti-submarine warfare, the British, French, and Italians agreed to compile lists of their naval vessels in the Mediterranean so they could ascertain the actual number and quality of ships, which each navy would put at the disposal of the admiral commanding patrols in the Mediterranean "for the accomplishment of the common task." This seemed to imply a common pool of destroyers and anti-submarine craft, which in fact never materialized. As for the Otranto barrage, the drifter or "moveable barrage," as it was designated, would be maintained, but two different types of a "fixed barrage," that is, permanent obstacles, would continue to be laid down. The "fixed barrage" had been consistently advocated by the French and Italians. The British and Italians promised to concentrate as many aircraft as possible at Otranto and all three Allies promised to study attacks by sea and land against Austrian bases in the Adriatic and then put all available means at the disposal of the Italians for this operation when required.[25] These operations were also destined to remain largely promises.

The disruption of the drifter patrols was regarded as very serious. Commodore Heneage, the commodore of Adriatic patrols, in his detailed report of the attack, which was subsequently printed and circulated in the Admiralty, reported that as of 3 June no drifters had been at sea at night since the raid because the necessary protection had not been given. This allowed German and Austrian submarines to pass through the Strait of Otranto "at will" in order to prey on shipping in the Mediterranean, and Heneage concluded "there is small doubt" the drifters had "proved themselves a serious menace to the activities of enemy submarines, and until they can again work in the narrow parts of the Straits the enemy can rely on saving a certain percentage of their submarine losses." Heneage believed that the resumption of the drifter barrage with adequate protection might even force the Austrians to send their heavier craft out, which would "certainly clear up the situation in the Adriatic to a very large extent," but at the moment "the enemy have had a very useful victory and are enjoying the fruits of it."[26]

Heneage's remarks eventually caught the eye of Sir Edward Carson, the First Lord of the Admiralty, who more than a month later queried if anything had been done about the situation, for "[i]t appears to be a serious matter affecting Allied shipping in the Mediterranean." Admiral Oliver, the chief of the naval staff, informed him that the drifters only went out at night when the Italians provided sufficient protection, but that it was hoped to eventually have British destroyers to protect the drifters. In addition, Australian destroyers were also on their way to the Mediterranean. Carson replied that he hoped "this matter will not be lost sight of."[27]

There is no question then that many on the British side believed the drifters were effective and that their disruption had serious consequences. The same belief was widely held by the Germans and Austrians and was indeed the primary reason why the Austrians had taken such risks in the raid. The Italians, in contrast, were inclined to be skeptical about the drifters and along with the French were intent on putting considerable effort into creating fixed defenses in the straits. This strongly held belief on both sides about the effectiveness of the drifters and the barrage was, however, erroneous. This can be demonstrated by examining the amount of tonnage sunk by the Mediterranean U-boat flotilla either directly or by submarine-laid mines. The figures cited below also include tonnage sunk by Austrian submarines, although given the small number of Austrian submarines operating outside of the Adriatic this was only a small proportion of the total.[28] Furthermore, while some of the sinkings might have been attributed to submarines entering the Mediterranean and proceeding to Austrian bases, the majority are credited to submarines that had passed in and out of the Strait of Otranto.

Shipping losses caused by submarines or
submarine-laid mines in the Mediterranean[29]

April 1917	277,948 tons
May 1917	180,896 tons
June 1917	170,473 tons
July 1917	107,303 tons
August 1917	118,372 tons
September 1917	111,241 tons

This survey of a six-month period before and after the Austrian raid shows that April 1917 was the worst month of the war for the Allies in the Mediterranean as, indeed, it was for Allied shipping throughout the war. Losses then declined, and in the period after the raid, when the Otranto barrage had been disrupted, they were actually less. This tends to demonstrate that for submarines the Otranto barrage was neither more nor less of a barrier after the raid than it had been before. The curtailment of drifter activity did not result in an increase in ships sunk. There were many reasons for the decline in losses to submarines, of which the most important is generally regarded to be the intro-duction of the convoy system in the Mediterranean. On 22 May the British in-augurated a Malta-Alexandria convoy, and the system, confined at first to the eastern Mediterranean, would be steadily expanded to the point where on 18 September Admiral Sir Somerset Gough-Calthorpe, the British com-mander in chief in the Mediterranean, issued printed instructions for all pa-trol commanders and shipping control officers to place merchant ships in the Mediterranean in escorted convoys on all open sea routes.[30] These convoys took some time to be established and necessitated the placement of shipping control officers in various Mediterranean ports to provide intelligence, collect ships for convoys, and expedite the discharging of cargos. In the autumn of 1917 so-called through Mediterranean convoys, from Port Said to Gibraltar and on to Great Britain, were also established. This was a major innovation, for it meant traffic from India would be spared the long voyage around Africa. This costly diversion had been forced on the British in 1916 when the subma-rine danger had closed the Mediterranean route for traffic bound for east of Suez. The savings in time and tonnage after the Mediterranean route re-opened was considerable. The French, for their part in the defense of traffic, tended to concentrate, understandably, on regular convoys between France and Algeria and Tunisia.

In addition to the establishment of convoys, the organization for countering submarines became more elaborate. There was not only a British Mediterra-nean commander in chief but also a Mediterranean admiral of patrols and a *Direction Générale des Routes* established at Malta. The *Commission de Malte* was an inter-Allied committee that coordinated shipping movements and routing in the Mediterranean. The French and Italians also developed their own specialized anti-submarine organizations, the *Direction Générale de la guerre sous-marin* for the French and the *Ispettorato della Difesa Traffico* for the Italians. Some of this looked better on paper than it was in practice. For example, the inter-Allied pools of destroyers and escorts never materialized. Moreover, inter-Allied cooperation often left much to be desired, especially in matters regarding the Italians. But whatever the problems, in the long run the resources devoted to anti-submarine warfare by the British, French, and Ital-ians steadily increased. These included escorts of all types, aircraft for both pa-trols and attacks on Austrian bases, wireless interception stations, and an elab-oration of the Otranto barrage with minefields and fixed obstructions. A British experimental fixed-net barrage of around two and a half miles laid in October 1917 was a failure, wrecked by continuous rough seas and high winds in only seventeen days. Nevertheless the British continually rejected Franco-Italian schemes for fixed barrages for which they would have been expected to

provide most of the material. The Admiralty regarded the schemes as impracticable and preferred to bar the straits by means of surface, air, or submarine
patrols. The most they would agree to was to furnish material for a trial. The
British did, however, provide the Italians with 2,000 mines to be laid off
Otranto. The French, after much delay, would eventually lay a mine-net barrage from Fano Island to a point eight miles distant from Otranto, but this was
not finished until less than a month before the war ended.[31]

Life became progressively harder for German and Austrian submarines, and
their losses increased. By the end of 1917 the Allies were able to use the destroyers and torpedo boats of the Greek navy, and by 1918 American warships would
also be employed in the Mediterranean. The submarine danger would never
be eliminated and there were months when losses would go up. There were
many factors to account for this, including the number of submarines the Germans and Austrians were able to keep at sea, the availability of escorts, and the
extent that traffic could be placed in convoys (as opposed to coastal routes or
independent sailings) or in other ways be closely protected. However, the
overall trend in losses to submarines was down. The heady days of 1916, when
submarine commanders like Arnauld de la Perière were able to run up record
scores, were gone for good. The submarine would not win the war for Germany and Austria.

Austrian surface forces also found it difficult to repeat their success of 15 May
1917. Much as the British might have complained of the apparent lack of protection given to the drifters, the balance of force remained heavily weighted
against the Austrians. The drifters may have been out of their reach, but the
Austrians did make occasional sorties directed against the lines of communication between Brindisi and Valona. Admiral Hansa, however, warned the Austrian commanders to avoid encounters with equal or superior Allied forces in
the vicinity of enemy bases. The Austrian sorties were frustrated either by bad
weather or failure to encounter any Allied transports. The latter was the experience, for example, of the *Helgoland* and the I Torpedo Division (six *Tátra*-
class destroyers) on the night of 18–19 October 1917. As part of the operation,
the Austrian submarines *U.32* and *U.40* were posted off Saseno and Brindisi to
attack any Allied warships that might sortie in pursuit.[32] The Austrians on their
return were attacked by Italian seaplanes from Brindisi while off the Albanian
coast and the engagement was joined by Austrian seaplanes from Durazzo and
Kumbor. The bombs directed at the *Helgoland* missed, but an hour later she
was attacked unsuccessfully by a submarine. This was almost certainly the
French submarine *Coulomb*, although the submarine commander later reported firing at the accompanying destroyer *Lika* rather than at the cruiser.
Substantial Allied forces came out from Brindisi in pursuit, initially Contrammiraglio Biscaretti with his flag in the light scout *Pepe*, accompanied by the *Poerio* of the same class and three Italian destroyers. They were followed by the

scouts *Aquila* and *Sparviero,* the British light cruisers *Gloucester* and *Newcastle,* and three French and three Italian destroyers. The *Weymouth* and two Italian destroyers en route from Valona to Brindisi were ordered to join them at sea. The surface forces of both sides were informed of enemy movements by aircraft, but beyond distant smoke saw nothing of each other. Austrian seaplanes bombed the *Pepe* group without success, but the presence of aircraft as well as aggressive depth charge attacks by destroyers thwarted any attacks by the Austrian submarines. On the Allied side, the small (361 tons) Italian submarine *H.2* sighted the Austrians, but was not in a position to attack.[33] These events are largely forgotten in the annals of the war, for in the end nothing happened and there were no losses on either side. Nevertheless the experience of 18–19 October demonstrated the large disparity between the opposing forces that now worked to inhibit offensive activity by the *k.u.k. Kriegsmarine* at the southern entrance to the Adriatic.

Bad weather again frustrated attempts to sweep by the *Novara* and three torpedo boats on the night of 12–13 November, as well as a subsequent sortie by three torpedo boats on 22 November. The *Novara* actually penetrated to within twenty-three miles of Brindisi but found no targets. Allied forces frustrated another sortie without firing a shot on the night of 13–14 December when the destroyers *Tátra, Balaton,* and *Csepel* detected four enemy destroyers. *Tátra* launched a torpedo against one of the enemy destroyers, but the torpedo missed. The Austrians, mindful of orders not to become engaged with stronger forces in the vicinity of enemy bases, turned for home. The unsuccessful torpedo attack was apparently never detected by the Allied destroyers. It is not clear exactly what Allied ships were involved because there were substantial numbers at sea that night, the result of the Italians believing on the basis of wireless interceptions that an enemy ship was in the area where the Italian submarine *H.4* was operating.

The intercept seemed to indicate the unknown target was not moving and might therefore be a ship that had broken down. Consequently Contrammiraglio Biscaretti sortied with the light scouts *Racchia, Poerio,* and *Bixio* and the British light cruisers *Dartmouth* (flying the flag of Commodore Howard Kelly, commanding the 8th Light Cruiser Squadron at Brindisi) and *Gloucester,* together with six Italian destroyers. The British light cruisers *Weymouth* and *Liverpool* and the Italian scout *Riboty* were held ready in reserve at Brindisi. After daybreak the Allies also had the use of dirigibles and reconnaissance aircraft, but although the *Racchia* and *Poerio* came within sight of Cape Rodoni, neither they nor the aerial reconnaissance saw anything of the enemy.[34] It is uncertain what, if anything, provoked the sortie of such a substantial number of Allied warships, but Thaon di Revel considered the size of the operation to be unjustified.[35] The incident also reveals the uncertainties of operating at night in an age before radar and how easily the advantage of numbers could be lost in the darkness. However, the incident also reveals how great the odds against the Austrians now were and how lucky the three destroyers had been to escape unscathed.

The *k.u.k. Kriegsmarine* had been relatively lucky in the war at sea, fighting against superior forces and escaping with relatively minor losses. This changed, however, in December 1917 with the development by the Italian navy of the *Mas*, which stood for *motobarca armata silurante*. These were fast motor torpedo boats powered with gasoline engines with a crew of about eight and capable of carrying two torpedoes. They may have been short-ranged and on the whole fragile, but they were well suited to Adriatic conditions. On the night of 10 December 1917, two *Mas* succeeded in penetrating the defenses of the harbor of Trieste, and Tenente di vascello Luigi Rizzo torpedoed and sank the old coast defense battleship *Wien*.[36] The success came at a critical moment for the Italians, who had suffered their worst defeat in the war on 24 October when Austrian and German forces broke through the Italian lines at Caporetto, starting a long Italian retreat of more than seventy miles that halted only at the Piave River. There was real concern that Venice might fall and the British even feared that the Italians might be compelled to drop out of the war.[37]

The Italian army held along the Piave, and in the aftermath of Caporetto the Italians experienced what amounted to a national revival. It would be Austria-Hungary that showed severe strains in the early months of 1918, and this would not fail to be reflected in the navy. There was a warning that the *k.u.k. Kriegsmarine* was not immune to the nationality problems that would eventually tear the Dual Monarchy apart on 5 October 1917, when some of the crew of the small torpedo boat *Tb.11* stationed at Sebenico locked their officers in their cabins and brought the boat across the Adriatic to surrender to the Italians. There was certainly an undercurrent of dissatisfaction in the Austrian navy by the beginning of 1918, and this was particularly marked in the larger ships, whose relative inactivity meant boredom and unvarying routine coupled with strict naval discipline for their crews. To this was added growing labor agitation in the dockyards on shore and concern over families facing hardships at home. The small craft, notably destroyers and torpedo craft as well as submarines and the small number of elite fast light cruisers like *Helgoland*, experienced far less of these problems. The destroyers and torpedo boats, after all, had much work escorting convoys through the channels between the maze of islands on the Adriatic coast and countering the threat of French, British, and Italian submarines. The bigger ships, notably battleships and armored cruisers, were in contrast relatively idle.

The real trouble came in the Gulf of Cattaro, where discontent was magnified by the attitude of many officers. They enjoyed relative luxury compared to their men, even to the point of bringing wives and families to the Bocche, where naval rations could be purchased at low prices compared to the hinterlands, where some commodities were unavailable. Leave was infrequent and travel facilities from the Bocche to the rest of the Monarchy were uncertain. There was growing war weariness, and an outside stimulus in the form of President Woodrow Wilson's "Fourteen Points" speech outlining the basis for a peace served as a catalyst for trouble. Barely three weeks after the speech, a mutiny began in the ships at the Bocche on 1 February, centered in the armored cruiser *Sankt Georg*. The men of the light cruisers and destroyers remained loyal for the most part and the army manning artillery positions overlooking the gulf was unaffected. The mutiny collapsed after a few days, particularly when three *Erzherzog*-class battleships arrived at the Bocche to reinforce the authority of the high command.[38]

The mutiny was enough to bring to a climax the growing sentiment that the navy needed "rejuvenation," that is, younger and more aggressive officers with fresh ideas in command. The result was that in March 1918 Kaiser Karl chose the forty-nine-year-old Horthy, still a Linienschiffskapitän in command of the dreadnought *Prinz Eugen* swinging around her buoy in relative idleness at Pola, to be Flottenkommandant. Horthy was promoted to Kontreadmiral but was still way down on the seniority list, and his elevation to command of the fleet caused considerable grumbling among some of those passed over. His conduct during the raid in May 1917 was probably the major reason for his elevation. He was one officer who had commanded a group of ships in combat at sea with some success. There was optimism among some, like the German naval attaché, that the more able commanders would no longer have their hands tied in "refloating the ship which had been stuck deeply in the mud."[39]

Certainly the fleet seemed to be stripping down for action, with older and obsolete ships, including the *Sankt Georg*, taken out of service. The core of the battle fleet in commission at Pola was now the four dreadnoughts of the *Tegetthoff* class and the semi-dreadnought *Radetzkys*. However, it was one thing to talk about "young blood" and another to find some real employment for the big ships of the navy. What could they really do given the forces arrayed against them at the entrance to the Adriatic? Horthy claims to have recognized this and had been reluctant to accept the appointment, pointing out to Kaiser Karl that he could not be expected to perform miracles in the fourth year of the war.[40]

The situation was indeed growing more serious, with shortages of coal and increased Allied aerial activity against Pola and Cattaro. The Italians were also becoming more aggressive, as evidenced by the famous raid associated with the poet and author Gabriele D'Annunzio in which three *Mas* boats managed to reach the Gulf of Buccari near Fiume on the night of 10–11 February and attacked laid-up steamers. Their torpedoes were faulty and no ships were sunk, but the achievement was impressive.[41] Not even the major naval base at Pola was absolutely secure.

A series of three attacks by *Grillo*-class "jumping boats" equipped with cater-pillar chains to climb over harbor obstacles resulted in one actually penetrat-ing some of the obstructions on the night of 13–14 May before it was discovered and sunk.[42]

Any repetition of the May 1917 raid on the part of the Austrians was to be-come progressively harder. This was not necessarily a good thing from the point of view of the Allied campaign against the submarine, for some at the Admiralty as well as the British Mediterranean commander in chief Admiral Calthorpe were still seduced by the idea of the Otranto barrage. The objective was to extend the minefields out from the Italian coast to the 100-fathom line and add more destroyers, trawlers, hydrophones, motor launches, CMBs (high speed coastal motor boats similar to the Italian *Mas*), and aircraft to create a zone sixty-five miles deep that a submerged submarine would be unable to traverse in a single night. The British secured the agreement of the Italians on 11 February 1918 to the general control of the barrage being placed under the British commander in chief, although this did not necessarily mean addi-tional Italian destroyers would be provided for the barrage. Calthorpe pro-posed solving the problem of finding sufficient destroyers by at least tempo-rarily withdrawing patrols from the Dardanelles and the Aegean and diverting destroyers from convoys. In hindsight, it can be seen that weakening the pro-tection of the convoys for the sake of the Otranto barrage would have been a mistaken policy, but that was not necessarily how it appeared to people like Calthorpe at the time, especially as continued losses in convoys shook his faith in the system.[43] Calthorpe's proposals regarding the convoys found more op-position than support at the Admiralty, notably from Rear Admiral A. L. Duff, director of the anti-submarine division, who was inclined to doubt the abso-lute effectiveness of even a strengthened barrage, although he acknowledged its value as a deterrent and also as a provocation to force the Austrian cruisers to come out. Duff, however, was strongly opposed to withdrawing forces for the barrage from trade protection but thought Calthorpe's plan might be at least partially put into effect by making economies in the way existing escorts were used in the Mediterranean and gradually increasing forces allocated to the barrage as forces became available from home waters.[44]

While the full plans for the Otranto barrage were never realized, the height-ened attention given to it as well as the presence of British and Australian de-stroyers made it much more difficult for the Austrians to raid the southern Adriatic. This was again demonstrated on the night of 22–23 April 1918. Five *Tátra*-class destroyers (*Triglav, Uzsok, Dukla, Lika,* and *Csepel*) under the command of Fregattenkapitän Karl Herkner in the *Triglav* swept southward into the Strait of Otranto seeking to disrupt Allied traffic between the Italian and Albanian coasts. They represented the newest and best Austrian destroy-ers; with the exception of the *Csepel* all had been laid down and completed during the war. *Uzsok* was destined to be the last destroyer ever to be commissioned by the *k.u.k. Kriegsmarine*. This night, however, there were six Allied destroyers on advanced patrol before the barrage, notably the British *Jackal*, *Hornet*, *Alarm*, and *Comet*, the Australian *Torrens*, and the French *Cimeterre*. The *Jackal*, *Hornet*, and *Alarm* were of the "I" (*Acheron*) class and *Torrens*, the slightly different Australian "I" class. The *Comet* belonged to the preceding "H" (*Acorn*) class. They were 720- to 810-ton oil-burning ships, armed with two four-inch and two twelve-pounder guns and two twenty-one-inch torpedo tubes and capable of twenty-seven knots. With the exception of *Torrens*, launched in 1915, they were pre-war ships, having been launched in 1910 and 1911.[45] The destroyers were divided into three subdivisions, each with a ten-mile beat with orders to commence their patrol from the easternmost portion of the beat and adjust course and speed to turn simultaneously at the end of their beat every fifty minutes. In addition, there were two British destroyers at Brindisi at six hours' notice (the "H"-class *Redpole* and *Rifleman*) and another two Australian destroyers (*Swan* and *Warrego*) and a British destroyer (*Acorn*) at lesser degrees of readiness. Two more British destroyers (*Larne* and *Lizard*) were attached to the Corfu division of the barrage destroyer patrol.

The *Jackal*, under the command of Lieutenant Commander A. M. Roberts, and *Hornet* had been assigned to patrol the western beat. At approximately 2110 the commander of the *Hornet* observed a number of vessels abaft the starboard beam, but because of the lighting conditions he mistook them for two small Italian troop-carrying vessels that had frequently been encountered between Brindisi and Valona. He also mistook smaller vessels in the distance for drifters. *Hornet* signaled *Jackal* by shaded lamp, drawing attention to the unidentified craft. The captain of the *Hornet* then noticed that the two leading ships had large bow waves and immediately rang the alarm bell for action stations. *Jackal* and *Hornet* both turned toward the unidentified ships and *Jackal* made the challenge. While still indistinct to the British and about 3,000 yards distant, the leading Austrian ship opened fire on the *Jackal*. The two British destroyers returned fire and the action became general. On the bridge of the *Hornet*, it seemed as if they were dealing with two light cruisers and four destroyers, although *Jackal's* report subsequently made no mention of cruisers and spoke only of five destroyers in line abreast. *Jackal* and *Hornet* altered course sixteen points and began making smoke with the intention of drawing the enemy to the south. The Austrians seemed to concentrate their fire on the *Hornet*. The British destroyer fired about twenty rounds and thought one or two hits were observed on the first or second enemy ship. In turn, an Austrian salvo hit the *Hornet*, with one shell penetrating the forward shell room and passing through to the forward magazine, starting fires in both compartments. This led to the ignition of some of the cordite and an explosion in the magazine that killed or wounded most of the ammunition supply parties and twelve-pounder crews. A second shell hit the fore bridge, blowing an officer and midshipman off the platform and killing two ratings. A third shell brought the mast down, injuring the captain in both arms and resulting in both sirens blowing continuously for about ten minutes, which made it impossible for orders to be heard. *Hornet's* helm then jammed "hard over" to starboard causing the ship to steam in a circle at twenty knots while receiving further damage aft in the tiller flat. The *Jackal* was also hit. Her mainmast and wireless aerial came down, preventing the first of her alert messages and emergency report from getting through, although subsequent messages appear to have been received. Another shell penetrated and exploded in the wardroom, killing a rating, and yet another exploded just above the wardroom hatch, mortally wounding another rating. The injured captain tried in vain to fire two torpedoes at the Austrians by means of the fore bridge firing gear as they approached to about 1,800 yards, but his injuries prevented him from doing this in time.

Commander Roberts gradually brought the *Jackal* around to the east and observed the Austrians altering course to the north. His opponent, Herkner, estimated that the encounter lasted approximately a quarter of an hour at ranges varying between 1,400 and 3,000 meters, but he decided to break off the combat given the proximity of enemy bases and the fact that the alarm had undoubtedly been raised. Moreover, he claimed to have discerned smoke approaching from the west. Roberts followed the Austrians at full speed, firing the *Jackal's* forward four-inch gun and signaling his position frequently as well as firing green rockets to show his position to the British destroyers coming up astern. *Jackal's* fire appeared to cause the Austrian destroyers to fan out from their line-ahead formation, making it impossible for Roberts to follow their movements. He therefore checked fire, but the Austrians steadily pulled ahead and by 0020 he had lost sight of them in the position latitude 41° 20′ north, longitude 19° 08′ east. At 0043 Roberts slowed to allow the *Torrens, Alarm,* and *Cimeterre* to catch up and then continued the pursuit, again increasing speed. There was no real chance of catching the Austrians, and at 0135 Roberts gave up the pursuit and turned to the south. The Allied destroyers had gone as far as 41° 49′ north and 19° 03′ east. Herkner, for his part, believed he had been pursued by three ships but had not been sure of their size or type.

The *Jackal* and *Hornet* had initially borne the weight of the five Austrian destroyers by themselves. They were not left unaided. The commander of the patrol, Lieutenant Commander Pridham-Wippell in the *Comet*, together with the *Torrens,* was on the central beat and had seen the flashes of gunfire and heard the sound of heavy firing. He ordered full speed, rang the alarm bell for action stations, and steamed toward the encounter. As the apparent fight appeared at this stage to be heading southward, Pridham-Wippell assumed that the Austrians were trying to reach the drifter line. He altered course slightly to permit the *Alarm* and *Cimeterre* from the easternmost beat to join, which they eventually did, forming line astern of the *Torrens*. Ascertaining that the firing seemed to be moving to the north, Pridham-Wippell altered his own course accordingly and worked up to full speed in an attempt to cut off the enemy. The intensity of the firing at first led Pridham-Wippell to believe cruisers were present, and his first signal indicated this fact. He quickly annulled it when he received *Jackal*'s message that only destroyers were involved. Shortly after 2200 he sighted smoke to the northwest and altered course again in an attempt to close the enemy, passing the damaged *Hornet* making for Valona. At 2210 the *Jackal* was in sight, and at 2254 the *Comet* fired a trial shot from her forward four-inch gun to see if the Austrians were in range. They were not, and they seemed to be drawing ahead. At 0027 *Comet*'s discharge pipe to the port air pump fractured at the flange due to the vibration. Pridham-Wippell was forced to reduce speed but ordered the *Torrens*, *Cimeterre*, and *Alarm* to continue to follow the *Jackal* in pursuit. There was a limit, however, to how far the pursuit would follow. Commodore Kelly at Brindisi ordered the destroyers not to proceed nearer than ten miles to the enemy coast because of the danger of mines.

With her speed reduced, the *Comet* altered course to the southwest. Her adventures were not over, for at 0143 a submarine was spotted on the surface. Pridham-Wippell promptly attacked, delivering a depth-charge attack after the submarine had dived. He then employed the destroyer's explosive sweep, but with the approach of daybreak and with his speed reduced and the closeness of Austrian ports thought it wise to abandon the search. At 0130 he ordered his destroyers to resume their regular patrol. The message did not get through at first, but by 0500 *Comet* had returned to her beat and was joined by *Torrens*, *Cimeterre*, and *Alarm* at 0550. *Jackal* returned to Brindisi for repairs at 0535 and was ready for sea by 1600 on the 24th. The submarine may have been the Austrian *U.28*. The submarine commander reported he had to crash dive and that two depth charges had been dropped, but he had been on his way out of the Adriatic on the start of a cruise to the central Mediterranean, whereas Pridham-Wippell had reported the submarine when sighted was apparently steering northward.

Hornet, with fires in the magazine and shell room burning, water in the oil reducing speed, and the helm continually jamming, made for Valona for repairs, arriving at 0400. The fires were finally extinguished by completely flooding both compartments, but the *Hornet* reported that two torpedoes had been fired at her by a submarine while entering Valona. The submarine may have been the Austrian *U.27* at the beginning of a Mediterranean cruise. The submarine was off Valona about this time but did not report attacking enemy destroyers until 1615 on the afternoon of the 23rd.

Captain George Chetwode, the Captain (D) or commander of the British destroyers at Brindisi, had, on receiving the first erroneous message that Austrian cruisers were involved, ordered all five British destroyers at Brindisi to raise steam, and at 2355 proceeded to sea in the *Rifleman* in company with *Redpole*. He set a course for Cattaro with the objective of cutting off any enemy vessels that might have been damaged and forced to steam at a reduced speed, but at 0130 he was ordered by Commodore Kelly to return. He encountered no Austrian or German forces. The British losses in the night action were seven dead and twenty-five wounded. It was estimated that repairs to the *Hornet* would require around fourteen days.[46]

The Italian navy had also reacted to the Austrian raid. The destroyer *Bronzetti* sailed from Brindisi, followed by the scout *Mirabello* with Contrammiraglio Biscaretti (commander of the IV Division) in company with the scout *Poerio* and followed shortly afterward by the destroyer *La Masa*. On the other side of the Adriatic, the British light cruiser *Gloucester* had been at Valona for exercises and had also put to sea.[47] None of these substantial Allied forces were in a position to actually intercept the Austrian destroyers, but it confirms why the Austrians were wise not to linger in the southern Adriatic.

Although gunners in the *Jackal* and *Hornet* were sure they had observed at least a few hits, the Austrians, although straddled, had not been hit and suffered no losses. Heyssler had recently replaced Admiral Hansa as leader of the Austrian light forces at Cattaro and was convinced that Herkner could have sunk the damaged British destroyer if he had energetically pushed the attack. Nevertheless, Heyssler could not attach any reproach to Herkner, for it had been the first operation of his division on what Heyssler claimed was a training mission, and he realized the Austrian destroyers had been in the vicinity of Valona on a night with bright moonlight and had to avoid being cut off by superior forces. The Austrian gunners had also used tracer shells (*Flugbahnanzeiger*), which had greatly assisted spotting the fall of shells. The British destroyers apparently lacked this advantage in spotting.[48]

At the Admiralty, Captain Coode, the director of operations division (foreign), agreed with Heyssler that the *Jackal* and *Hornet* ought to have been sunk or completely crippled before British reinforcements could arrive. He believed that the action had demonstrated that a covering force of six destroyers patrolling by subdivisions was not enough and that they needed a minimum of eight destroyers patrolling by divisions. Nevertheless, although the actual losses were lopsided, the British were well satisfied with the results of the engagement. As Commodore Kelly put it, "The enemy were sighted well north of the drifter line, and after being engaged by a subdivision of the patrol destroyers withdrew at once to the north." The British Mediterranean commander in chief, Admiral Calthorpe, agreed: "Your late destroyer scrap showed that a good lookout was being kept which undoubtedly saved the Barrage being raided."[49] These assumptions were not strictly correct. The Austrian objective had been traffic in the Strait of Otranto and not specifically the drifters on the barrage. Nevertheless, the implications of the strengthened Allied patrol were the same. The action of the night of 22–23 April 1918 has largely been forgotten by historians. It is probably similar to a number of German destroyer raids in the Strait of Dover during the war, raids that were hard to counter and that resulted in short, sharp actions with all the difficulties of fighting in the dark in an age before radar, but raids that ultimately failed to disrupt British communications with the Continent. The action for the Austrians had a similar effect. If they were going to disrupt the barrage, they might have to risk something more potent that the light forces at Cattaro.

With an aggressive new commander like Horthy in charge with the promise to bring new vigor to the naval war, and with the strengthened Allied defenses in the Strait of Otranto, the action Horthy planned for June 1918 is not all that surprising. The Cattaro mutiny in February had shown the dangers of leaving the large ships unemployed. Horthy had a use for them. Although the ostensible purpose of the raid was to facilitate the passage of submarines through the Strait of Otranto, one suspects questions of morale and the need "to do something" played an equally important role. The operation set for dawn on 11 June was to be a repeat of the May 1917 raid. The light cruisers *Novara* and *Helgoland*, in company with four *"Tátra"*-class destroyers, would attack along the Fano–Santa Maria di Leuca line. The light cruisers *Saida* and *Admiral Spaun*, accompanied by four 250-ton high-seas torpedo boats, would simultaneously sweep the waters off Otranto and attack the seaplane station at this port. When the expected swarm of Allied cruisers and destroyers sortied to take advantage of the opportunity that the elusive Austrians had apparently given them, they would meet Austrian heavy ships. The four *Tegetthoff*-class dreadnoughts from Pola and three small battleships of the *Erzherzog* class from Cattaro were divided into seven separate groups, each protected by destroyers and/or torpedo boats. The seven groups were to be deployed in different positions in the southern Adriatic. Austrian and German submarines were to be deployed off Brindisi and Valona, and Austrian aircraft would bomb Brindisi and Otranto and also support the surface warships. The submarine deployment included the Austrian *U.28, U.29, U.31* off the Italian coast, and *U.27* and the German *UC.52* off the Albanian coast. It was an ambitious scheme and might have resulted in the heaviest fighting in the Adriatic during the war. There were ten British, Australian, and French destroyers on patrol north of the drifter line that night. However, the raid was destined not to take place.

The Austrian dreadnoughts proceeded south from Pola in two echelons, Horthy in *Viribus Unitis* together with *Prinz Eugen* in the first. It was the second echelon, however, that met disaster. As the second echelon (*Szent István* and *Tegetthoff*) passed a point roughly nine nautical miles southwest of the island of Premuda, it was attacked at around 0330 by two Italian motor torpedo boats, Mas.15 and Mas.21, and Capitano di corvetta Luigi Rizzo with Mas.15 succeeded in putting his two torpedoes into the *Szent István*. The ship could not be saved, although she did not sink until after dawn so that the incident could be filmed, a sequence frequently used in documentaries though the ship involved is not usually identified. It was probably the high point of the war for the Italian navy and it meant the end of the planned raid. Horthy cancelled the operation for fear that with the loss of the essential element of surprise and the Allies' knowledge that the Austrian heavy ships were at sea, he might meet the superior numbers of Italian and French dreadnoughts located near the entrance to the Adriatic as well as a swarm of submarines and *Mas*.[50]

The Austrians may not have been able to shake the Allied grip on the entrance to the Adriatic, but the Adriatic itself and the Austrian coastline remained unscathed. The success of Luigi Rizzo had demonstrated once again that the relatively confined waters of the Adriatic were unhealthy for large warships, and the Allies were certainly reluctant to risk their larger ships far into the Adriatic. However, the gravest potential threat to the Austrian coast in 1918 probably came from the United States. The Americans were anxious to use maritime power to deny the German and Austrian submarines the use of bases in the Adriatic. The planning section of the staff of Vice Admiral William S. Sims, commander of U.S. naval forces in European waters, even weighed the possibilities of a raid on the Gulf of Cattaro using the older and by implication expendable pre-dreadnoughts of the United States Navy. A more feasible and serious plan involved a landing on the Sabbioncello peninsula, which would be secured and from which raids could be launched inland to sever communications to Cattaro. At the same time, a base would be established between Curzola Island and the Sabbioncello peninsula. U.S. Marines would have played a leading role in the operation. The Americans were also seduced by the Otranto barrage and, once the extensive barrage planned for the North Sea had been finished, proposed a mid-Adriatic barrage from Gargano Head on the mainland running across the Adriatic to Curzola. The Americans had other extensive mining projects for the Mediterranean, but the war ended before they could be implemented. As for the landing on the Sabbioncello peninsula, Ludendorff's offensive on the western front in France, which began on 21 March 1918, meant all available troops had to be diverted to France to help stop the Germans, and the American Adriatic projects became another "what might have been" of military history.[51]

There was nevertheless an American naval presence at the Strait of Otranto by June 1918. It took the form of thirty-six 110-foot wooden-hulled "submarine chasers." They were usually armed with a three-inch gun and carried depth charges. Most important of all in the plans of the Americans, they were equipped with hydrophone listening devices on which the Americans placed great faith. The submarine chasers would work in groups of three and seek to detect a submarine through the listening devices and then fix its position by means of triangulation. Despite the great hopes placed in these vessels, the war ended without their having accounted for a single submarine, and the majority of the extensive mining and barrage programs the Americans had planned for the Mediterranean remained unrealized. The barrage itself claimed one of its few confirmed victims on 3 August when *UB.53*, in the middle of the strait about twenty-five miles from Otranto on the parallel of Fano Island, fouled a mine net and detonated two mines.[52] The submarine's commander apparently did not realize the fixed barrage had been extended to the east. It was a momentary triumph, however. The Austrians and Germans, on learning of the loss via an Italian communiqué, promptly altered their routes and methods of passing through the strait. The submarine campaign was thwarted, but not by barrages and nets or listening devices.

In the closing weeks of the war, as Austrian land forces began their retreat from Albania and the Dual Monarchy headed toward collapse, there was a sizeable Allied naval effort directed against the Albanian port of Durazzo. The operation was shielded against possible intervention by large Austrian warships by the Italian dreadnought *Dante Alighieri*, together with large numbers of British, Australian, and Italian warships as well as American sub chasers. British, French, and Italian submarines were also deployed off Austrian bases. The actual bombardment was carried out by three Italian armored cruisers and three British light cruisers on 2 October. British and Italian aircraft also bombed Durazzo throughout the operation. In the port were only two old Austrian destroyers, a torpedo boat, and a handful of steamers, one of which was sunk. The Austrian warships escaped largely unharmed. The same could not be said for the Allies. There were two Austrian submarines in the vicinity and one, *U.31*, torpedoed the British cruiser *Weymouth*. The cruiser's stern was blown off and four ratings killed, but the ship survived.[53] The Adriatic until the very end of the war remained dangerous for larger warships. This had been the third British cruiser torpedoed in the Adriatic during the war. It was, however, the final action of the *k.u.k. Kriegsmarine*.

The war in the Adriatic ended at the beginning of November following the collapse of the Austro-Hungarian army after the battle commencing 24 October and commonly known as Vittorio Veneto. This would lead to the signing of the armistice at the Villa Giusti on 4 November ending hostilities on the Italian front. The entire monarchy by then was in a state of dissolution, and on the afternoon of 31 October Horthy received orders from Kaiser Karl to turn over the fleet and all naval property to the South Slav National Council that had recently been established in Agram. The red-white-red naval ensign of the *k.u.k. Kriegsmarine* was lowered for the last time in the flagship *Viribus Unitis* at around 1645, to be replaced by red-white-blue Slavic colors. A Croatian as-

sumed command of the fleet on a provisional basis, but that night, with precautions at Pola relaxed or non-existent, a pair of daring Italian officers wearing rubber suits and using a self-propelled mine-torpedo dubbed the
"mignatta" or "leech" managed to attach explosive charges to the hull of the
Viribus Unitis. The charges detonated and capsized the ship.[54] A second group
of explosives that had been left aboard the "mignatta" after it been abandoned
also exploded and probably caused the sinking of the Austrian Lloyd steamer
Wein. The *Wein* before the war had maintained the Trieste-Alexandria service
and in 1918 was in use as an accommodation ship for German U-boat crews.
The Germans, however, were no longer around, for when they sensed their
Austrian allies were seeking an armistice, the German naval high command
ordered all U-boats ready for sea to leave Austrian bases, while those at sea
were ordered by wireless to return home. Accordingly, a dozen submarines
sailed from Pola or the Bocche and ten submarines not ready for the voyage
were blown up or scuttled off Austrian ports. None of the submarines trying to
escape back to Germany were intercepted in the Otranto barrage nor, for that
matter, were they caught passing through the Strait of Gibraltar, despite
heightened vigilance. Once again it was demonstrated that barrages were not
an effective way to catch submarines.

EPILOGUE

WITH THE END OF the war and the disintegration of the Habsburg Monarchy, the seagoing warships of the *k.u.k. Kriegsmarine* were divided among the victorious Allies, and many of the older ones were quickly scrapped. With the exception of Horthy's *Novara*, all the cruisers and destroyers that had proved so hard to catch during the Battle of the Otranto Straits ended their lives in the Italian navy. Not surprisingly, all received new names. Heyssler's old command, the *Helgoland*, became the *Brindisi*, while Purschka's *Saida* became the *Venezia*. The destroyers *Csepel* and *Balaton* became the *Muggia* and *Zenson*, respectively. The *Zenson*, considered in bad condition, saw no service in the Italian navy except as a source of spares and was struck from the navy list in 1923. The *Muggia* ended her days far from the Adriatic, wrecked off the coast of China in 1929. *Brindisi* and *Venezia* lasted until 1937, but, considered to be worn-out and too lightly armed for fleet work and ill-adapted for employment outside the Adriatic, they were primarily used on special missions to Italian colonies or the Levant and as flagships for torpedo boat divisions. The *Novara* went to the French navy, where she became the *Thionville* and was technically the longest lived of the Austrian ships in the battle. Despite an inauspicious beginning, sinking near Brindisi while under tow to Bizerte in 1920, the *Thionville* found useful employment as an artillery and torpedo school ship in the Mediterranean training ship division. Although disarmed and relegated to the status of hulk in 1932, the *Thionville* remained in use as a stationary accommodation ship at Toulon and was not finally sold for scrapping until 1941.

The two opposing commanders in the Strait of Otranto on 15 May 1917 had long though differing careers. Acton followed a traditional path, eventually reaching the rank of *Ammiraglio d'Armata*. He served as *Capo di stato maggiore* from December 1919 to February 1921 and again from May 1925 to December 1927. Acton would be relatively well known in international naval circles, for he was an Italian delegate at both the Washington naval conference of 1921–22 and the London naval conference of 1930. He died in 1934 and was thus spared the disasters which befell his country and service during the Second World War.

Horthy had a much longer and unconventional, though controversial, career. In 1919 he would lead a counter-revolution against the Communist regime in Hungary and become Regent, although the pressure of the succession states would prevent any actual restoration of the Habsburgs. In 1941 he brought Hungary into the war on the side of Germany during the attack on Russia. His attempt to escape from the disastrous war in 1944 led to his overthrow by the rabidly fascist Arrow Cross party and imprisonment first by the Germans and then by the Allies. He avoided, however, being charged as a "war criminal," primarily because he had finally tried to take Hungary out of the war. Horthy completed his *Memoirs* (1956) before his 1957 death in exile in Portugal. The memoirs were not very informative, possibly because he did not have extensive records at his disposal. Horthy throughout his political career was usually addressed as "Admiral" and frequently seen in naval uniform. The Nazis, when courting Hungary, brought him to Germany in 1938 for the launching of the heavy cruiser *Prinz Eugen* because of the Austrian and Habsburg memories the ship's name invoked. The incongruous spectacle of landlocked Hungary under an admiral resulted in the common inter-war joke that "Hungary was a kingdom without a king ruled by an admiral without a fleet." The jokes were unfair. Horthy, however controversial and whatever his defects as a politician and statesman, had been a real sailor and a bold and dashing one at that. He owed his initial fame to his leadership in the Otranto battle, even though this was little known outside of Hungary. Horthy was also distinct. His fellow captains at Otranto, like Heyssler, saw their naval careers ended by the disappearance of the Habsburg Monarchy and its fleet, and they retired to private life.

On the British side, Captain Addison of the *Dartmouth*, who had borne so much of the battle, would eventually command the Australian fleet from 1922 to 1924 and as a rear admiral, the destroyer flotillas in the Mediterranean Fleet from 1924 to 1926. He ended his career as director of dockyards at the Admiralty from 1928 to 1937. Addison died in 1952. Captain Vivian, the frustrated

British senior naval officer at Brindisi, did not survive the war for long, dying in 1921. Admiral Kerr, commander of the British Adriatic Force, followed his love of flying and became a major general in the Royal Air Force and deputy chief of air staff in 1918. He retired in 1918 and in 1919 attempted a transatlantic flight. But for a faulty radiator in the engines of his Handley Page, he and his crew might well have beaten the Vickers Vimy of Alcock and Brown in making the first non-stop flight across the Atlantic, which would have made Kerr one of the more famous names in aviation history. Before his death in 1944 he also wrote two volumes of interesting memoirs, notably *Land, Sea and Air* (1927) and *The Navy in My Time* (1933). None of these careers on the British and Italian side, however worthy, could compare with that of Horthy, who remains by far the best known of the leaders at the Battle of the Otranto Straits.

Otranto was the largest battle fought at sea between rival warships in the Mediterranean area during the First World War. It is true that the sortie of the Austrian fleet against the Italian coast on Italy's entrance into the war might have involved more ships, as did the British and French operations at the Dardanelles in 1915. However, these were for the most part naval operations against targets on land, not encounters between squadrons. There is a temptation therefore to consider Otranto the "Mediterranean Jutland" in the sense that it was the largest battle at sea in this area during the war. It might seem at first glance a gross exaggeration to compare Otranto, a battle involving a relative handful of ships, none larger than a light cruiser, with Jutland, a battle involving hundreds of ships including some of the largest and most powerful afloat. There can also be no comparison between the handful lost in one action and the thousands of casualties in the other. Yet, curious as it may seem, there are in a very broad sense certain similarities. Both battles involved a weaker fleet sallying against a stronger fleet. At Jutland, neither the British nor German commanders realized at first the other was at sea in full strength. At Otranto, the British and Italians had at least some confusion at first over whether they were dealing with destroyers or cruisers, and Horthy may well have underestimated the type of British cruiser opposing him, regarding it as the weaker *Blanche* class instead of the more powerful *Dartmouth*. This in turn may have led him to accept an encounter he might possibly have avoided.

The other broad similarity between Jutland and Otranto is that the weaker fleet was able to escape after inflicting more damage than it suffered itself. This was certainly true in regard to the Austrians at Otranto, who succeeded with their German ally in sinking two destroyers, a transport, and fourteen drifters with no losses of their own. While this is true, it also emphasizes another great similarity between the two encounters. Neither encounter resulted in a change in the strategic situation. In the case of Jutland, the common saying allegedly from an American newspaper was that the German fleet had assaulted its jailor and was back in jail. The Austrians had done the same thing, but the exit from the Adriatic remained closed to them and their fleet. Except for a handful of modern submarines they could not really think of operations outside the Adriatic. Moreover, the great disparity in strength between the resources available to the Allies and the Austrians made any successful repetition of 15 May 1917 increasingly difficult.

Otranto exceeded Jutland in complexity in at least one sense. It was far more of a battle in three dimensions than Jutland had been in that both aircraft and submarines on both sides played a real though not decisive role. Otranto was also far more of a multi-national encounter, with the forces of Austria and Germany involved on one side and the British, Italian, and French on the other. This was demonstrated also by the unusual aspect of an Italian admiral directing operations from the bridge of a British warship. That the Allied force was multi-national appears also to have been responsible for the difficulties in signaling and reporting that were encountered, demonstrating that much practice is necessary for ships of different nationalities to work together effectively. The encounter on the Austrian side also suggested that aviators needed practice in communicating with ships and, for that matter, correctly identifying them.

Otranto was also a battle fought to a certain extent under misapprehensions. The Austrians believed they had to act against the Otranto barrage, which in their eyes threatened to cut off submarine exit and entry into the Adriatic. This was coupled with the need for action, the very human factor that ships and men could not be kept indefinitely in idleness as a fleet-in-being. The Austrians were wrong in not realizing how ineffective in stopping submarines the Otranto barrage actually was. The barrage may have been an inconvenience to submarine commanders and may even have caused them jangled nerves and uncomfortable moments during its passage, but it was more of an inconvenience than an absolute obstacle. However, the Austrian raid reinforced misconceptions on the Allied side as well, leading them to believe the barrage must have been effective if the Austrians had taken the effort and risk to raid it. Consequently, the Otranto barrage throughout the war maintained its strong attraction for the British, French, Italians, and eventually the Americans. They were tempted to pour resources into it which might well have been used to better effect elsewhere. This reached its most dangerous stage in late 1917 and early 1918, when the British commander in chief was, despite the experience of the preceding six to eight months, actually tempted to withdraw escorts from convoys to reinforce the barrage. Neither side realized that the anti-submarine war was being decided far from the Strait of Otranto in dozens of small actions involving convoys and their escorts and that these actions were reducing the amount of tonnage sunk by submarines and preventing them from fulfilling the German Admiralstab's promise that unrestricted submarine warfare would bring the Allies to their knees.

There is value in looking at the 15 May 1917 battle in the Strait of Otranto. Not all naval actions will be major encounters between large fleets. In the Adriatic there were sudden clashes between fast, light forces, glancing blows rather than pitched battles, with aircraft and submarines complicating matters. In the naval war in the Adriatic, one can also see how a stronger side is prevented from using its full power by the constraints of geography and by new weapons like submarines. This does not mean, however, that the weaker side would be able to gain the freedom of the open seas or exercise its naval power beyond certain well-defined limits. Otranto also had great symbolic value for the Austrians and Hungarians as well as Croatians and the other ethnic groups who made up the navy. The Habsburg Monarchy was a relative newcomer to late-nineteenth-century navalism, and there was some debate over whether the navy was an artificial and unnatural creation. The Austrian navy was also not without success, as Admiral Tegetthoff's victory at Lissa in 1866 demonstrated. During the First World War, however, it was opposed not only by one power—Italy—but by the major maritime powers of Great Britain and France, and finally the United States. On 15 May 1917, the *k.u.k. Kriegsmarine* accredited itself well in the face of three of those powers, and Otranto represents the high point of Austria-Hungary at sea in the 1914–1918 war. Sadly, the Austro-Hungarian navy had less than a year and a half left to exist before becoming a historical curiosity.

GLOSSARY OF GEOGRAPHICAL NAMES

Italian or German Name	Current Name
Antivari	Bar
Bocche di Cattaro	Boka Kotorska
Buccari	Bakar
Castelnuovo	Hercegnovi
Cattaro	Kotor
Curzola	Korčula
Drin (Gulf of)	Drinit (Gjiri)
Durazzo	Durrës
Fano	Óthoni
Fiume	Rijeka
Gjenović	Denovići
Gravosa	Gruz
Lesina	Hvar
Linguetta (Kap)	Gjuhezës (Kepi)
Lissa	Vis
Menders (Kap)	Mendre (Rat)
Merlera	Errikoúsa
Pelagosa	Palagruza
Planka (Kap)	Ploca (Rat)
Pola	Pula
Punta/Spitze d'Ostro	Oštri (Rat)
Ragusa	Dubrovnik
Rodoni (gulf)	Rodonit (Gjirit)

Italian or German Name	Current Name
Rondoni	Mamula
Sabbioncello	Pelješac
San Giovanni di Medua	Shëngjin
Santi Quaranta	Sarandës/Sarande
Saseno	Sazan
Scutari/Skutari	Skadar/Shkodra
Sebenico	Šibenik
Spalato	Split
Teodo	Tivat
Valona	Vlore/Vlonës

EQUIVALENT RANKS

British	French	Italian	Austrian
Admiral of the Fleet	—	—	Großadmiral
Admiral	—	Ammiraglio	Admiral
Vice Admiral	Vice Amiral	Viceammiraglio	Vizeadmiral
Rear Admiral	Contre Amiral	Contrammiraglio	Kontreadmiral
Commodore (1st & 2nd Class)	—	—	Kommodore
Captain	Capitaine de vaisseau	Capitani di vascello	Linienschiffskapitän
Commander	Capitaine de frégate	Capitano de fregata	Fregattenkapitän
Lieutenant Commander	Capitaine de corvette	Capitano de corvetta	Korvettenkapitän
Lieutenant	Lieutenant de vaisseau	Tenente di vascello	Linienschiffsleutnant
Sub Lieutenant	Enseigne de vaisseau	Sottotenente di vascello	Fregattenleutnant
	Aspirant de 1ère et 2e classe	Guardiamarina	Seefähnrich
Midshipman	—	Aspirante	Seekadett
Naval Cadet	Eleve de l'ecole navale	Allievo di marina	Seeaspirant

Note: The subject of equivalent ranks between different navies is far more complicated than it seems and certainly not as neat as a chart like this seems to imply. For example, there is disagreement about exact gradations, some authorities ranking a Fregattenkapitän and Capitano di fregata as equivalent to a junior Captain in the Royal Navy, and a Korvettenkapitän as the equal of a Royal Navy Commander. The rank of Lieutenant Commander in the Royal Navy and Capitaine de corvette in the French navy was only introduced during the war. Prior to this a distinction was made between Junior and Senior Lieutenants, the latter with more than eight years' seniority. The only German rank mentioned in the text, that of Kapitänleutnant, is the equivalent of an Austrian Linienschiffsleutnant and a pre-war Royal Navy Senior Lieutenant. Post-war, the rank seems to have been accepted as equivalent to a Lieutenant Commander.

In addition to the ranks of line officers there were a wide variety of technical, administrative, and medical ranks. The varieties of warrant officers, petty officers, and ratings were even more numerous. The only petty officer ranks mentioned in the text are usually pilots or observers.

NOTES

1. THE NAVAL WAR IN THE ADRIATIC

1. On Austro-Hungarian naval development in the late nineteenth century, see Lawrence Sondhaus, *The Naval Policy of Austria Hungary, 1867–1918: Navalism, Industrial Development and the Politics of Dualism* (West Lafayette, Ind.: Purdue University Press, 1994).

2. The Triple Alliance naval convention is discussed in Paul G. Halpern, *The Mediterranean Naval Situation, 1908–1914* (Cambridge, Mass.: Harvard University Press, 1971), chapter VIII, and in great detail with full texts of treaties in Mariano Gabriele, *Le convenzioni navali della Triplice* (Rome: Ufficio Storico della Marina Militare, 1969).

3. These points are discussed in Paul G. Halpern, *The Naval War in the Mediterranean, 1914–1918* (London and Annapolis: Allen & Unwin and Naval Institute Press, 1987), pp. 17–20, and idem, *Anton Haus: Österreich-Ungarns Grossadmiral* (Graz: Verlag Styria, 1998), pp. 147–57.

4. The most detailed account of French operations remains A. Thomazi, *La guerre navale dans l'Adriatique* (Paris: Payot, 1925).

5. A good introduction to the Adriatic naval war is Charles W. Koburger, Jr., *The Central Powers in the Adriatic, 1914–1918: War in a Narrow Sea* (Westport, Conn.: Praeger, 2001). See also Ezio Ferrante, *La grande guerra in Adriatico: Nel LXX anniversario della vittoria* (Rome: Ufficio Storico della Marina Militare, 1987).

6. For the opposition of General Joffre, chief of the army general staff, see J. J. C. Joffre, *Mémoires du Maréchal Joffre*. 2 volumes (Paris: Plon, 1932), vol. I, pp. 484–86; see also Adolphe Laurens, *Le Commandement naval en Méditerranée, 1914–1918* (Paris: Payot, 1931), pp. 52–56; and Thomazi, *Guerre navale dans l'Adriatique*, pp. 52–57. A summary of the arguments is in Halpern, *Naval War in the Mediterranean*, pp. 31–37.

7. The subject is thoroughly examined in Halpern, *Naval War in the Mediterranean*, pp. 69–75, 102–106.

8. Haus's memorandum is a classic exposition of a defensive strategy and printed in full in Hans Hugo Sokol, *Österreich-Ungarns Seekrieg* (Vienna: Amalthea Verlag,

1933), pp. 164–69. See also Erwin Sieche, "Die diplomatischen Aktivitäten rund um das Haus-Memorandum vom März 1915," *Marine—Gestern, Heute* 9, no. 3 (Sept. 1982), pp. 93–103; and Halpern, *Haus*, pp. 199–214.

9. German submarine operations in the Mediterranean can be followed in exhaustive detail in the relevant chapters of Rear Admiral Arno Spindler, *Der Handelskrieg mit U-Booten*, 5 volumes (Berlin [volume 5, Frankfurt am Main]: E. S. Mittler, 1932–66. Full accounts of the activities of all small *UB* and *UC* (minelayer) submarines are in Harald Bendert, *Die UB-Boote der Kaiserlichen Marine 1914–1918* (Hamburg, Berlin, and Bonn: E. S. Mittler, 2000) and idem, *Die UC-Boote der Kaiserlichen Marine 1914–1918* (Hamburg, Berlin, and Bonn: E. S. Mittler, 2001). Similar detail for Austrian submarines is in Wladimir Aichelburg, *Die Unterseeboote Österreich-Ungarns*, 2 vols. (Graz: Akademische Druck- u. Verlagsanstalt, 1981).

10. The British light cruiser *Dublin* had also been torpedoed and badly damaged by *U.4* on 9 June.

11. Revel's policy is given in Revel to Abruzzi, 30 July and 27 August 1915, Ufficio Storico della Marina Militare, Rome [hereafter cited as USM], Cartella 356/3.

12. There is detailed coverage of the action from the perspective of the different navies in Sokol, *Österreich-Ungarns Seekrieg*, pp. 250–63; Ufficio Storico, *La marina italiana nella grande guerra*, 8 vols. (Florence: Vallecchi, 1935–42), vol. 2, chap. 15; Naval Staff (Training and Staff Duties Division), *The Mediterranean, 1914–1915* (Admiralty [London], March 1923), pp. 216–25; Julian S. Corbett and Henry Newbolt, *History of the Great War: Naval Operations*, 5 vols. in 9 (London: Longmans, Green, 1920–31), vol. 4, pp. 106–17; and Thomazi, *Guerre navale dans l'Adriatique*, pp. 110–14.

13. Halpern, *Naval War in the Mediterranean*, p. 214.

14. See the discussion in Lothar Baumgartner, "Österreich-Ungarns Dünkirchen? Ein Gegenüberstellungen von Berichten zum Abtransport der serbischen Armee aus Albanien im Winter 1915/16," *Marine-Gestern, Heute* 6, no. 2 (June 1982), pp. 46–53.

15. Haus to AOK (*Armeeoberkommando*, the Austrian military high command), 28 February and 12 March 1916, Kriegsarchiv, Vienna, OK/MS VIII-1/1 ex 1917, no. 1118. See also Sokol, *Österreich-Ungarns Seekrieg*, pp. 394–400; and Halpern, *Naval War in the Mediterranean*, pp. 285–87.

16. Peter Schupita, *Die k.u.k. Seeflieger* (Koblenz: Bernard & Graefe Verlag, 1983), p. 192.

17. Extensive detail on the craft is in Erminio Bagnasco, *I Mas e le motosiluranti italiane, 1906–1966* (Rome: Ufficio Storico della Marina Militare, 1967). The operations are described in Ufficio Storico, *Marina italiana*, vol. 3, pp. 50–55.

18. Ufficio Storico, *Marina italiana*, vol. 4, pp. 378–83.

19. These totals include submarines in the Black Sea, en route or preparing to leave Germany. Halpern, *Naval War in the Mediterranean*, pp. 249–53. Dates of *U.35*'s cruise and tonnage sunk is taken from Spindler, *Handelskrieg mit U-booten*, vol. 3, pp. 155–56, 161–63.

20. The Austrian record of the Schloss Pless conference is in Note to Neutrals and Maritime-Technical Portion of the Agreement of Pless, 26 Jan. 1917, OK/MS VIII-1/19 ex 1917, no. 473; memorandum by Rodler [Haus's chief of staff], 31 Jan. 1917, ibid., no. 662. The German record is in National Archives and Records Service [hereafter cited as NARS]. Microfilm publication T-1022, Roll 804, PG 75268. Summaries are in Halpern, *Haus*, pp. 323–30; and idem, *Naval War in the Mediterranean*, pp. 308–10.

21. On the death of Haus, see Halpern, *Haus*, pp. 330–31. For a brief biography of Njegovan, see Heinrich Bayer von Bayersburg, *Unter der k.u.k. Kriegsflagge, 1914–1918* (Vienna: Bergland Verlag, 1959), pp. 21–26.

22. Figures are from Spindler, *Handelskrieg mit U-booten*, vol. 5, pp. 88, 390; Aichelburg, *Unterseeboote Österreich-Ungarns*, vol. 2, pp. 490–91.

2. THE ALLIES IN THE SOUTHERN ADRIATIC

1. These ideas were forcibly expressed by Thaon di Revel (*Capo di stato maggiore*) in Revel to Abruzzi, 8 May 1915, USM, Cartella 356/1.

2. The negotiations are examined in depth in Paul G. Halpern, "The Anglo-French-Italian Naval Convention of 1915," *Historical Journal* 13, no. 1 (1970), pp. 106–29; and Mariano Gabriele, "Le convenzione navale italo-franco-britannica del 10 maggio 1915," *Nuova antologia*, vols. 492–94, fasc. 1972–73 (Apr.–May 1965). The negotiations are summarized in Halpern, *Naval War in the Mediterranean*, pp. 96–99; and Ferrante, *Grande guerra in Adriatico*, pp. 20–24.

3. The text of the treaty (seven articles and an eight-point codicil) is reproduced in Ufficio storico, *Marina italiana*, vol 1, pp. 435–39; and Thomazi, *Guerre navale dans l'Adriatique*, pp. 82–85.

4. Thursby to Admiral Sir Henry B. Jackson [first sea lord], n.d. [late May 1915], in Paul G. Halpern, ed., *The Royal Navy in the Mediterranean, 1915–1918*, Publications of the Navy Records Society, no. 126 (Aldershot: Temple Smith, 1987), document no. 4, p. 17.

5. Midshipman Charles F. Drage, diary, 26 June 1915, *Royal Navy in the Mediterranean*, document no. 8, p. 22.

6. Details from R. A. Burt, *British Battleships, 1889–1904* (Annapolis, Md.: Naval Institute Press, 1988), pp. 172–73, 192–93, 227–28.

7. Thursby to Limpus, 12 June 1915, *Royal Navy in the Mediterranean*, document no. 7, p. 22. *Topaze*, a third ship of the "Gem" class, also saw service in the Adriatic.

8. Thursby to Jackson, 12 May 1916, *Royal Navy in the Mediterranean*, document no. 75, pp. 143–45.

9. Kerr to Jackson, 16 June 1916, ibid., document no. 83, p. 157.

10. Kerr to Limpus, 10 Sept. 1916, ibid., document no. 94, p. 173; Kerr to Jackson, 27 Oct. 1916, ibid., document no. 98, p. 183; Kerr to Jellicoe, 12 March 1917, Jellicoe MSS., British Library, London, Addl. MSS. 49036.

11. Cited in Halpern, *Naval War in the Mediterranean*, p. 28.

12. French order of battle is in Thomazi, *Guerre navale dans l'Adriatique*, pp. 220–23; data on French warships is in Jean Labayle-Couhat, *French Warships of World War I* (London: Ian Allan, 1974), pp. 101–15, 140–43. An exhaustive study of the *Pluvoîse* class is in Gérard Garier, *L'Odyssée technique et humaine du sous-marin en France*, vol. 2: *Des* Emeraude *(1905–1906) au* Charles Brun *(1908–1913)* (Nantes: Marines édition, 1998), chapter III.

13. On de Cacqueray and Franco-Italian relations at Brindisi, see Thursby to Jackson, 12 May 1916, *Royal Navy in the Mediterranean*, document no. 75, pp. 143–45; and Halpern, *Mediterranean Naval Situation*, pp. 271–72, 281–84.

14. Thursby to Jackson, 12 May 1916, *Royal Navy in the Mediterranean*, document no. 75, p. 143.

15. A. Thomazi, *La guerre navale dans la Méditerranée* (Paris: Payot, 1929), pp. 51–58.

16. A sixth dreadnought, the *Leonardo da Vinci*, capsized and sank at Taranto on 2 August 1916 following a fire and explosion, possibly as a result of sabotage. The Italians lost three battleships within a year. The pre-dreadnought *Benedetto Brin* was lost to a fire and explosion at Brindisi on 27 September 1915, and her sister ship the *Regina*

Margherita was mined and sunk off Valona on 11 December 1916. Ferrante, *La grande guerra in Adriatico,* pp. 62–63.

17. Aldo Fraccaroli, *Italian Warships of World War I* (London: Ian Allan, 1970), pp. 49–50.

18. Ibid., pp. 51–54.

19. Italian dispositions taken from Ufficio Storico, *Marina italiana,* vol. 4, pp. 429–35. Brindisi also had two squadriglie of *Mas* boats and approximately fourteen mine-sweepers.

20. Ufficio Storico, *Marina italiana,* vol. 4, pp. 378–81. The *Poerio* class, completed in 1915, were classified by the Italians as *esploratori*. Approximately 911–1,028 tons, they would in other navies be considered destroyers. The *Nullos* were 770-ton destroyers, completed in 1915; the *Ardito* class 595-ton destroyers, completed in 1913–1914.

21. Naval Staff (Training and Staff Duties Division), *The Mediterranean, 1914–1915,* Naval Staff Monographs (Historical) no. 21 (March 1923), pp. 204–205. Copy in Public Record Office, Kew [hereafter referred to as PRO], ADM 186/618.

22. E. Keble Chatterton, *Seas of Adventures: The Story of the Naval Operations in the Mediterranean, Adriatic and Aegean* (London: Hurst & Blackett, 1936), p. 65.

23. Ibid., pp. 66–67.

24. Thursby to Limpus, 28 Sept. 1915, *Royal Navy in the Mediterranean,* document no. 11, pp. 25–26.

25. Chatterton, *Seas of Adventures,* p. 22. It is not clear if this was the second ship referred to as *Adriatico* by Thursby.

26. Thursby to Limpus, 28 Sept. and 17 Oct. 1915, *Royal Navy in the Mediterranean,* documents nos. 11 and 12, pp. 26–27; Naval Staff, *Mediterranean 1914–1915,* p. 205. The exact organization changed somewhat in October when eighteen drifters were detached for work at the Dardanelles.

27. Chatterton, *Seas of Adventure,* pp. 74–75.

28. Thursby to Limpus, 17 Oct. 1915, *Royal Navy in the Mediterranean,* document no. 12, p. 27; Thursby to Admiralty, 5 January 1916, ibid., document no. 32, pp. 74–75.

29. Naval Staff, *Mediterranean, 1914–1915,* pp. 206–207; Thursby to Jackson, 19 Oct. 1915, *Royal Navy in the Mediterranean,* document no. 14, pp. 31–32; Chatterton, *Seas of Adventures,* pp. 99–100.

30. Thursby to Jackson, 10 Mar. 1916, *Royal Navy in the Mediterranean,* document no. 58, p. 114.

31. Thursby to de Robeck, 16 Mar. 1916, *Royal Navy in the Mediterranean,* document no. 62, p. 120; Halpern, *Mediterranean Naval Situation,* pp. 278–79.

32. Thursby to Limpus, 6 May 1916, *Royal Navy in the Mediterranean,* document no. 74, p. 142.

33. For the argument that Kerr's relationship with the King and his desire not to compromise him may have had some role in the escape of the *Goeben* and *Breslau* to Turkish waters at the beginning of the war, see Geoffrey Miller, *Superior Force: The conspiracy behind the escape of the* Goeben *and* Breslau (Hull: University of Hull Press, 1996), chapter XII. Kerr's bias in favor of Constantine is most evident in his writings. See Admiral Mark Kerr, *Land, Sea and Air* (London: Longmans, Green, 1927) and idem, *The Navy in My Time* (London: Rich & Cowan, 1933).

34. Wemyss to Keyes, 17 July 1916, in Paul G. Halpern, ed., *The Keyes Papers,* vol. I: *1914–1918,* Publications of the Navy Records Society, vol. 117 (London: Navy Records Society, 1972), document no. 162, p. 366.

35. Kerr to Jackson, 29 May 1916, *Royal Navy in the Mediterranean,* document no. 79, pp. 150–51.

36. Kerr to Jackson, 2 and 8 June 1916, ibid., document nos. 80 and 81, pp. 151–55. On the Austrian raid, see Sokol, *Österreich-Ungarns Seekrieg*, p. 361.

37. Antonio Casale and Marina Cattaruzza, *Sotto i mari del mondo: La Whitehead, 1875–1900* (Rome and Bari: Editori Laterza, 1990), pp. 107–108; and Edwyn Gray, *The Devil's Device: Robert Whitehead and the History of the Torpedo.* Revised edition (Annapolis: Naval Institute Press, 1991), p. 165.

38. Kerr to Jackson, 8 June 1916, ibid., document no. 81, p. 154.

39. Kerr to Limpus, 10 Sept. 1916, ibid., document no. 94, p. 174; Chatterton, *Seas of Adventure*, pp. 225–26; Corbett and Newbolt, *Naval Operations*, vol. 4, p. 288. Data on the MLs is from F. J. Dittmar and J. J. Colledge, *British Warships, 1914–1919* (London: Ian Allan, 1972), p. 136.

40. These events are summarized in Halpern, *Naval War in the Mediterranean*, p. 280; full accounts are in Thomazi, *Guerre navale dans l'Adriatique*, pp. 127, 135; Ufficio Storico, *Marina italiana*, vol. 3, pp. 301–302, 313–14; Sokol, *Österreich-Ungarns Seekrieg*, pp. 362–63, 427–28.

41. Kerr to Limpus, 10 Sept. 1916, *Royal Navy in the Mediterranean*, document no. 94, p. 174.

42. The Otranto conference is summarized in Halpern, *Naval War in the Mediterranean*, pp. 281–84. For Kerr's reactions, see also Kerr to Jackson, 27 Oct. and 4 Nov. 1916, *Royal Navy in the Mediterranean*, document no. 98 and 99, pp. 182–85. Italian views are in Ufficio Storico, *Marina italiana*, vol. 3, pp. 322–26.

43. Halpern, *Naval War in the Mediterranean*, pp. 284–85.

44. Illustrative of the polyglot nature of the *k.u.k. Kriegsmarine*, Nowotny after the war became the first head of the navy in the newly independent Poland. Sondhaus, *Naval Policy of Austria-Hungary*, p. 370.

45. Quoted in Corbett and Newbolt, *Naval Operations*, vol. 4, p. 64.

46. Summarized from accounts in Sokol, *Österreich-Ungarns Seekrieg*, pp. 367–75; Thomazi, *Guerre navale dans l'Adriatique*, pp. 138–39; Ufficio Storico, *Marina italiana*, vol. 3, pp. 520–33.

47. Agenda and Conclusions, Allied Naval Conference, London, 23–24 Jan. 1917, pp. 3–4, PRO, ADM 137/1420.

48. Ibid.

49. On these and other questions at the conference, see Halpern, *Naval War in the Mediterranean*, pp. 326–33.

50. On Revel, see Ezio Ferrante, *Il Grande Ammiraglio Paolo Thaon di Revel* (Rome: *Rivista Marittima* [Supplement to No. 8/9, August/September], 1989), pp. 68–76; idem, *La grande guerra in Adriatico*, pp. 62–65, 70–75; and Halpern, *Naval War in the Mediterranean*, pp. 333–38. Revel summarized his policy to the King's aide-de-camp General Ugo Brusati in: "Compiti impellenti che debbono prevalere su ogni considerazione di ordine politico o di altri ordini," n.d., and Revel to Brusati, 20 February 1917, Rome, Archivio Centrale dello Stato, Carte Brusati/2 (VIII-17-61). See also Thaon di Revel, "Il primi cinque mesi dal ritorno alla carica di capo di stato maggiore della marina," n.d., USM, Cartella 738/2.

51. Kerr to Admiralty, 20 April 1917, *Royal Navy in the Mediterranean*, document no. 123, pp. 242–43.

52. For detailed description, see Directions for "De-Quillacq-Fromaget's Sweep" and "Project for Deep Water Barrage" [translation] with extensive minutes by staff officers at the Admiralty, 26 Feb.–4 Apr. 1917, PRO, ADM 137/1416. See also Hubert de Blois, *La Guerre des Mines dans la Marine Française* (Brest and Paris: Editions de la Cité, 1982), pp. 44–45.

53. Chatterton, *Seas of Adventure*, p. 260.

54. Minutes by Learmonth, 26 and 27 Feb. and 12 Mar. 1917, Duff, 3 Mar. 1917, and Oliver, 4 Apr. 1917; Admiralty to Lostende, 13 Mar. 1917, PRO, ADM 137/1416.

55. Commodore Heneage, "Better Protection of Ships in the Mediterranean Sea," n.d., Minutes of the Corfu Conference (30 April 1917), Appendix II, PRO, ADM 137/1421.

56. Minutes of the Corfu Conference, 29 and 30 April 1917, ibid.

57. Heneage to de Robeck, 3 April 1917, *Royal Navy in the Mediterranean*, document no. 120, p. 237.

58. Kerr to Admiralty, 20 April 1917 and minute by G. Hope, 26 April 1917, ibid., document no. 123, pp. 242–43.

59. Admiralty to Admiral de Lostende [French naval attaché], 13 Mar. 1917, PRO, ADM 137/1416.

60. Minutes by Hope and Oliver, 26 April 1917, and by Jellicoe, 27 April 1917, *Royal Navy in the Mediterranean*, document no. 123, pp. 243–45.

3. THE AUSTRIANS PREPARE AN ATTACK

1. On indicator nets, trawlers, and drifters, see Archibald Hurd, *History of the Great War: The Merchant Navy*, 3 vols. (London: John Murray, 1921–29), vol. 1, pp. 369, 372–73.

2. Chatterton, *Seas of Adventures*, pp. 63–64.

3. There are no losses besides the Austrian *U.6* actually credited to indicator nets in the analyses of losses given by Professor Grant, although certainly those nets might have been a contributing factor in other losses. See Robert M. Grant, *U-Boats Destroyed: The Effect of Anti-Submarine Warfare, 1914–1918* (London: Putnam, 1964), pp. 159–63.

4. *U.6* under Falkhausen had been responsible for sinking the French destroyer *Renaudin* off Cape Durazzo on 18 March.

5. Austrian accounts are in Aichelburg, *Die Unterseeboote Österreich-Ungarns*, vol. 2, pp. 302–303, and Sokol, *Österreich-Ungarns Seekrieg*, pp. 357–58. British versions are in Hurd, *The Merchant Navy*, vol. 2, pp. 169–70, and Chatterton, *Seas of Adventures*, pp. 147–50. The Italian report is in Ufficio Storico, *Marina italiana*, vol. 3, pp. 299–301. There is also a discrepancy in the location of the sinking. Austrian sources place it in the middle of the Otranto Straits at 40° 10′ N in a depth of 800 meters. British and Italian sources say twelve nautical miles east-northeast of Cape Otranto.

6. Ufficio Storico, *Marina italiana*, vol. 3, p. 291.

7. The only other victim, the German *UB.53*, was mined and subsequently sunk on 3 August 1918 because the submarine commander did not realize the Franco-Italian fixed mine-net had recently been extended. This might be considered a failure of intelligence. Had the commander known of the recent extension, he might easily have avoided it. Spindler, *Handelskrieg mit U-booten*, vol. 5, p. 201, and Grant, *U-Boats Destroyed*, pp. 132–33.

8. Bendert, *Die UB-Boote der Kaiserlichen Marine*, p. 118, and Paul Kemp, *U-Boats Destroyed: German Submarine Losses in the World Wars* (Annapolis: Naval Institute Press, 1997), p. 20.

9. Heneage to Rear Admiral commanding British Adriatic Squadron, 22 April 1917, PRO, ADM 137/1414; Procès Verbale, Corfu Conference, 30 Apr. 1917, ADM 137/1421. See also Chatterton, *Seas of Adventure*, pp. 256, 259.

10. Linienschiffsleutnant Gaston Vio, "Bericht über Mission mit *U.39*," 4 July 1916, OK/MS VIII-1/14 ex 1916, no. 4219, Kriegstagebuch *U.39*, ibid.

11. Report of Linienschiffsleutnant Dürrigl and copy of Kriegstagebuch *UB.46*, 23 July 1916, OK/MS VIII-1/14 ex 1916, no. 5052.

12. Kophamel to Admiralstab, 13 July 1916, and endorsement by Kophamel to Kriegstagbuch *UB.42*, 8–30 June 1916, NARS, T-1022, Roll 12, PG 61801.

13. Admiralstab, "Tätigkeit der Unterseeboote im Mittelmeer," 9 Feb. 1917, NARS, T-1022, Roll 804, PG 75268.

14. Figures are culled from Spindler, *Handelskrieg mit U-booten*, vol. 3, pp. 388, 390; ibid., vol. 4, pp. 194–95, 376–77.

15. See Halpern, *Naval War in the Mediterranean*, pp. 307–12.

16. Njegovan to Armeeoberkommando, 24 Feb. 1917, OK/MS VIII-1/1 ex 1917, no. 1046.

17. Njegovan to Kailer, 7 March 1917, Kriegsarchiv, Nachlass Kailer, B/242.

18. See Aichelburg, *Unterseeboote Österreich-Ungarns*, vol. I, pp. 92–100, 110–17.

19. Erich Heyssler, "The Memoirs of Erich Heyssler," translated by Inge Baker, unpublished memoir in the possession of the family (Graz, 1935, English translation, 1997), p. 237.

20. The plan is discussed in Halpern, *Naval War in the Mediterrranean*, pp. 69–70.

21. Biographical details are from Heinrich Bayer von Bayersburg, *Unter der k.u.k. Kriegsflagge*, pp. 27–30, and Thomas Sakmyster, *Hungary's Admiral on Horseback: Miklós Horthy, 1918–1944* (Boulder, Colo.: East European Monographs, 1994), pp. 1–9.

22. Heyssler, "Memoirs," p. 237.

23. Admiral Nicholas Horthy, *Memoirs* (London: Hutchinson, 1956), pp. 80–81.

24. Ibid., p. 81.

25. Sokol, *Österreich-Ungarns Seekrieg*, pp. 355, 363.

26. Heyssler, "Memoirs," p. 237.

27. Ibid., p. 250.

28. Ibid.

29. Ship's data are culled from *Conway's All the World's Fighting Ships, 1906–1921* (London: Conway Maritime Press, 1985), p. 336; René Greger, *Austro-Hungarian Warships of World War I* (London: Ian Allan, 1976), pp. 33–35; Erwin Sieche, *Kreuzer und Kreuzerprojekte der k.u.k. Kriegsmarine, 1889–1918* (Hamburg: E. S. Mittler & Sohn, 2002), pp. 140–45; and Lothar Baumgartner and Erwin Sieche, *Die Schiffe der k.u.k. Kriegsmarine im Bild*, Vol. 2: *1896–1918* (Vienna: Verlagsbuchhandlung Stöhr, 2001), pp. 104–106. Heyssler's delighted impressions of handling the *Helgoland* are in his "Memoirs," p. 252.

30. Heyssler, "Memoirs," pp. 251–52.

31. During the summer of 2002 excerpts from what is presumably this film were being shown on a continuous basis in the Marinesaal of the Heeresgeschichtliches Museum in Vienna. They provide the visitor with an interesting view of the *Helgoland* in motion shortly before the raid. See also Roger Smither, ed., *Imperial War Museum Film Catalogue*. Vol. 1: *The First World War Archive* (Westport: Greenwood Press, 1994), p. 266.

32. Kreuzerflottillenkommando [Kontreadmiral Hansa], "Angriff auf die Überwachungslinie LEUCA-FANO," 13 May 1917, OK/MS VIII-1/1 ex 1917, no. 2716. An abbreviated version of the order is reproduced in Sokol, *Österreich-Ungarns Seekrieg*, p. 376.

33. See short sketch in Heinrich Bayer von Bayersburg, *Österreichs Admirale, 1867–1918* (Vienna: Bergland Verlag, 1962), pp. 111–12.

34. Baumgartner and Sieche, *Schiff der k.u.k. Kriegsmarine*, pp. 132–33; Franz F. Bilzer, *Die Torpedoschiffe und Zerstörer der k.u.k. Kriegsmarine 1867–1918* (Graz: H. Weishaupt Verlag, 1990), pp. 108–15, 124–27.

35. Kreuzerflottillenkommando, "Angriff auf die Überwachungslinie."

36. Ibid.; on German participation, see Kophamel to Admiralstab, 11 May 1917, NARS, T-1022, Roll 731, PG 75298; submarine data is from Bendert, *Die UC-Boote der Kaiserlichen Marine 1914–1918*, pp. 102–103, 197. As a minor historical note, for approximately six months in 1918 *UC.25* would be commanded by then Kapitänleutnant Karl Dönitz, the future commander of German submarines and Hitler's chosen successor in the Second World War.

37. Sieche, *Kreuzer und Kreuzerprojekte der k.u.k. Kriegsmarine*, pp. 89–97; Franz F. Bilzer, *Die Torpedoboote der k.u.k. Kriegsmarine von 1875–1918* (Graz: H. Weishaupt Verlag, 1984), pp. 115–27.

38. Kontreadmiral Hansa to Flottenkommando, 17 May 1917, OK/MS -1/1 ex 1917, no. 2716.

39. Sketch in Bayer von Bayersburg, *Unter der k.u.k. Kriegsflagge*, pp. 42–47.

40. Heyssler, "Memoirs," p. 253.

4. THE ATTACK ON THE DRIFTERS

1. Corsi to Capitano di fregata Villarey [Italian naval attaché in London], 25 March 1917, and Corsi to Baron Sonnino [Italian foreign minister], 25 March 1917, USM, Cartella 740/1.

2. Memorandum by Admiral Corsi [translated by the Italian naval attaché], 6 April 1917, PRO, ADM 137/1414.

3. Ibid. The six *Calliope*-class (3,750 tons) ships had been launched between December 1914 and March 1916 and were the first class of light cruisers to be oil burners. They were capable of twenty-nine knots and armed with two six-inch and eight four-inch guns or four four-inch and one four-inch anti-aircraft guns. Dittmar and Colledge, *British Warships, 1914–1919*, p. 48.

4. Minutes by Oliver, 8 April, and Jellicoe, 9 and 11 April 1917; Admiralty to Villarey, 12 April 1917, ADM 137/1414. On the question of hospital ships in the Mediterranean, see Halpern, *Naval War in the Mediterranean*, pp. 316–24.

5. Information on British ships is from Captain G. W. Vivian [senior naval officer Brindisi] to Rear Admiral commanding British Adriatic Squadron, 18 May 1917, PRO, ADM 137/782, f.331b. Information on Italian forces is from Ufficio Storico, *Marina italiana*, vol. 4, pp. 496–97.

6. Ufficio del Capo di Stato Maggiore della Marina (Ufficio Storico), *Cronistoria Documentata della Guerra Marittima Italo-Austriaca, 1915–1918*. Collezione: *Preparezione dei mezzi e loro impiego*. Fascicolo VII: *L'Aviazione marittima durante la guerra* ([Rome], n.d.), pp. 89–90. Copy in PRO, ADM 137/798.

7. Lucien Morareau et al., *L'Aviation Maritime Française Pendant la Grande Guerre (hydravions et avions)* (Paris: Association pour la researche de documentation sur l'histoire de l'aéronautique navale, 1999), pp. 257–63.

8. Carlo De Risio, *L'Aviazione di Marina* (Rome: Ufficio Storico della Marina Militare, 1995), pp. 43–45; Morareau et al, *L'Aviation Maritime Française*, pp. 362–70.

9. Ufficio Storico, *Marina italiana*, vol. 4, pp. 497–98.

10. Ibid., pp. 493–98; Thomazi, *La guerre navale dans l'Adriatique*, pp. 147–49.

11. A. N. Heneage [Commodore of Adriatic Patrols] to Rear Admiral commanding British Adriatic Squadron, 3 June 1917, and Appendix II, PRO, ADM 137/782, ff.314–16.

12. Signals officer, HMS *Liverpool* to Captain G. W. Vivian, 17 May 1917, ADM 137/782; Vivian to Kerr, 18 May 1917, *Royal Navy in the Mediterranean*, document no. 127, pp. 256–57. On *Sommerzeit*, see Wladimir Aichelburg, "Zeitrechnung im Krieg 1914–

1918," *Marine-Gestern, Heute* 5, no. 1 (March 1978), pp. 29–30. The *k.u.k. Kriegsmarine* also followed the British practice of using the twelve-hour clock and A.M. and P.M., v.M and n.M respectively, rather than the modern military twenty-four-hour clock used for consistency in this text.

13. Sokol gives the times as: 0306 commencement of attack; 0315 end of attack; and 0405 the Austrian destroyers in a position fifteen nautical miles west of Saseno. The Italian official history puts the times at: 0306 Austrian course alteration to 241°; 0326 commencement of attack; 0345 end of attack; and 0445 Austrians west of Saseno. See Ufficio Storico, *Marina italiana*, vol. 4, pp. 498–99, note 1; and Sokol, *Österreich-Ungarns Seekrieg*, pp. 377–78.

14. Liechtenstein to Kreuzerflottillenkommando, 16 May 1917, and Kriegs-Tage-buch of *Csepel* and *Balaton*, 14–15 May 1917, OK/MS VIII-1/1 ex 1917, no. 2716. The logs of both *Csepel* and *Balaton* state they opened fire at 0326. Liechtenstein in his Ge-fechtsbericht merely states that he sighted and engaged the convoy shortly after mak-ing the course alteration at 0306 and this vagueness may be the source of the discrep-ancy in Sokol. I am indebted to Mr. Erwin Sieche for providing me with photocopies of the log entries.

15. Details of the attack on the convoy are drawn from Ufficio Storico, *Marina itali-ana*, vol. 4, pp. 498–504; Sokol, *Österreich-Ungarns Seekrieg*, pp. 377–78.

16. Ufficio Storico, *Marina italiana*, vol. 4, pp. 504–505.

17. Ibid., pp. 505–506, 514–15; Ufficio Storico, *Cronistoria Documentata*, Fascicolo VII, pp. 136–37; Sokol, *Österreich-Ungarns Seekrieg*, p. 381; Horthy, *Memoirs*, p. 81. The time of the FBA's return is given as 0730 in the *Cronistoria Documentata*.

18. Ufficio Storico, *Marina italiana*, vol. 4, pp. 503, note 1, 506.

19. Heneage to Rear Admiral commanding British Adriatic Squadron, 3 June 1917, PRO, ADM 137/782.

20. Heyssler gives the time of separation as 0215 in his memoirs; Sokol gives 0310. Heyssler states that in writing his memoirs he used the notes of his navigation officer who stood next to him on the bridge, watch in hand carefully noting the time of each phase of the action, as ordered. He may also have been able to consult Sokol's semi-official history published in 1933. Heyssler, "Memoirs," p. 255; Sokol, *Österreich-Ungarns Seekrieg*, p. 379.

21. Once again this does not coincide with the times provided in Commodore He-neage's report. They seem to indicate it was both "N" and "C" divisions that were at-tacked first at 0315. In Heyssler's account the attack on "C" came first. This sequence is supported by the reports from the three cruisers cited in Sokol. Here the times they opened fire on the drifters were given as: *Helgoland* about 0433; *Saida* about 0420; and *Novara* 0507. See Sokol, *Österreich-Ungarns Seekrieg*, pp. 379–81.

22. The account of the action is drawn from the report of the Commodore of Adri-atic Patrols, A. W. Heneage, to Rear Admiral commanding British Adriatic Squadron, 3 June 1917, PRO, ADM 137/782; Sokol, *Österreich-Ungarns Seekrieg*, pp. 379–81; Ufficio Storico, *Marina italiana*, vol. 4, pp. 507–11; and Heyssler, "Memoirs," pp. 253–55.

23. Corbett and Newbolt, *Naval Operations*, vol. 4, p. 300. Newbolt's account is based heavily on Heneage to Rear Admiral commanding British Adriatic Squadron, 3 June 1917, Appendix V, "Recommendations sent to Admiralty respecting action of cer-tain drifters," PRO, ADM 137/782.

24. In Austrian naval parlance, the GDO or *Gesamtdetailoffizier*.

25. Details of the drifter's armament taken from Dittmar and Colledge, *British War-ships, 1914–1919*, pp. 243, 255, 262. *Young Linnett* is also listed as having a 25mm gun.

26. Chatterton, *Seas of Adventures*, p. 264. The author also reproduces interesting photographs of the damage to the *Floandi*, *Gowan Lea*, and *Jean*.

27. The account of actions of the drifters is based on "Recommendations sent to Admiralty respecting action of certain drifters," Appendix V of Commodore Heneage's report, loc. cit.

28. Horthy, *Memoirs*, p. 81.

29. Heneage to Rear Admiral commanding British Adriatic Squadron, 3 June 1917, PRO, ADM 137/782.

30. Ufficio Storico, *Marina italiana*, vol. 4, p. 509. A much higher and surely excessive figure of one officer and seventy men killed is given in Chatterton, *Seas of Adventures*, p. 263.

31. Heneage to Rear Admiral commanding British Adriatic Squadron, 3 June 1917, PRO, ADM 137/782.

5. THE PURSUIT

1. Ufficio Storico, *Marina italiana*, vol. 4, pp. 512–13.

2. Ibid., p. 512; Thomazi, *La guerre navale dans l'Adriatique*, p. 149.

3. Giorgio Giorgerini and Augusto Nanni, *Gli incrociatori italiani, 1861–1964* (Rome: Ufficio Storico della Marina Militare, 1964), pp. 159–64.

4. Ufficio Storico, *Marina italiana*, vol. 4, p. 513. There is a discrepancy between the time given for signals in the text and that given in Appendix A, a list of the principal signals transmitted during the action. This is possibly due to the difference between the time the signal was sent and the time it was subsequently decoded and logged, ibid., p. 572.

5. Ammiraglio Luigi Slaghek-Fabbri, *Con gl'inglesi in Adriatico* (Rome: Edizioni Ardita, 1934), pp. 183–84. There is a discrepancy between Italian and British accounts as to the time of sailing. The British give 0503.

6. Acton to Comando in Capo [Thaon di Revel], 19 May 1917, copy and translation in PRO, ADM 137/782.

7. Douglas Morris, *Cruisers of the Royal and Commonwealth Navies* (Liskeard, Cornwall: Maritime Books, 1987), pp. 120–22; Robert Wall, *The Story of H.M.S. Bristol* (Bristol: City of Bristol District Council, 1986), pp. 26–30.

8. Vivian to Rear Admiral Mark Kerr, 11 June 1917, with enclosed report from *Liverpool*'s engineer lieutenant commander, PRO, ADM 137/782.

9. Paul G. Halpern, *A Naval History of World War I* (Annapolis and London: Naval Institute Press, 1994), p. 372.

10. Ammiraglio di Squadra Giuseppe Fioravanzo et al., *I cacciatorpediniere italiani, 1900–1966* (Rome: Ufficio Storico della Marina Militare, 1966), pp. 125–32, 140–42.

11. Morris, *Cruisers of the Royal and Commonwealth Navies*, pp. 124–25.

12. HMS *Dartmouth*, log, 15 May 1917, PRO, ADM 53/39501.

13. Ufficio Storico, *Marina italiana*, vol. 4, p. 513; Slaghek-Fabbri, *Con gl'inglesi*, p. 183.

14. Addison to Crampton, 28 May 1917, reproduced in *Royal Navy in the Mediterranean, 1915–1918*, document no. 129, p. 260. There is a discrepancy between British and Italian sources. In his report Acton states he did fly his flag. Acton to Comando in Capo, 19 May 1917, PRO, ADM 137/782.

15. Fioravanzo et al., *I cacciatorpediniere italiani*, pp. 149–51, 153–54. Both *Schiaffino* and *Acerbi* were destined to be lost in the Second World War.

16. *Bristol*'s log lists *Aquila* as leaving Brindisi in company with the other ships at 0536. The Italian official history indicates she sailed later, at 0600, and joined the oth-

ers after an hour and forty minutes. However, the Ufficio Storico then states that Acton's force had also joined with *Bristol* by 0640. The logs of *Dartmouth* and *Bristol* seem to indicate this juncture took place at 0712 or 0715. Ufficio Storico, *Marina italiana*, vol. 4, p. 519; HMS *Dartmouth*, log, 15 May 1917, ADM 53/39501; HMS *Bristol*, log, 15 May 1917, ADM 53/36144.

17. Franco Bargoni, ed., *Esploratori, fregate, corvette ed avvisi italiani* (Rome: Ufficio Storico della Marina Militare, 1970), pp. 249–66. The ship was secretly transferred to the Spanish nationalist navy in October 1937.

18. HMS *Bristol*, log, 15 May 1917, ADM 53/36144; Ufficio Storico, *Marina italiana*, vol. 4, p. 519.

19. Bargoni, *Esplatori, fregate, corvette ed avvisi italiani*, pp. 221–42. The *Mirabello* was also a long-lived ship, surviving the Second World War and not struck from the naval list until 1946.

20. Labayle-Couhat, *French Warships of World War I*, pp. 101–11. For a full account from a technical point of view of the different "800-ton" French destroyers, see Henri Le Masson, *Histoire du torpilleur en France* (Paris: Academie de la Marine, n.d. [1966]), chapter IX.

21. Thomazi, *Guerre navale dans l'Adriatique*, pp. 97, 138.

22. Ufficio Storico, *Marina italiana*, vol. 4, pp. 513–16, 573; Sokol, *Österreich-Ungarns Seekrieg*, pp. 381–82, 391; Aichelburg, *Die Unterseeboote Österreich-Ungarns*, vol. 2, p. 276.

23. Heyssler, "Memoirs," p. 255. Heyssler also reported the enemy destroyers as having turned on a parallel course before the exchange of fire.

24. Heyssler, "Memoirs," pp. 257–58. Heyssler mentions two aircraft coming from astern. The Ufficio Storico account mentions only one. Sokol, writing from Austrian reports, also cites two. See Sokol, *Österreich-Ungarns Seekrieg*, p. 382.

25. I am indebted to Robert Feuilloy, Secrétaire Général de l'ARDHAN [Association pour la recherche de documentation sur l'histoire de l'Aéronautique Navale] for this information. See also Morareau et al., *L'aviation maritime française pendant la grande guerre*, pp. 261–63.

26. Walter Zanoskar, "Die Aktion S.M.S. *Novara* vom 14–15 Mai 1917," Oedl MSS., copy in possession of Mr. Erwin Sieche.

27. Data from Schupita, *Die k.u.k. Seeflieger*, pp. 72, 89, 256. For a critical analysis of Austro-Hungarian aviation, although not strictly naval, see John H. Morrow, *German Air Power in World War I* (Lincoln and London: University of Nebraska Press, 1982), chapter VIII.

28. Linienschiffsleutnant Konjović, "Fliegertätigkeit," 16 May 1917, OK/MS VIII-1/1 ex 1917, no. 2716.

29. Fregattenkapitän Liechtenstein to Kreuzerflottillenkommando, 16 May 1917, ibid.

30. Acton to Comando in Capo, 19 May 1917, PRO, ADM 137/782.

31. Ibid. See also Ufficio Storico, *Marina italiana*, vol. 4, pp. 526–29.

32. Schupita, *Die k.u.k. Seeflieger*, pp. 34, 71, 256. On Weichmann's subsequent activity with army aviation, see Peter M. Grosz, George Haddow, and Peter Schiemer, *Austro-Hungarian Army Aircraft of World War One* (Mountain View, Calif.: Flying Machines Press, 1993), pp. 191, 264, 339, 458.

33. Ufficio Storico, *Marina italiana*, vol. 4, p. 530. See also Vivian to Rear Admiral Kerr, 24 May 1917, PRO, ADM 137/782. Vivian corrected earlier reports that it had been *Aquila*'s after oil tanks that were on fire.

34. Ufficio Storico, *Marina italiana*, vol. 4, pp. 530–31.

35. Gérard Garier, *L'odyssée technique et humaine du sous-marin en France*.Vol. 3 (part 2): *A l'épreuve de la Grande Guerre* (Nantes: Marines édition, 2002), pp. 91–92, 116. *Bernouilli's* luck ran out the following year. The submarine did not return from a patrol in February 1918, probably mined off Durazzo sometime between the 10th and 13th.

36. Konjović, "Fliegertätigkeit"; Liechtenstein to Kreuzerflottillenkommando, 16 May 1917, OK/MS VIII-1/1 ex 1917, no. 2716.

37. Schupita, *Die k.u.k. Seeflieger*, pp. 68–70, 87–88.

38. Horthy, Gefechtsbericht, 17 May 1917, OK/MS VIII-1/1 ex 1917, no. 2716.

39. Nikolaus A. Sifferlinger, *Auslaufen verspricht Erfolg: Die radiotelegraphie der k.u.k. Kriegsmarine* (Vienna: Verlag Österreich, 2000), p. 121.

40. Horthy, Gefechtsbericht; Sifferlinger, *Auslaufen verspricht Erfolg*, p. 121.

41. Heyssler, "Memoirs," p. 256.

42. Karl von Lukas, "Das Gefecht in der Otrantostraße am 15 Mai 1917: Versuch einer kritischen Betrachtung," *Marine-Gestern, Heute* 4, no. 2 (June 1977), p. 36.

43. The class was more generally known as the *Boadica* class, named after the lead ship of two in the 1907 program. *Blanche* was one of two virtually identical ships in the 1909 program. The *Active* of a very similar class of three in the 1910 and 1911 programs was in the Mediterranean in 1918. See Dittmar and Colledge, *British Warships, 1914–1919*, p. 45; and Morris, *Cruisers of the Royal and Commonwealth Navies*, pp. 114–16.

44. Acton to Comando in Capo, 19 May 1917, ADM 137/782.

45. Captain Vivian [SNO Brindisi] to Kerr, 18 May 1917, PRO, ADM 137/782.

46. Acton to Comando in Capo, 19 May 1917, ibid.

47. Heyssler, "Memoirs," p. 257.

48. Lieutenant [illegible] to Captain A. P. Addison, gunnery narrative of HMS *Dartmouth*, 25 May 1917, PRO, ADM 137/1950.

49. Ufficio Storico, *Marina italiana*, vol. 4, pp. 536–37.

50. Horthy, Gefechtsbericht; Heyssler, "Memoirs," p. 258.

51. Gunnery narrative of HMS *Dartmouth*.

52. Heyssler, "Memoirs," pp. 257–58; Heyssler to Kreuzerflottillenkommando, "Ausführlicher Gefechtsbericht, 15.5.1917," OK/MS VIII-1/1 ex 1917, no. 2716. Horthy's report makes no mention of the near collisions in the smoke.

53. Ufficio Storico, *Marina italiana*, vol. 4, pp. 537–38; Konjović, "Fliegertätigkeit"; Ufficio del Capo di Stato Maggiore della Marina (Ufficio Storico), *Cronistoria Documentata della Guerra Marittima Italo-Austriaca, 1915–1918. Collezione: Impiego delle Forze Navali. Fascicolo VI: Azione Navale del 15 Maggio 1917 nel Basso Adriatico* ([Rome], n.d.), pp. 65–67. Copy in USM.

54. Schupita, *Die k.u.k. Seeflieger*, pp. 73, 89.

55. Konjović, "Fliegertätigkeit."

56. Ufficio Storico, *Marina italiana*, vol. 4, p. 539.

57. Ibid., pp. 538–41.

58. Gunnery narrative of HMS *Dartmouth*.

59. Horthy, *Memoirs*, pp. 82–83; Horthy, Gefechtsbericht. Jure Dunay to Dr. Ing. Robert Oedl, 13 May 1937; Iván Bosnyák to Oedl, 13 May 1937; Walter Zanoskar to Oedl, 11 May 1937. Dunay, Bosnyák, and Zanoskar had been cadets in the *Novara* during the action. Copies of these letters in the collection of Mr. Erwin Sieche, Vienna.

60. Heyssler, "Memoirs," p. 258.

61. Ibid.; Heyssler, "Ausführlicher Gefechtsbericht."

62. HMS *Bristol*, log, 15 May 1917, PRO, ADM 53/36144.

63. Gunnery narrative of HMS *Dartmouth*.

64. Heyssler, "Memoirs," p. 259.

65. Acton to Comando in Capo, 19 May 1917; Gunnery narrative of HMS *Dart-*

mouth, ibid. To further muddle the issue, *Bristol*'s log indicates she reopened fire with her 6-inch guns at maximum range at 1035. HMS *Bristol,* log, 15 May 1917, ADM 53/36144.

66. Konjović, "Fliegertätigkeit."

67. Gunnery narrative of HMS *Dartmouth;* HMS *Bristol,* log, 15 May 1917, PRO, ADM 53/36144.

68. Addison to Crampton, 28 May 1917, *Royal Navy in the Mediterranean, 1915–1918,* document no. 129, p. 259.

69. Heyssler, "Memoirs," p. 259.

70. Horthy, *Memoirs,* p. 83; Heyssler, "Ausführlichen Gefechtsbericht." In his memoirs, Heyssler claims no warning of *Novara*'s slowing was given, Heyssler, "Memoirs," p. 259.

71. Acton to Comando in Capo, 19 May 1917.

72. Extract from Kriegstagebuch, I Flottillenkommando, 15 May 1917, OK/MS VIII-1/1 ex 1917, no. 2716.

73. Ufficio Storico, *Marina italiana,* vol. 4, pp. 544–45; Sokol, *Österreich-Ungarns Seekrieg,* p. 385 and note 265.

74. Sokol, *Österreich-Ungarns Seekrieg,* p. 391.

75. Ufficio Storico, *Marina italiana,* vol. 4, pp. 545–46. The times for aircraft departures and arrivals at Brindisi given in the text do not match those given in Appendix B: "Movimenti del naviglio a Brindisi durante la giornata del 15 maggio," ibid. See also *Cronistoria Documentata,* Fascicolo VI: *Azione Navale del 15 Maggio 1917,* pp. 27–28. Copy in USM.

76. Extract from Kriegstagebuch, I Torpedoflottillenkommando, 15 May 1917, OK/MS VIII-1/1 ex 1917, no. 2716; Sokol, *Österreich-Ungarns Seekrieg,* p. 387; Sifferlinger, *Auslaufen verspricht Erfolg,* p. 123. According to figures cited in the Italian official history, *Sankt Georg* received the verbal order to sortie at 0915 but took from 0920 to 1040 to clear the harbor obstructions and assume her southerly course, increasing speed to a maximum twenty knots. Ufficio Storico, *Marina italiana,* vol. 4, pp. 552–53.

77. Hansa to k.u.k. Flottenkommando, 17 May 1917, OK/MS VIII-1/1 ex 1917, no. 2716; Sokol, *Österreich-Ungarns Seekrieg,* p. 387, note 269; Sifferlinger, *Auslaufen verspricht Erfolg,* p. 123.

78. Lukas, "Das Gefecht in der Otrantostraße . . . ," p. 38.

79. Sokol, *Österreich-Ungarns Seekrieg,* p. 386.

80. Heyssler, "Ausführlicher Gefechtsbericht"; Extract from Kriegstagebuch I Torpedoflottillenkommando, 15 May 1917; Heyssler, "Memoirs," p. 259

81. Sokol, *Österreich-Ungarns Seekrieg,* p. 386.

82. Ufficio Storico, *Marina italiana,* vol. 4, pp. 550–51; Heyssler, "Ausführlicher Gefechtsbericht"; Extract from Kriegstagebuch I Torpedoflottillenkommando, 15 May 1917. The latter gives the time of the "*Quarto*"'s attack as 1124 at a range of 9,900 to 8,800 meters.

83. Extract from Kriegstagebuch, I Torpedoflottillenkommando, 15 May 1917.

84. Ibid.

85. Acton to Comando in Capo, 19 May 1917.

86. Ufficio Storico, *Marina italiana,* vol. 4, pp. 550–52; Sokol, *Österreich-Ungarns Seekrieg,* pp. 386–87. Both clearly differentiate the *Acerbi*'s from the *Racchia*'s action but contain no mention of a third separate attack by a lone destroyer.

87. S.M.S. *Saida,* "Operationsjournal über die Aktion in der Strasse von Otranto, am 14 und 15.5.17," OK/MS VIII-1/1 ex 1917, no. 2116.

88. Sokol, *Österreich-Ungarns Seekrieg,* p. 386.

89. Heyssler, "Ausführliche Gefechtsbericht"; idem, "Memoirs," pp. 259–60.

90. I am indebted to Mr. Nikolaus Sifferlinger for this clarification of Austrian naval usage.

91. *Saida*'s log gives no specific time for the union with *Sankt Georg*, merely listing it on the line below that noting the beginning of the tow. *Helgoland* times the union at 1230. S.M.S. *Saida*, "Operationsjournal über die Aktion in der Strasse von Otranto, am 14 und 15.5.17," OK/MS VIII-1/1 ex 1917, no. 2716; Horthy, "Gefechtsbericht," ibid.; I Torpedoflottillenkommando [*Helgoland*], Kriegstagebuch, ibid. There is no mention of *Saida*'s 1145 signal to *Sankt Georg* in the logs of the other two cruisers or in the list of signals cited by Sifferlinger, *Auslaufen verspricht Erfolg*, pp. 123–24. The times of other signals also differ slightly.

92. H.M.S. *Dartmouth*, log, 15 May 1917, ADM 53/39501; H.M.S. *Bristol*, log, 15 May 1917, ADM 53/36144.

93. Acton to Comando in Capo, 19 May 1917, PRO, ADM 137/782.

94. This point is raised in Lukas, "Das Gefecht in der Otrantostraße . . . ," p. 35.

95. Slaghek-Fabbri, *Con gl'inglesi*, pp. 196–97.

96. Addison to Crampton, 28 May 1917. Addison after the war corresponded with Heyssler and claimed that he did not realize the Austrian cruisers had stopped and that if he had, "I think I shall have disobeyed orders." This claim may be difficult to accept, for Admiral Acton was on the bridge of the *Dartmouth* and had received *Acerbi*'s report that at least one of the Austrian cruisers was motionless. It is possible, however, that this information was not translated and given to Addison at the time when he was busy conning his ship. Addison to Heyssler, 19 Nov. 1921, Heyssler MSS.

6. THE FORCES RETURN

1. Sieche, *Kreuzer und Kreuzerprojekte die k.u.k. Kriegsmarine*, pp. 162–63.

2. Sifferlinger, *Auslaufen verspricht Erfolg*, p. 124. See also Lothar Baumgartner and Nikolaus A. Sifferlinger, *"Abgelauscht": Die Funkaufklärung der K.U.K. Kriegsmarine*. Part 1: *1917: Depeschen, Dechiffrierung und Technik* (Vienna: Verlagsbuchhandlung Stöhr, 2002), pp. 13–14.

3. I Torpedoflottillenkommando, "Auszug aus dem Kriegstagebuch für die Zeit vom 14 bis 15 Mai 1917"; Hansa to Flottenkommando, 17 May 1917, OK/MS VIII-1/1 ex 1917, no. 2716.

4. Hansa to Flottenkommando, excerpts from log, 18 May 1917, ibid.

5. Heyssler, "Memoirs," p. 260.

6. Hansa to Flottenkommando, excerpts from log, 18 May 1917, OK/MS VIII-1/1 ex 1917, no. 2716.

7. Kriegstagebuch Dr. Peter Freiherr von Handel-Mazzetti, 15 May 1917, Kriegsarchiv, Vienna, Nachlasse Handel-Mazzetti. I am indebted to Mr. Erwin Sieche for providing me with a transcript of this source. The events of 15 May are not mentioned in the chronicle of *UC.34* in Bendert, *Die UC-Boote der Kaiserlichen Marine*, p. 115, or Spindler, *Handelskrieg mit U-Booten*. Vol. 4, p. 179.

8. Ufficio Storico, *Marina italiana*, vol. 4, pp. 562–63.

9. Ibid., p. 261.

10. Walter Zanoskar, "Die Aktion S.M.S. *Novara* vom 14–15 Mai 1917," p. 8. Oedl MSS. Copy in the possession of Mr. Erwin Sieche, Vienna.

11. Jure Dunay to R. Oedl, 13 May 1937, Oedl MSS. Copy in possession of Mr. Erwin Sieche.

12. Data is taken from diagram prepared by Dip.Ing. Dr. Robert Oedl (1937) repro-

duced in Karl von Lukas, "Skizze zum Otranto-Gefecht vom 15.5.1917," *Marine-Gestern Heute* 7, no. 3 (September 1980), p. 101.

13. Zanoskar to Oedl, 24 April 1937. Oedl MSS. Copy in the possession of Mr. Erwin Sieche.

14. Hansa to Flottenkommando, excerpts from log, 18 May 1917; Heyssler, "Memoirs," pp. 260–61.

15. Heyssler, "Memoirs," p. 261.

16. Linienschiffsartz Dr. Rudolph Kobal [Sanitätschef, Kreuzerflottillenkommando], Beitrag zum Operationsbericht, 17 May 1917, OK/MS VIII-1/1 ex 1917, no. 2716; Greger, *Austro-Hungarian Warships of World War I*, p. 123; Wladimir Aichelburg, *Die Handelsschiffe Österreich-Ungarns im Weltkrieg 1914–1918* (Graz: H. Weishaupt Verlag, 1988), pp. 41–42.

17. Horthy, *Memoirs*, pp. 85–86; Heyssler, "Memoirs," pp. 261–62; Sakmyster, *Hungary's Admiral on Horseback*, pp. 8–9; Sieche, *Kreuzer und Kreuzerprojekte der k.u.k. Kriegsmarine*, p. 155.

18. Präsidialkanzlei, Marinesektion to Flottenstabschef, Pola [telephone despatch] 16 May 1917, 16:05; Flottenstabschef to Präsidialkanzlei, Marinesektion [telegram], 16 May 1917, 17:20; OK/MS VIII-1/1 ex 1917, no. 3310; Marinesektion to AOK [*Armeeoberkommando*] Marinereferent [telegram], 16 May 1917, 16:00, OK/MS VIII-1/1 ex 1917 no. 2605.

19. Fritz Bratusch-Marrain to R. Oedl, 10 May 1937, Nachlasse Oedl.

20. Sieche, *Kreuzer und kreuzerprojekte der k.u.k. Kriegsmarine*, p. 155; details of decorations from *Marineverordnungsblatt*, nos. 31–33.

21. Handel-Mazzetti to [?], 30 May 1917, Kriegsarchiv, Vienna, Nachlasse Handel-Mazzetti. Handel-Mazzetti's record of wireless messages during the battle is reproduced in Baumgartner and Sifferlinger, "*Abgelauscht*," pp. 11–18. See also Lukas, "Das Gefecht in der Otrantostraße," p. 40.

22. Hansa to Flottenkommando, 17 May 1917, OK/MS VIII-1/1 ex 1917, no. 2716; Heyssler, "Ausführlicher Gefechtsbericht," ibid.

23. Lukas, "Das Gefecht in der Otrantostraße," p. 40. See also F. Bratusch-Marrain, 10 May 1937, Nachlasse Oedl. Bratusch-Marrain states that the *Saida*'s handling party had not been in place and the noise of the battle, especially the nasty crack of the Austrian 10cm guns that others such as Heyssler have remarked on, deafened the crew and made orders difficult to hear.

24. This material is in the Oedl MSS, copies in the possession of Mr. Erwin Sieche.

25. Acton to Comando in Capo, 19 May 1917, PRO, ADM 137/782; Ufficio Storico, *Marina italiana*, vol. 4, p. 556; Thomazi, *Guerre navale dans l'Adriatique*, p. 151.

26. Bendert, *Die UC-Boote der Kaiserlichen Marine*, pp. 102–103; Eberhard Rössler, *The U-Boat: The evolution and technical history of German submarines*. Translated by Harald Erenberg (London: Arms and Armour Press, 1981), pp. 50–53. The submarine was designated *U.89* in the Austrian naval list.

27. Ufficio Storico, *Marina italiana*, vol. 4, p. 557.

28. Vivian to Kerr, 18 May 1917, PRO, ADM 137/782.

29. Ufficio Storico, *Marina italiana*, vol. 4, pp. 556–57; Acton to Comando in Capo, 19 May 1917; Addison to Kerr, 16 May 1917 and Vivian to Kerr, 24 May 1917, PRO, ADM 137/782. There are minor discrepancies between Acton's original report and the detailed account in the Italian official history as to the time of *Dartmouth*'s torpedoing, 1335 in the former and approximately 1330 in the latter. Acton also places *Acerbi* on *Dartmouth*'s starboard bow.

30. Ufficio Storico, *Marina italiana*, vol. 4, p. 557.

31. H.M.S. *Bristol*, log, 15 May 1917, PRO, ADM 53/36144.

32. Acton to Comando in Capo, 19 May 1917; Addison to Kerr, 16 May 1917, ADM 137/782.

33. Addison to Kerr, 16 May 1917, ibid.; H.M.S. *Dartmouth*, log, 17 May 1917, ADM 53/39501.

34. Acton to Comando in Capo, 19 May 1917, ADM 137/782.

35. Ufficio Storico, *Marina italiana*, vol. 4, Appendix A.

36. Vivian to Kerr, 18 May 1917, ADM 137/782.

37. Ufficio Storico, *Marina italiana*, vol. 4, pp. 560–61; Thomazi, *Guerre navale dans l'Adriatique*, p. 152. Lieutenant Chauvin's report is reproduced in Ufficio Storico del Capo di Stato Maggiore, *Cronistoria Documentata*, Fascicolo VI: *Azione Navale del 15 Maggio 1917*, pp. 68–69. Copy in USM.

38. Vivian to Kerr, 21 May 1917, ADM 137/782.

39. Ibid.; see also Ufficio Storico, *Marina italiana*, vol. 4, p. 561.

40. Acton to Comando in Capo, 19 May 1917, Addison to Kerr, 16 May 1917, Vivian to Kerr, 18 May 1917, ADM 137/782; Ufficio Storico, *Marina italiana*, vol. 4, p. 561.

41. Addison to Kerr, 16 May 1917, ADM 137/782; Interim report by Commander F. Gifford enclosed in Kerr to Admiralty, 21 May 1917, ibid.

42. Ufficio Storico, *Marina italiana*, vol. 4, p. 568.

43. Linienschiffsleutnant Sauter, "Meldung über Einvernahme der von S.M.S. *Novara* und *Helgoland* eingebrachten englischen Kriegsgefangenen der Fischerdampfer," n.d. [21 May 1917], OK/MS VIII-1/1 ex 1917, no. 2828.

44. F. Bratusch-Marrain to R. Oedl, 10 May 1937, Nachlasse Oedl.

45. Heyssler, "Memoirs," p. 262.

46. Ibid. For further comments on the wife and family problem, see ibid., pp. 265–66; Richard Georg Plaschka, *Cattaro-Prag: Revolte und Revolution* (Graz: Verlag Böhlau, 1963), p. 25; and Paul G. Halpern, "The Cattaro Mutiny, 1918," in Christopher M. Bell and Bruce A. Elleman, eds., *Naval Mutinies of the Twentieth Century: An International Perspective* (London: Frank Cass, 2003), chapter III.

47. Acton to Comando in Capo, 19 May 1917.

48. Addison to Crampton, 28 May 1917, in *Royal Navy in the Mediterranean*, document no. 129, p. 259; and Vivian to Kerr, 18 May 1917, ibid., document no. 127, pp. 254–55; Kerr to Admiralty, 21 May 1917, ADM 137/782.

49. Acton to Comando in Capo, 19 May 1917, ADM 137/782.

50. Admiralty to Rear Admiral commanding British Adriatic Squadron, 23 May 1917, ADM 137/782.

51. Addison to Crampton, 28 May 1917.

52. Major W. L. Huntingford, Royal Marine Artillery, "The Austrian Raid on the Drifter Line on 15th May 1917," 20 June 1917, ADM 137/782.

53. Ibid.

54. Vivian to Kerr, 18 May 1917, *Royal Navy in the Mediterranean*, document no. 128, pp. 256–57.

55. Ibid.

56. Signals officer H.M.S. *Liverpool* to Vivian, 17 May 1917, ADM 137/782; Vivian to Kerr, 18 May 1917, *Royal Navy in the Mediterranean*, document no. 128, pp. 256–57.

57. Ibid.

58. Todd to Admiral Kerr, 24 May 1917, ADM 137/782.

59. Kerr to Admiralty, 21 May 1917, *Royal Navy in the Mediterranean*, document no. 128, p. 258.

60. Kerr to Jellicoe, 29 May 1917, ibid., document no. 130, p. 261.

61. Pipon to F. T. Hamilton, 30 May 1917, ibid., document no. 133, p. 264.

62. Kerr to Admiralty, 29 May 1917 (telegram); and minute by J. W. S. Anderson, 25 June 1917, ADM 137/782.

63. Minutes by Everett, 2 July 1917, and C. Burney [second sea lord], 3 July 1917, ibid. Everett had proposed a Distinguished Service Cross for Skipper Watt and a Conspicuous Gallantry Medal for Deck Hand Lamb with promotions in rank if either were eligible, and Italian medals which had been placed at the disposal of the Admiralty.

64. Minutes by Jellicoe, 3 July 1917; Carson, 5 July 1917; and G. Steel, 15 August 1917, ibid. See also Stephen Snelling, *VCs of the First World War: The Naval VCs* (Stroud, Gloucestershire: Sutton Publishing, 2002), pp. 171–72.

65. Minute by Everett, 9 July 1917; Admiralty to Kerr, 16 July 1917, ADM 137/782. The names and awards are published in *Supplement to the London Gazette*, 29 August 1917, ibid.

66. For the application of "scale" in awards for the Dardanelles campaign as well as Jutland, see for example Keyes to his wife, 4 February 1916, in Halpern, ed., *The Keyes Papers*, vol. I: *1914–1918*, document no. 148, pp. 338–39; de Robeck to Keyes, 14 August 1916, ibid., document no. 164, pp. 367–68; Keyes to de Robeck, 12 Oct. 1916, ibid., document no. 165, pp. 368–70, 370.

67. *Supplement to the London Gazette*, 29 August 1917, ADM 137/782.

68. A. Lyall to D. Masters, 30 December 1935; D. Masters to A. Lyall, 30 Dec. 1935, Imperial War Museum, London, Department of Documents, VC/GC Collection, Chief Skipper Joseph Watt file.

69. Heneage to Kerr, 3 June 1917, ADM 137/782.

70. Snelling, *The Naval VCs*, pp. 173–74.

71. Ibid., p. 171. The author refers to the *Floandi* as "among those vessels" Watt assisted.

72. Admiralty to Kerr, 10 November 1917; E. Earle, Notes on Rear Admiral Mark Kerr's visit to N. Branch on the 12th of November in regard to the Conspicuous Gallantry Medal awarded to Watt, 13 Nov. 1917; Kerr to Admiralty, 15 Nov. 1917, ADM 137/782.

73. Minute by Everett, 17 November 1917, ibid.

74. Kerr to Admiralty, 30 May 1917, ibid.

75. Minute by Carson, 5 July 1917, ibid.

76. Minutes by Burney, 7 July, and Jellicoe, 9 July 1917; Admiralty to Kerr, 17 July 1917, ibid.

7. THE RESULTS OF THE BATTLE

1. Halpern, *Naval War in the Mediterranean*, p. 364; Thomazi, *Guerre navale dans l'Adriatique*, pp. 153–54.

2. Kerr to Admiralty, 21 May 1917, reproduced in *Royal Navy in the Mediterranean*, document no. 128, pp. 257–58.

3. Ibid.

4. Minutes by Hope, 25 May, Oliver, 27 May, and Jellicoe, 27 May 1917, ibid., pp. 258–59.

5. Kerr to Admiralty, 21 May 1917, ibid., p. 258.

6. Minute by Hope, 25 May 1917, ibid.

7. Addison to Crampton, 28 May 1917, ibid., document no. 129, p. 259.

8. Vivian to Kerr, 18 May 1917, ibid., document no. 127, pp. 254–56.

9. Kerr to Admiralty, 21 May 1917, PRO, ADM 137/782.

10. Ibid.

11. Vivian to Kerr, 18 May 1917, *Royal Navy in the Mediterranean*, document no. 127, p. 254; Addison to Crampton, 28 May 1917, ibid., p. 259.

12. Vivian to Kerr, 24 May 1917, PRO, ADM 137/782.

13. Ibid.

14. Vivian to Kerr, 18 May 1917, *Royal Navy in the Mediterranean*, document no. 127, pp. 254–55.

15. Vivian to Kerr, 23 May 1917, ADM 137/782.

16. Admiralty to Under Secretary of State, Colonial Office, 6 and 18 May 1917; Colonial Office to Admiralty, 12 May 1917; Admiralty to Vice Admiral commanding Eastern Mediterranean Squadron, senior naval officer Malta and Rear Admiral commanding British Adriatic Squadron, 4 June 1917, ADM 137/1414; Halpern, *Naval War in the Mediterranean*, p. 365; A. W. Jose, *The Royal Australian Navy, 1914–1918*, 11th edition (Sydney: Angus and Robertson, 1943, reprinted St. Lucia, Queensland: University of Queensland Press, 1987), pp. 310–17.

17. Walter Raleigh and H. A. Jones, *The War in the Air*, 6 volumes (Oxford: Clarendon Press, 1922–37), vol. 5, pp. 391–93; Owen Thetford, *British Naval Aircraft since 1912*, revised edition (London: Putnam, 1977), pp. 272–77, 282–83, and 290–97.

18. Minute by Jellicoe, 27 May 1917, *Royal Navy in the Mediterranean*, document no. 128, p. 259.

19. The British had replaced the *Dartmouth* with her sister ship *Weymouth*. The week of 7–14 July the cruisers at Brindisi were *Newcastle, Bristol, Gloucester,* and *Weymouth*. The *Newcastle* and *Gloucester* were sister ships of the *Bristol*. Kerr to Admiralty, 14 July 1917, ADM 137/496.

20. Memorandum from Italian ambassador, 26 June 1917, *Royal Navy in the Mediterranean*, document no. 135, pp. 167–269.

21. W. Graham Greene [Permanent Secretary of the Admiralty] to Foreign Office, 6 July 1917, *Royal Navy in the Mediterranean*, document no. 136, pp. 269–70. The memorandum was for communication to the Italian ambassador.

22. Ibid., p. 271.

23. Cited in Halpern, *Naval War in the Mediterranean*, p. 365. The original with Revel's annotation is in USM, Cartella 740/1.

24. Minute by C. Coode, 15 July 1917, ADM 137/496.

25. Ministry of Marine, General Staff, 4th Section, "Decisions at Paris Conference, 1917, 24–26 July 1917," copy in ADM 137/1420; Ufficio Storico, *Marina italiana*, vol. V, pp. 304–13.

26. A. W. Heneage, "Attack by Austrian Warships on the Drifters in the Straits of Otranto, May 15, 1917," 3 June 1917, ADM 137/782.

27. Minutes by Carson, 16 and 18 July, and Oliver, 16 July 1917, ibid.

28. A striking example of this may be seen in the bar graph with Austrian contribution darkened to set it apart in Erwin Sieche, "La guerra sottomarina tedesca nel Mediterraneo, 1915–1918," in Achille Rastelli and Alessandro Massignani, eds., *La Guerra Navale 1914–1918: Un contributo internazionale alle operazioni in Mediterraneo* (Novale-Valdagno: Gino Rossato Editore, 2002), p. 88.

29. Summarized from figures given in Halpern, *Naval War in the Mediterranean*, pp. 312, 396. These figures were based on the data given for German submarines in Spindler, *Handelskrieg mit U-Booten*, vol. 3, pp. 388, 390; vol. 4, pp. 194–95, 376–77, 496–97. The Austrian data is from Aichelburg, *Die Unterseeboote Österreich-Ungarns*, vol. 2, pp. 490–92.

30. Halpern, *Naval War in the Mediterranean*, pp. 386–87.

31. Ibid., pp. 408–409, 565. A favorable view of the Franco-Italian proposals is in Thomazi, *Guerre navale dans l'Adriatique*, pp. 164–65.

32. Both were built to the plans of the German *UB.II* class and relatively new, having entered into service in June and August of 1917. Aichelburg, *Die Unterseeboote Österreich-Ungarns*, vol. 2, pp. 412, 421–22.

33. Hansa, "Aktionen gegen feindliche Transporte nach Valona," 17 Oct. 1917, Heyssler to Hansa, 20 Oct. 1917, OK/MS VIII-1/1 ex 1917, no. 5757; see also the sometimes differing accounts in Sokol, *Österreich-Ungarns Seekrieg*, pp. 548–50; Thomazi, *Guerre navale dans l'Adriatique*, pp. 165–66; Ufficio Storico, *Marina italiana*, vol. 6, pp. 105–10; Aichelburg, *Die Unterseeboote Österreich-Ungarns*, vol. 2, pp. 412–13, 423; and Garier, *L'odyssée technique et humaine du sous-marin en France*, vol. 3, p. 124.

34. Hansa to Marinesektion, 14 and 23 Nov. and 14 Dec. 1917, OK/MS VIII-1/1 ex 1917, nos. 6128, 6319, and 6684; Sokol, *Österreich-Ungarns Seekrieg*, pp. 549–50; Ufficio Storico, *Marina italiana*, vol. 6, pp. 465–67.

35. Ufficio Storico, *Marina italiana*, vol. 6, p. 467.

36. For details see Marco Gemignani, "I Mas nel primo conflitto mondiale," in Rastelli and Massignani, *La Guerra Navale 1914–1918*, pp. 278–81.

37. On British contingency planning in the event Italy would be compelled to leave the war, see Halpern, *Naval War in the Mediterranean*, pp. 403–406.

38. The most thorough modern account of the Cattaro mutiny remains Plaschka, *Cattaro-Prag: Revolte und Revolution*. Shorter accounts are in Sondhaus, *The Naval Policy of Austria-Hungary, 1867–1918*, pp. 317–25; René Greger, "Die Marinemeuteri in Cattaro und Franz Rasch," *Marine Rundschau* 85, no. 6 (November/December, 1988), pp. 351–57; David Woodward, "Mutiny at Cattaro, 1918," *History Today* 26, no. 12 (December 1976), pp. 804–10; and Halpern, "Cattaro, 1918," in Bell and Elleman, eds., *Naval Mutinies of the Twentieth Century: An International Perspective*, chapter III.

39. Cited in Halpern, *Naval War in the Mediterranean*, p. 449.

40. The claim is made in Horthy, *Memoirs*, pp. 88–89.

41. Gemignani, "I Mas nel primo conflitto mondiale," pp. 281–83.

42. Full details are in Bagnasco, *I Mas e le Motosilurante italiane*, pp. 619–27; Ufficio Storico, *Marina Italiana*, vol. 7, chapter XX; Sokol, *Österreich-Ungarns Seekrieg*, pp. 624, 627–30; and Marco Gemignani, "I mezzi d'assalto italiani nella prima guerra mondiale," in Rastelli and Massignani, *La Guerra Navale 1914–1918*, pp. 295–305.

43. Calthorpe to Admiralty, 27 and 28 Nov. 1917, in *Royal Navy in the Mediterranean*, document nos. 150 and 151, pp. 313–21; Calthorpe to Admiralty, 9 and 16 Jan. 1918, ibid., document nos. 157, 160, pp. 363–64, 367–73. The argument over the question is summarized in Halpern, *Naval War in the Mediterranean*, pp. 409–10.

44. Naval staff minutes on Otranto barrage proposals, 21 Jan.–1 Feb. 1918, *Royal Navy in the Mediterranean*, document no. 164, pp. 383–88; memorandum by Calthorpe, 20 Feb. 1918, ibid., document no. 174, pp. 409–12.

45. Dittmar and Colledge, *British Warships 1914–1919*, pp. 61–62.

46. Documents relating to the action between British and Austrian destroyers on the night of 22–23 April 1918, *Royal Navy in the Mediterranean*, document no. 160 (a)-(f), pp. 450–59. This includes the reports of *Jackal*, *Hornet*, and *Comet*. Summary accounts are in Corbett and Newbolt, *Naval Operations*, vol. 5, pp. 287–88; Sokol, *Österreich-Ungarns Seekrieg*, pp. 550–51; Ufficio Storico, *Marina italiana*, vol. 7, pp. 754–57; Thomazi, *Guerre navale dans l'Adriatique*, pp. 184–85; and Halpern, *Naval War in the Mediterranean*, p. 452. Movements of Austrian submarines are in Aichelburg, *Die Unterseeboote Österreich-Ungarns*, vol. 2, pp. 382, 394.

47. Ufficio Storico, *Marina italiana*, vol. 7, p. 757.

48. Heyssler to Horthy, 24 April 1918, and report by Herkner with comments by Heyssler, 25 April 1917, OK/MS VIII-1/1 ex 1918, no. 2071. Unfortunately, Heyssler does not comment on this action in his memoirs.

49. Remarks by D.O.D. (F) [Coode], 6 May 1918, *Royal Navy in the Mediterranean*, document no. 190 (f), pp. 458–59; Calthorpe to Kelly, 3 May 1918, ibid., document no. 193, p. 465.

50. Sokol, *Österreich-Ungarns Seekrieg*, pp. 553–63; Ufficio Storico, *Marina italiana*, vol. 7, chapter XXIV; Edgar Tomicich, "Die Versenkung des k.u.k. Schlachtschiffes *Szent István* am 10 Juni 1918," *Marine-Gestern, Heute* 6, nos. 1 and 2 (March and June 1979). On possible forewarning to the Allies through wireless intercepts and the subject of betrayal and intelligence, see the secret diary of a former wireless officer in the Austrian navy, Linienschiffsleutnant Peter Handel-Mazzetti in Lothar Baumgartner, ed., "*Abgelauscht*": *Die Funkaufklärung der K.U.K. Kriegsmarine. Part 2: 1918 Verschlüsselung, Verrat und Verluste* (Vienna: Verlagsbuchhandlung Stöhr, 2002), pp. 68–72.

51. On American plans for the Adriatic, see Halpern, *Naval War in the Mediterranean*, pp. 434–41; David F. Trask, *Captains and Cabinets: Anglo-American Naval Relations, 1917–1918* (Columbia: University of Missouri Press, 1972), pp. 240–51; and Michael Simpson, ed., *Anglo-American Naval Relations, 1917–1919*, Publications of the Navy Records Society, vol. 130 (Aldershot: Scholar Press, 1991), documents nos. 310–19, pp. 406–15.

52. Kemp, *U-Boats Destroyed: German Submarine Losses in the World Wars*, p. 53; Bendert, *Die UB-Boote*, p. 134; Thomazi, *Guerre navale dans l'Adriatique*, p. 181.

53. Documents relating to the bombardment of Durazzo [4 October 1918], *Royal Navy in the Mediterranean*, document no. 256 (a)-(c), pp. 557–66; Ufficio Storico, *Marina italiana*, vol. 8, pp. 380–97; Sokol, *Österreich-Ungarns Seekrieg*, pp. 636–45.

54. Short account is in Ferrante, *La Grande Guerra in Adriatico: Nel LXX Anniversario della Vittoria*, pp. 116–21. Submarine details in Spindler, *Handelskrieg mit U-Booten*, vol. 5, pp. 226–28. See also Halpern, *Naval War in the Mediterranean*, pp. 566–68.

SELECT BIBLIOGRAPHY

UNPUBLISHED MATERIALS

Specific file, volume, or cartella references are given in the notes for material from the following sources:

Archivio Centrale dello Stato, Rome.
British Library, London.
Imperial War Museum, London.
Kontreadmiral Erich Heyssler, "Memoirs." In private possession.
National Archives and Records Service, Washington, Microfilm Publication T-1022,
    Records of the German Navy, 1850–1945.
Naval Historical Branch, Ministry of Defence, London.
Österreichisches Staatsarchiv/Kriegsarchiv, Vienna.
Public Record Office, Kew.
Ufficio Storico della Marina Militare, Rome.

PUBLISHED MATERIALS

Aichelburg, Wladimir. *Die Unterseeboote Österreich-Ungarns.* 2 vols. Graz: Akademische Druck-u. Verlagsanstalt, 1981.
———. *Die Handelsschiffe Österreich-Ungarns im Weltkrieg 1914–1918.* Graz: H. Weishaupt Verlag, 1988.
Bagnasco, Erminio. *I Mas e le Motosilurante italiane, 1906–1966.* Rome: Ufficio Storico della Marina Militare, 1967.
———. *La Portaerei nella Marina italiana: Idee, progetti e realizzazioni dalle origini ad oggi.* Rome: *Rivista Marittima* [Supplement to no. 12, December], 1989.
Bagnasco, Erminio, and Achille Rastelli. *Navi e marinai italiani nella Grande Guerra.* Parma: Ermanno Albertelli Editore, 1997.
Bargoni, Franco, ed. *Esploratori, fregate, corvette ed avvisi italiani.* Rome: Ufficio Storico della Marina Militare, 1970.

Baumgartner, Lothar. *"Abgelauscht": Die Funkaufklärung der K.U.K. Kriegsmarine.* Part 2: *1918: Verschlüssellung, Verrat und Verluste.* Österreichische Militärgeschichte Sonderband 2002-2. Vienna: Verlagsbuchhandlung Stöhr, 2002.

——. "Österreich-Ungarns Dünkirchen? Ein Gegenüberstellungen von Berichten zum Abtransport der serbischen Armee aus Albanien im Winter 1915/16." *Marine-Gestern, Heute* 6, no. 2 (June 1982): pp. 46–53.

Baumgartner, Lothar, and Erwin Sieche. *Die Schiffe der k.u.k. Kriegsmarine im Bild.* Vol. 2: *1896–1918.* Vienna: Verlagsbuchhandlung Stöhr, 2001.

Baumgartner, Lothar, and Nikolaus A. Sifferlinger. *"Abgelauscht": Die Funkaufklärung der K.U.K. Kriegsmarine.* Part 1: *1917: Depeschen, Dechiffrierung und Technik.* Österreichische Militärgeschichte Sonderband 2002-1. Vienna: Verlagsbuchhandlung Stöhr, 2002.

Bayer von Bayersburg, Heinrich. *Unter der k.u.k. Kriegsflagge, 1914–1918.* Vienna: Bergland Verlag, 1959.

——. *Österreichs Admirale und bedeutende Persönlichkeiten der k.u.k. Kriegsmarine, 1867–1918.* Vienna: Bergland Verlag, 1962.

——. *'Schiffe verlassen!' 1914–1918.* Vienna: Bergland Verlag, 1965.

——. *Die Marinewaffen im Einsatz, 1914–1918.* Vienna: Bergland Verlag, 1968.

Bendert, Harald. *Die UB-Boote der Kaiserlichen Marine 1914–1918.* Hamburg, Berlin, and Bonn: E. S. Mittler & Sohn, 2000.

——. *Die UC-Boote der Kaiserlichen Marine 1914–1918.* Hamburg, Berlin, and Bonn: E. S. Mittler & Sohn, 2001.

Bilzer, Franz F. *Die Torpedoboote der k.u.k. Kriegsmarine von 1875–1918.* Graz: H. Weishaupt Verlag, 1984.

——. *Die Torpedoschiffe und Zerstörer der k.u.k. Kriegsmarine, 1867–1918.* Graz: H. Weishaupt Verlag, 1990.

Blois, Hubert de. *La Guerre des mines dans la marine française.* Brest and Paris: Editions de la Cité, 1982.

Brauzzi, Alfredo. *I Mezzi D'Assalto della Marina Italiana.* Rome: *Rivista Marittima* [Supplement to no. 6, June], 1991.

Burt, R. A. *British Battleships, 1889–1904.* Annapolis: Naval Institute Press, 1988.

Casale, Antonio, and Maria Cattaruzza. *Sotto i mari del mondo: La Whitehead 1875–1990.* Rome and Bari: Editori Laterza, 1990.

Chatterton, E. Keble. *Seas of Adventures: The Story of the Naval Operations in the Mediterranean, Adriatic and Aegean.* London: Hurst & Blackett, 1936.

Coletta, Paolo E. *Allied and American Naval Operations in the European Theater, World War I.* Lewiston, N.Y.: Edward Mellon, 1996.

Conway's All the World's Fighting Ships, 1906–1921. London: Conway Maritime Press, 1985.

Corbett, Julian S., and Henry Newbolt. *History of the Great War: Naval Operations.* 5 vols. in 9. London: Longmans, Green, 1920–31.

De Risio, Carlo. *L'Aviazione di Marina.* Rome: Ufficio Storico della Marina Militare, 1995.

Dittmar, F. J., and J. J. Colledge. *British Warships, 1914–1919.* London: Ian Allan, 1972.

Doisy, J. Pelletier. "Le combat d'Otrante 15 mai 1917." *Cols Bleus*, no. 2235 (6 November 1993), pp. 11–15.

Ferrante, Ezio. *La Grande Guerra in Adriatico: Nel LXX Anniversario della Vittoria.* Rome: Ufficio Storico della Marina Militare, 1987.

——. *Il Grande Ammiraglio Paolo Thaon di Revel.* Rome: *Rivista Marittima* [Supplement to No. 8/9, August/September], 1989.

Fioravanzo, Ammiraglio di Squadra Giuseppe, et al. *I Cacciatorpediniere italiani, 1900–1966*. Rome: Ufficio Storico della Marina Militare, 1966.

Fraccaroli, Aldo. *Italian Warships of World War I*. London: Ian Allan, 1970.

Gabriele, Mariano. "Le convenzione navale italo-franco-britannica del 10 maggio 1915." *Nuova antologia*, vols. 492–494, fasc. 1972–73 (April–May 1965).

——. *Le Convenzioni navali della Triplice*. Rome: Ufficio Storico della Marina Militare, 1969.

Garier, Gérard. *L'odyssée technique et humaine du sous-marin en France*. Vol. 2: *Des Emeraude (1905–1906) au Charles Brun (1908–1933)*. Nantes: Marines édition, 1998.

——. *L'odyssée technique et humaine du sous-marin en France*. Vol. 3 (part 2): *À l'épreuve de la Grande Guerre*. Nantes: Marines édition, 2002.

Giorgerini, Giorgio, and Augusto Nanni. *Gli incrociatori italiani, 1861–1964*. Rome: Ufficio Storico della Marina Militare, 1964.

Grant, Robert M. *U-Boats Destroyed: The Effect of Anti-Submarine Warfare, 1914–1918*. London: Putnam, 1964.

——. *U-Boat Intelligence, 1914–1918*. London: Putnam, 1969.

Gray, Edwyn. *The Devil's Device: Robert Whitehead and the History of the Torpedo*. Revised edition. Annapolis: Naval Institute Press, 1991.

Greger, René. *Austro-Hungarian Warships of World War I*. London: Ian Allan, 1976.

——. "Die Marinemeuterei in Cattaro und Franz Rasch." *Marine Rundschau* 85, no. 6 (November/December, 1988): pp. 351–57.

Grosz, Peter M., George Haddow, and Peter Schiemer. *Austro-Hungarian Army Aircraft of World War One*. Mountain View, Calif.: Flying Machines Press, 1993.

Halpern, Paul G. "The Anglo-French-Italian Naval Convention of 1915." *Historical Journal* 13, no. 1 (March 1970): pp. 106–29.

——. *The Naval War in the Mediterranean, 1914–1918*. London and Annapolis: Allen & Unwin and Naval Institute Press, 1987.

——. *A Naval History of World War I*. Annapolis: Naval Institute Press, 1994.

——. *Anton Haus: Österreich-Ungarns Großadmiral*. Graz: Verlag Styria, 1998.

——. "Cattaro, 1918." In Christopher M. Bell and Bruce A. Elleman, eds., *Naval Mutinies of the Twentieth Century: An International Perspective*. London: Frank Cass, 2003.

——, ed. *The Keyes Papers*. Vol. 1: *1914–1918*. Publications of the Navy Records Society, vol. 117, London: Navy Records Society, 1972; reprint, Allen & Unwin, 1979.

——, ed. *The Keyes Papers*. Vol. 2: *1919–1938*. Publications of the Navy Records Society, vol. 121, London: Allen & Unwin, 1980.

——, ed. *The Royal Navy in the Mediterranean, 1915–1918*. Publications of the Navy Records Society, vol. 126, Aldershot: Temple Smith for the Navy Records Society, 1987.

Heyssler, Erich. "Les croiseurs autrichiens dans le canal d'Otrante." In Vice Amiral E. von Mantey, ed., *Les Marins allemands au combat*, pp. 293–304. Paris: Payot, 1930.

Horthy, Admiral Nicholas. *Memoirs*. London: Hutchinson, 1956.

Hurd, Archibald. *History of the Great War: The Merchant Navy*. 3 vols. London: John Murray, 1921–29.

Joffre, J. J. C. *Mémoires du Maréchal Joffre*. 2 vols. Paris: Plon, 1932.

Jose, Arthur W. *The Royal Australian Navy, 1914–1918*. The Official History of Australia in the War of 1914–1918, vol. 9. 11th ed. Sydney: Angus and Robertson, 1943. Reprint, St. Lucia: University of Queensland Press in association with the Australian War Memorial, 1987.

Kemp, Paul. *U-Boats Destroyed: German Submarine Losses in the World Wars.* Annapolis: Naval Institute Press, 1997.

Kerr, Admiral, and Major General Mark. *Land, Sea, and Air: Reminiscences of Mark Kerr.* London: Longmans, Green and Co., 1927.

——. *The Navy in My Time.* London: Rich & Cowan, 1933.

King, Brad. *Royal Naval Air Service, 1912–1918.* Aldershot: Hikoki Publications, 1997.

Koburger, Charles W. *The Central Powers in the Adriatic, 1914–1918: War in a Narrow Sea.* Westport, Conn.: Praeger, 2001.

Labayle-Couhat, Jean. *French Warships of World War I.* London: Ian Allan, 1974.

Laurens, Adolphe. *Le Commandement naval en Méditerranée, 1914–1918.* Paris: Payot, 1931.

Layman, R. D. *Before the Aircraft Carrier: The Development of Aviation Vessels, 1849–1922.* Annapolis: Naval Institute Press, 1989.

——. *Naval Aviation in the First World War: Its Impact and Influence.* Annapolis: Naval Institute Press, 1996.

Le Masson, Henri. *Histoire du torpilleur en France.* Paris: Academie de la Marine [1966].

——. *Du Nautilus (1800) au Redoutable (Histoire critique du sous-marin dans la marine française).* Paris: Presses de la Cité, 1969.

Lukas, Karl von. "Das Gefechte in der Otrantostraße am 15 Mai 1917: Versuch einer kritischen Betrachtung." *Marine-Gestern, Heute* 4, no. 2 (June 1977): pp. 34–40.

——. "Skizze zum Otranto-Gefecht vom 15.5.1917." *Marine-Gestern, Heute* 7, no. 3 (September 1980), pp. 94–101.

Manfroni, Camillo. *I Nostri Alleati Navali: Ricordi della guerra Adriatica, 1915–1918.* Milan: A. Mondadori, 1927.

Martiny, Nikolaus von. *Bilddokumente aus Österreich-Ungarns Seekrieg, 1914–1918.* 2nd edition. 2 vols. Graz: Akademische Druck- u. Verlagsanstalt, 1973.

Masson, Philippe. *Histoire de la marine.* Vol. 2: *De la Vapeur à l'Atome.* Paris and Limoges: Charles Lavauzelle, 1983.

——. "La Marine dans la première guerre mondiale." In Guy Pedroncini, ed., *Histoire Militaire de la France.* Vol. 3: *De 1871 à 1940.* Paris: Presses Universitaires de France, 1992.

Miller, Geoffrey. *Superior Force: The conspiracy behind the escape of the* Goeben *and* Breslau. Hull, Humberside: University of Hull Press, 1996.

Morareau, Lucien, et al. *L'Aviation maritime française pendant la grande guerre (hydravions et avions).* Paris: Association pour la researche de documentation sur l'histoire de l'aéronautique navale, 1999.

Morris, Douglas. *Cruisers of the Royal and Commonwealth Navies.* Liskeard, Cornwall: Maritime Books, 1987.

Morrow, John H. *German Air Power in World War I.* Lincoln and London: University of Nebraska Press, 1982.

Oedl, Franz Robert. "50 Jahre Otranto." *Österreichische Militärische Zeitschrift* (1967): pp. 244–48.

Pawlik, Georg, and Lothar Baumgartner. *S.M. Unterseeboote.* Graz: H. Weishaupt Verlag, 1986.

Plaschka, Richard Georg. *Cattaro-Prag: Revolte und Revolutionen.* Graz and Cologne: Verlag Böhlau, 1963.

Raleigh, Walter, and H. A. Jones. *History of the Great War: The War in the Air.* 6 vols. Oxford: Clarendon Press, 1922–37.

Rastelli, Achille, and Alessandro Massignani, eds. *La Guerra Navale 1914–1918: Un contributo internazionale alle operazioni in Mediterraneo.* Novale-Valdagno: Gino Rossato Editore, 2002.

Rauchensteiner, Manfried. *Der Tod des Doppeladlers: Österreich-Ungarn und der Erste Weltkrieg.* Graz, Vienna, and Cologne: Verlag Styria, 1997.

Roskill, Captain S. W., ed. *The Naval Air Service.* Vol. 1: *1908–1918.* Publications of the Navy Record Service, Vol. 113. London: Navy Records Society, 1969.

Rössler, Eberhard. *The U-Boat: The Evolution and Technical History of German Submarines.* Translated by Harald Erenberg. London and Melbourne: Arms and Armour Press, 1981.

Sakmyster, Thomas. *Hungary's Admiral on Horseback: Miklós Horthy, 1918–1944.* Boulder, Colo.: East European Monographs, 1994.

Salaun, Vice-Amiral. *La Marine française.* Paris: Les Editions de France, 1934.

Schupita, Peter. *Die k.u.k. Seeflieger: Chronik und Dokumentation der Österreichisch-ungarischen Marineluftwaffe 1911–1918.* Koblenz: Bernard & Graefe Verlag, 1983.

Sieche, Erwin. "Die diplomatischen Aktiväten rund um das Haus-Memorandum vom März 1915." *Marine-Gestern, Heute* 9, no. 3 (September 1982): pp. 93–103.

———. *Kreuzer und Kreuzerprojekte die k.u.k. Kriegsmarine, 1889–1918.* Hamburg, Berlin, and Bonn: Verlag E. S. Mittler & Sohn, 2002.

Sifferlinger, Nikolaus A. *Auslaufen verspricht Erfolg: Die Radiotelegraphie der k.u.k. Kriegsmarine.* Vienna: Verlag Österreich, 2000.

Simpson, Michael, ed. *Anglo-American Naval Relations, 1917–1919.* Publications of the Navy Records Society, vol. 130. Aldershot: Scholar Press for the Navy Records Society, 1991.

Slaghek-Fabbri. Ammiraglio di divisione Luigi H., *Con gl'inglesi in Adriatico.* Rome: Edizioni Ardita, 1934.

Smither, Roger, ed. *Imperial War Museum Film Catalogue.* Vol. 1: *The First World War Archive.* Westport: Greenwood Press, 1994.

Snelling, Stephen. *VCs of the First World War: The Naval VCs.* Thrupp, Stroud, Gloucestershire: Sutton Publishing, 2002.

Sokol, Anthony E. *The Imperial and Royal Austro-Hungarian Navy.* Annapolis: Naval Institute Press, 1968.

Sokol, Hans Hugo. *Österreich-Ungarns Seekrieg.* 2 vols. Vienna: Amalthea Verlag, 1933. Reprint, Graz: Akademische Druck- u. Verlagsanstalt, 1967.

———. "Vor 20 Jahren: Das Seegefecht in der Otranto-Straße am 15 Mai 1937." *Marine Rundschau* 1937, no. 5 (May 1937).

Sondhaus, Lawrence. *The Naval Policy of Austria-Hungary, 1867–1918: Navalism, Industrial Development and the Politics of Dualism.* West Lafayette, Ind.: Purdue University Press, 1994.

Spindler, Rear Admiral Arno. *Der Handelskrieg mit U-Booten.* 5 vols. Berlin (Vol. 5, Frankfurt am Main): E. S. Mittler, 1932–66.

Thetford, Owen. *British Naval Aircraft since 1912.* Revised edition. London: Putnam, 1977.

Thomazi, A. *La Guerre navale dans l'Adriatique.* Paris: Payot, 1925.

———. *La Guerre navale dans la Méditerranée.* Paris: Payot, 1929.

Tomicich, Edgar. "Die Versenkung des k.u.k. Schlachtschiffes *Szent István* am 10 Juni 1918." *Marine-Gestern, Heute* 6, nos. 1–2 (March and June 1979).

Trapp, Georg von. *Bis zum letzten Flaggenschuss: Erinnerungen eines Österreichischen U-Boots-Kommandanten.* Salzberg and Leipzig: Verlag Anton Pustet, 1935.

Trask, David F. *Captains & Cabinets: Anglo-American Naval Relations, 1917–1918.* Columbia: University of Missouri Press, 1972.

Ufficio Storico della R. Marina. *La Marina italiana nella grande guerra.* 8 vols. Florence: Vallecchi, 1935–42.

Usborne, Vice Admiral C. V. *Smoke on the Horizon: Mediterranean Fighting, 1914–1918.* London: Hodder & Stoughton, 1933.

———. *Blast and Counterblast: A Naval Impression of the War.* London: John Murray, 1935.

Wall, Robert. *The Story of H.M.S. Bristol.* Bristol: City of Bristol District Council, 1986.

Wilson, Michael, and Paul Kemp. *Mediterranean Submarines.* Wilmslow, Cheshire: Crécy Publishing, 1997.

Woodward, David. "Mutiny at Cattaro, 1918." *History Today* 26, no. 12 (December 1976): pp. 804–10.

INDEX

Note: Officers are usually cited with the rank held when first mentioned.

ABOUT THE AUTHOR

PAUL G. HALPERN, Professor of History at Florida State University, is author of *A Naval History of World War I*; *The Naval War in the Mediterranean, 1914–1918*; *The Mediterranean Naval Situation, 1908–1914*; and *Anton Haus: Österreich-Ungarns Großadmiral*. He has served on the Council of the Navy Records Society (Great Britain) and is a Fellow of the Royal Historical Society.